An
Outline-History of
RUSSIA

BY

WALTHER KIRCHNER, Ph.D.

The University of Delaware

Second Edition

The Student's Private Tutor

TRADE MARK REG.

New York

BARNES & NOBLE, INC.

Printed in the United States of America

PREFACE

In his recent *Geschichte Russlands,* Professor Valentin Gitermann of Zürich, Switzerland, refers to the "special charm and attraction of the broadly flowing stream of Russian history." It has been my endeavor to preserve this very attraction in a book that by its nature must limit space and must treat only the factual information essential for an understanding and for a balanced judgment of past and present-day events in our great neighbor country, Russia.

In order to assure brevity and clarity without missing the spirit of Russia or losing a sense of the complexities of life (ever-present complexities which can be unraveled only in retrospect by historians), particular care has been taken to supplement the text with appropriate appendices. The chronological table, for instance, divulges by the very sequence of events the logical—and sometimes illogical—course of history and its influence on our lives. The maps reveal better than any description the causes and results of major trends. The index provides a biographical dictionary and a glossary of foreign terms, particularly useful, the writer hopes, in a book which cannot afford to identify persons or explain terms more than once. The bibliography directs attention to easily accessible material for more bibliographical information and for further study.

The book owes much to the untiring help of my friend Dr. Harold Bierck, of the Carnegie Institute of Technology, and of my wife. Neither of them being a Russian scholar, both have perused the manuscript from the point of view of the reader, leaving the responsibility for accuracy of information and fairness of emphasis to the author, but criticizing unsparingly and improving fundamentally the presentation of the material, its organization, and its comprehensibility. Thanks of the author are due also to Dr. W. O. Sypherd, University Professor of the University of Delaware, and to Dr. Raymond Lindgren of Vanderbilt University, who have offered many helpful suggestions. The assistance of Mr. Laurin Johnson, a graduate student at the University of Pennsylvania, who has contributed much research in the compilation of a number of historical maps, is herewith gratefully acknowledged.

The book does not intend either "to promote friendship" or "to voice warnings." It has no ulterior motive, good or bad. By a presentation of facts, it does hope to reduce ignorance and thereby prejudices of all shadings, and to enable the student of Russian affairs to arrive at conclusions and judgments of his own, based not on propaganda but upon investigation.

TABLE OF CONTENTS

MAPS AND CHARTS

CHAPTER I

BEGINNINGS AND FOUNDATIONS OF RUSSIAN HISTORY

On the steps of the National Archives in Washington are engraved these words: WHAT IS PAST IS PROLOGUE. Taking such a premise very literally, historians have investigated the remotest past, delving back ten, twenty, or thirty thousand years into periods which witnessed climate and geographic conditions in no direct way related to historical times. True, the strata formed in early ages have exercised an economic influence; but the "history" of a people begins properly with the appearance of man, and still more properly with his activities as known by us.

EARLIEST INHABITANTS

Primitive Man. The oldest traces of human life found in present-day European Russia date from the early Stone Age—from a time after the violent heat and cold of the Tertiary Period and the Ice Ages had given way to equable weather. Such traces occur in the regions of Kiev, in the Crimea, and on the banks of the Don River. In the later Stone Age, man, accompanied by his friend the dog, existed also farther north—on the Oka River, on the shores of Lake Ladoga, and even as far north as present-day Archangel. In-

1

struments indicating his cultural level have been found, and they reveal about the same accomplishments that prevailed in other northern European regions during the same era. But tools of the two succeeding periods, the Bronze and the Copper Ages are inferior in design to those discovered in Western Europe. ... gs from the Iron Age, from the seventh century B.C. on. ...se evidence a comparatively low degree of inventiveness ; ...nan of Eastern Europe. On the other hand, trading abili' ... to have supplemented what he lacked in art and craftsm' ...nd intercourse with other parts of the world is known to ' ...:loped. The distribution of objects uncovered in Eas' ... invites speculation as to trade connections which m'' ...i between its peoples and those in the Danube re' ....editerranean area, and in Persia, Babylon, and '' ...rses, and perhaps some agricultural products fr' ....r shores of the Black Sea were exchanged fo: ' ....iles, and other manufactured goods produced b' ...izations encircling the Mediterranean.

7 ... Peoples. Historical accounts are more pre- ...i Age on. Names have been given to the peoples ... regions north of the Black Sea, and we encounter suc- ...iy Cimmerians, Scythians (who are sometimes considered as ...:estors of the Germanic and Slavic races), Sarmatians (who are difficult to distinguish from their predecessors, the Scythians), and Alans, who were living at the beginning of the Christian era. Although these peoples seem to have supplemented their means of life by plowing the earth and cultivating the land, almost all were nomads occupied with hunting, fishing, and warring. All of them were cruel "barbarians" in the eyes of the Greeks and Romans. Their customs were primitive, their lives unstable. Asiatic influences on them proved stronger than is generally surmised, despite the infiltration of Greek ideas through Greek settlements on the northern shore of the Black Sea.

MIGRATIONS. The peoples moved back and forth, east as well as west. No general direction of their movement can be established. A real change occurred with the arrival of Germanic tribes in the first and second centuries A.D. These tribes, led by the Goths, brought more settled ways. They introduced a certain modicum of regional administration, and it is probable that the later capital of Kiev began its rise under them in the fourth century. They were also the first to accept the Christian faith, having been converted to it by Bishop Ulfilas.

But their achievements were destroyed in the fourth century with the arrival of the Huns, who promptly expelled them. The Huns were replaced by Avars in the sixth century, and these in turn by Magyars. Finally, in the eighth century, Turkish tribes—the Khazars—arrived, settling about the mouth of the Volga and farther west. Generally speaking, their upper class adopted the Jewish faith, their lower the Mohammedan; but some became Christians.

THE SLAVS. The movement of the Khazars came to a halt when they encountered Slavic peoples, speaking an Aryan language, who were spreading eastward and northward. Near the Baltic Sea, the Slavs came upon indigenous Lithuanians and, farther east, upon infiltrating Finns. Where the first settlement of these Slavs had been made, it is impossible to say; some students place it in the present-day Ukraine, others in the region of the Carpathian Mountains, still others in the lower Danube. Certainly, like all tribes, they were rovers, and very likely they wandered eastward again after recurring Asiatic invasions had pushed them west. Eventually the Slavs, whose descendants now inhabit Russia, split into three distinguishable groups: the Great Russians, the Little Russians, and the White Russians. Other Slavic tribes—the Wends, Czechs, Poles, and Slovaks—occupied more westerly regions. Still others settled in Serbia, Bulgaria, and Rumania.

The Slavs comprised numerous tribes, such as the Severyane, Polyane, Krivichi, Drevlyane, Dregovichi, and others now as little known. They established themselves around three great centers, Kiev in the southwest, Novgorod in the north, and Tmutorokan in the southeast, and mingled freely with the peoples living in these sections, particularly with the Finns, the Germans, and the Turks.

GEOGRAPHIC INFLUENCES ON RUSSIAN HISTORY

The Land.

PLAINS. In spreading over the southern and western parts of present-day European Russia, the Slavs met with few natural obstacles; vast level plains, which extend from the North Sea to the Pacific Ocean, lay before them and account, in great part, for the continuous "surging" back and forth of so many different races. These plains are generally divided into four belts: (1) the tundras in the Arctic region, frozen much of the year and having scant vegetation in the summer; (2) the forests and marshes south of them down to about 50 to 54 degrees latitude, with pine and birch trees and some cultivable soil; (3) the steppe, with extensive areas of fertile agricultural "black-earth" layers; and (4) a dry alkaline or saline desert zone from the Caspian Sea into the Asiatic highlands.

MOUNTAINS. No mountains interrupt the vast plains. A slight elevation in the center of European Russia marks the source of a mighty river system. A higher range, the Urals (the average elevation being only 1500 feet and the highest mountains hardly more than 5000 feet), connects rather than divides European and Asiatic Russia. Only on the southern borders of Russia do we find real mountains: the Carpathians and a range of majestic proportions, the Caucasus. Such paucity of mountains accounts for the perpetual sweep of strong winds and for the scanty rainfall in Russia. Despite the remarkable fertility of the soil in some regions, cultivation in general is difficult and crops are small, rewarding but insufficiently the work invested by the peasant.

Other Geographic Factors. Aside from the lack of natural boundaries which results from the unbroken extent of the plains, three geographical factors have given direction to the growth of the Russian nation: the forests, the rivers, and the sea.

FORESTS. Although Russia abounds in mineral wealth—including gold, oil, coal, and iron—the greatest wealth has consisted in the timber, which during certain periods in Russian history has been a bargaining point in political alliances and which has dominated Russia's economic welfare.

RIVERS. The rivers have stimulated the Russian trading activities. Having few natural obstructions and being interconnected by nature and by human ingenuity, they have formed the backbone of a superior communication system. In ancient times, the two chief watercourses were explored and used. Trade flowed from the north of Europe through the Baltic to the Neva River, then to Lake Ladoga and thence to Lake Ilmen; here boats and cargoes were put on wheels and the route divided. One course led by portage a short distance overland to the Volga River and down into the Caspian Sea—terminus of routes from Persia, India, and the Far East. The other ed by portage to the Duena River, which was followed to a second ortage connecting with the Dnieper; this river carried the ships to e Dnieper rapids, where a third portage became necessary to reach e Black Sea. From the Black Sea, ships made contact with the st Roman Empire and the rich Mediterranean lands. Goods transported along these routes included furs, honey, wax, timber, and in ancient times slaves, and were exchanged for salt, metals, armor, and luxury articles. This exchange of goods created what was for its period a well-developed public economy, with furs serving often as a monetary unit. It established a system of private property and capitalism at a time when the normal basis of capitalism, the private possession of land, was practically unknown.

THE SEA. The third factor, the sea, was equally important in furthering the growth of Russia, though in a negative way. In relation to maritime access, Russia is the most disadvantageously situated of all large powers. The Grand Duchy of Muscovy, which was to give rise eventually to modern Russia, had no access whatever to the sea. Russia in the nineteenth century, after having expanded for six hundred years, reached a seacoast extending thousands of miles on the Arctic but almost useless for transport purposes. She also secured ports on the Baltic and Black Seas which were suitable for peaceful trade but which lacked free exit. The straits connecting the Baltic with the open sea were dominated by Denmark, those of the Black Sea by Turkey; and England insisted on the independence of these two countries. Thus, strategically, the ports formed a liability rather than an asset. Finally, Russia in the nineteenth century had access to the northern Pacific Ocean in the east, but her ports there were ice-bound much of the year, and the Sea of Japan was dominated by the Japanese empire. The question of open ports was thus first an economic, later a strategic, driving force in Russian history.

THE RUSSIAN PEOPLE

The geography, climate, and landscape constitute a starting point for an interpretation of the "Russian character" upon which eloquent and clever essays have been written—essays that are often cited by historians. The vastness of the country has been brought into relationship with the broad outlook of Russian peoples; the climate, with such character traits as patience and humility; the nature of the soil and forests, with depth and peacefulness; the variety of regions and climates, with openness of mind and innate adaptability. But because of their vagueness and arbitrariness, the truth of such comparisons and generalizations must be seriously challenged; and in the light of fresh knowledge and more recent events, a re-evaluation of the various interpretations is necessary.

In ancient times, the Russian people possessed no cohesion, few common traits, and little state-building force. They were segregated into tribes, clans, or families, and sometimes into combinations of these, "ruled" by princes. Warfare made them a prey to their neighbors. Marriage hardly existed, and incestuous relationships were common. Matriarchal influence predominated as in many a primitive society. After the Germanic peoples, who introduced some elements of European civilization, had been evicted by the Huns, it was Byzantine influence and subsequently Christianity which brought about fundamental changes. Byzantine culture itself was, of course, an admixture of many elements. It suggested to the peoples in Russia a form of government along Asiatic lines, including despotism, bureaucracy, and centralization—the latter emphasizing also the predominance of the state over religious establishments. Maternal influence was broken to such an extent that eventually the women of the upper classes, much as in the Asiatic models, were confined to seclusion in the *terem*. Economic factors, however, precluded the spread of a like movement among the lower social strata.

Russia in the eighth century A.D. thus appears as neither a geographical expression, nor a people, nor a civilization. It is in the ninth century that her historical growth begins to become "one of the most remarkable features in modern history." Her lack of uniformity—geographic, racial, economic, and climatic—became an overruling factor for the future, accounting largely for her reverses and failures, yet ever constituting her greatest asset and strength.*

PROBLEMS

1. Discuss the significance of migrations in Russia's historical development.
2. Discuss the significance of the river system in Russia's economic life.
3. Discuss the position of Russia with regard to access to the sea.

* Careful examination of the map on p. 18 will serve to explain and supplement the discussion in this chapter of geopolitical features and the description of land, tribes, and trade routes.

CHAPTER II

FORMATION OF THE RUSSIAN STATE

Two events mark the importance of the ninth century in Russian history: the work of Cyril and Methodius, and the beginning of the rule of the Northmen, or Varangians.

CYRIL AND METHODIUS

The Slavic Alphabet. Cyril and Methodius were Christian missionaries sent out to preach the gospel to the heathen. Contrary to general assumption, they were not exclusively representatives of the Eastern rite: Methodius, at least, was appointed by the Roman Pope. To accomplish their task, they worked out an alphabet for the West Slavic tongues; for until then none had existed. Cyril, who died in 869, labored among the various Slavic tribes, penetrating as far east as the Crimea and Tmutorokan, where he apparently succeeded in firmly implanting the Christian faith. Methodius devoted most of his energy to the western regions. His main field of activity was Moravia, whither he was sent by the Pope to compete with the missionary work previously begun by Bavarian priests dispatched by the German kings. He tried to introduce the Slavonic liturgy and Orthodoxy, but the Bavarian missions proved the stronger. Ultimately neither achieved anything permanent, for invading Magyars put an end to Christianity in Moravia. Methodius died in 885. The significance of the work of the two clericals consists in their having forged a link for Slavic peoples by introducing an alphabet and composing in the vernacular a text of the gospel.

THE NORTHMEN

Disunity of Slavs. The second gre͏ the rule of the Northmen or Varangians—is reported by t͏ niclers to have been the outcome of disunity among the ͏ es and of their voluntary submission to a strong foreign͏ to lead them to peace, order, and prosperity. This beli͏ seriously to be doubted in its specific facts, is substantiall͏ ͏s to implications. The Slavic tribes were disunited. Their ve͏ ͏ce was threatened not only by foreign enemies, but also by ͏ se geographic conditions and the economic needs of the ͏ All these factors favored, indeed called for, the formation ͏ a state, lawful and unified, as the indigenous Slavic tribes at ͏ age of development had been unable to build up. Trade nec͏ in a land so little advanced on the road to contemporary civi͏ n did not admit the independence of small groups or allow for ͏ed action. The open plains and the length of the waterways su͏ d unification for the sake of engaging in trade with safety.

Rurik. The Northmen were qualifie͏ carry out the task. Their military prowess was known and fel͏ ir disciplinary system and order were respected. Following nat͏ waterways to Lake Ladoga, they had entered Slavic territory i͏ e eighth century and had penetrated it to the shores of the Black ͏ where they threatened the newly formed Khazar state west of the ͏ lga. Furthermore, by participating in many internal wars they had lent their arms to various tribes, and, as in other parts of Europe, the Northmen proved to be not only good warriors but also able administrators and shrewd traders. It is therefore possible that one of their leaders, a rather obscure figure named Rurik, was asked to assume the rulership; for it was realized that union, unless brought about voluntarily, was bound to be effected by force—and perhaps in an undesirable way.

Oleg. Rurik established himself in Novgorod on Lake Ilmen and placed relatives in charge of Pskov, Rostov, and other centers in the north. Two of his—perhaps legendary—companions, Askold and Dir, took possession of Kiev, which was strategically located on the border of the forest and steppe zone in the center of the waterways flowing north and south, and which was within easy reach of the great civilized metropolis Constantinople. They were treacherously murdered in 882 by Rurik's successor Oleg, who recognized the importance of the region and took their place in Kiev. By combining his own dominions in the north with the southern center, Oleg— through a crime—accomplished the task expected of the Northmen and benefited the country. He is regarded as the founder of "Russia," the root "Rus" being derived possibly from the Finnish *ruotsi* (or the German *Ruderer*) or from the name of some Ukrainian princes, and later extended to include the entire country.

ORGANIZATION OF RUSSIA

Influence of the Northmen. The Scandinavian newcomers were soon assimilated. As did the Normans in England after 1066, they formed an upper class which, because of its smallness, was easily absorbed and left few distinct traces. No specific influence on the future destiny of the country was exercised by them. Local government as found by them was retained, and the Scandinavians had to fit themselves into the general structure.

Kiev. Oleg's transfer of central authority to Kiev shifted the balance from Novgorod, with its dependence upon the Baltic Sea, to the south, with its Black Sea connections. Although the steppe country on the Black Sea could not be retained or recovered from invading Asiatic tribes, the mouth of the Dnieper was secured and the whole course of the river brought into "Russian" hands. From Kiev, trade routes were kept open, not only with Constantinople but also with the Volga region.

At this period, the future of Russia for the next three centuries becomes evident—the main tasks ahead consisting of internal consolidation, expansion of trade, and expansion of territory.

Political Consolidation. Consolidation was threatened by the lack of cohesion among the various Slavic tribes spreading from the Baltic to the Black Sea. It was also endangered by the inroads of foreigners (particularly of the Pechenegs, a tribe living in an adjoining territory to the east) although, indirectly, the very existence of the menace contributed also to a rallying of forces. Furthermore, the changes in the relationship with Constantinople, with which wars and treaties alternated, offered serious problems. Oleg had dealt successfully with all these questions; to preserve his work thus became the first important objective.

Trade. Expansion of trade was the next task, congenial to Slavs and Northmen alike. Its direction was south and southeast, neglecting both west and north though good prospects were offered there.

Expansion. Territorial expansion followed the direction of trade, but with little success. Numerous military campaigns were undertaken, leading as far as the Caspian coast, but most frequently directed against the East Roman emperor ruling in Constantinople. In 860 and 907, when thousands of troops were employed, and in 940, when a naval attack was tried, Constantinople itself was endangered. After each war a trade treaty was concluded, a particularly favorable one for Russia being negotiated in 911. In consequence, very lively intercourse between Russia and the Byzantine Empire developed, and just as contact with the Arabian world in the Caucasus region had led to an infiltration of Mohammedan ideas, so the trade with Constantinople led now to considerable knowledge and appreciation of Christian life. The Christian creed with its appeal to the lowly was adopted by many of the poor classes, yet spread also among the highborn. Olga, regent for Oleg's grandson Sviatoslav, was the first in the ruling house and perhaps the first in the entire noble class to profess it.

Sviatoslav. During Olga's regency the thirst for territorial expansion was suppressed, but when Sviatoslav came to the throne in 960 it was revised. His military expeditions took him to the northeast as well as to the southeast, where he subdued Tmutorokan and annexed the Volga mouth. His ambition also led him southwest towards the Danube, to the banks of which he planned to move his capital. His expedition, interrupted by a new invasion of the Pechenegs, who were probably incited by the frightened Byzantine Empire, led to disaster. It had to be given up; and on his return to Kiev, Sviatoslav was killed. His lands were divided among his sons; but they could not agree on the share of each, and internal war broke out which ended with the triumph of an illegitimate son, Vladimir. About 980, Vladimir established himself as sole ruler in Kiev.

Vladimir I. Like his predecessor, Vladimir engaged in ceaseless warfare. He even conquered the Crimea, which, however, he returned to Constantinople after his conversion to Christianity. He built frontier fortifications and improved the internal administration, to which he devoted himself during the later part of his reign. But his fame rests less with these deeds than with the introduction of the Christian faith into Russia. Common faith and resulting common culture belonged to the most important factors which ultimately succeeded in knitting the empire together, and which gave it homogeneity and a clearly defined national identity.

PROBLEMS

1. Discuss the significance of the work of the first Slavic apostles.
2. Discuss the importance of Kiev for the new united Russian Empire.
3. Discuss the relationship of Kiev-Russia with Byzance.

CHAPTER III

INTRODUCTION OF CHRISTIANITY

THE FAITH

Choice of Faith. Vladimir officially introduced Christianity into Russia about 988, and approximately twenty years later he issued the first "Church Statute." According to legend, he examined the faiths of the Jews, of the Roman Catholics, and of the Mohammedans, dispatching ambassadors to study the religious practices of these peoples before he finally accepted the Christian Orthodox faith as practiced in Constantinople. By choosing the Eastern ritual, he not only served the spiritual requirements of his country, but likewise served its political needs through closer contact with the Eastern parts of the Christian world. For centuries to come, Constantinople's culture and politics were to influence Russian life. It was from Byzance that Vladimir chose his wife, sister of the emperor—who in turn hoped to profit in his political schemes by this marriage alliance. From Byzance, Vladimir inherited the concepts underlying the political status of the church. Like the emperors of the East, he was to claim supreme authority over the church; and with this end in mind he promoted the autonomy of the Russian church, which was

12

to be as independent as possible of external influences including that of the Patriarch at Constantinople.

Acceptance of the Faith. Christianity was readily accepted in Russia. No prior faith or culture had existed which filled or could fill the spiritual needs of the people. In the veneration of Dashbog, god of heaven and light, of Perun, god of thunder, and of Stribog, god of winds, adoration of nature had been combined with ancestor cults. No temples and no priests, except Finnish seers and sorcerers, had inspired the people. Slavophil historians have always insisted that Christianity therefore had especial depth and meaning for the Russians, that it found virgin soil unspoiled by any pre-existing culture and was received with particular sincerity. Many historians, however, do not accept this view: they believe that because of the absence of a cultural basis among the people, Christianity failed to be truly understood, that it remained superficial, was wasted in displays and rituals, and left the converts as essentially pagan as before. In any case, many heathen customs were preserved for centuries or infiltrated the new faith which tolerated them.

By order of the grand duke, the inhabitants of Kiev were baptized in 990. Many had been converted to Christianity before this, and a Christian church is said to have existed in Kiev for more than a hundred years. Inhabitants of other regions, particularly those living on the great trade routes and engaged in business, had been in close contact with Christians from other countries; and most of them willingly followed Vladimir's orders. Only in a few regions, chiefly around Novgorod, was resistance offered. There it was overcome by force, though some seem to have taken to the woods rather than submit. On the whole, Vladimir's work was successful; but except in occasional instances, Christianity's true meaning and its demands on the conduct of daily life went unrealized at first and could be absorbed only gradually.

Dogma. Despite negotiations with the Pope in Rome, the Orthodox church derived its tradition from the early Christian church in the East—that region which claimed, through close contact with the origins of the faith, to preserve Christianity in its purest form. All the great church councils of early times had been held there. The West, led by Rome, had gone its own way, emancipating itself in more than material aspects from Eastern domination. Indeed, a definite break occurred less than fifty years after Vladimir's death when, in 1054, ambassadors of Pope Leo IX pronounced the excommunication of the Patriarch of Constantinople. From that time on, the Roman Catholic church seemed not less heretical to the Orthodox than the Waldenses, Albigenses, and Protestants later seemed to the Catholics.

CAUSES FOR CATHOLIC–ORTHODOX SCHISM

The differences between Catholicism and Orthodoxy lie in the political, theological, and sociological fields.

Political Differences. These had arisen before the schism of 1054, but increased thereafter. Jealousies existed between the church at Rome, which enjoyed considerable independence under a Pope, and that at Constantinople, which was under the supervision of an emperor residing close at hand. The position of a Pope or any head of the church was challenged in the East, the Patriarch at Constantinople or later at Moscow never enjoying dominating power. Jurisdiction over various dioceses was claimed by Rome as well as by Constantinople. In the eleventh and twelfth centuries, rival claims were brought forward by the Crusaders from East and West. The outrage of the Fourth Crusade, which instead of regaining the Holy Land attacked Constantinople and forced the Eastern church to submit to the rule of the Roman Popes, aroused the indignation of the Orthodox. In the sixteenth, seventeenth, and nineteenth centuries, invasions and oppression by Poles and French—both Catholic powers —contributed to the old antagonism in Russia.

Theological Differences. These were likewise irreconcilable. Disputes marking different concepts in East and West had arisen long before the separation. In the third century, the date and celebration of Easter were disputed; in the fourth, the divinity of Christ was an issue; in the seventh, the question of the double or single nature of Christ led to a split; and in the eighth and ninth centuries, the use of images was debated. Other points of difference were: celibacy, which was not prescribed (indeed, not even allowed) to the lower clergy of the Eastern church; the use of milk in the first week of Lent; the use of leavened or unleavened bread for communion; indulgences, the teaching of the immaculate conception and of salvation, and the ceremony of baptism; and the profound question of the double procession of the Holy Ghost, the Eastern church maintaining that the Holy Ghost proceeded from God alone and that the inclusion of Christ, the Son, by the Western church was the result of a falsification—of the interpolation of the word *filioque* ("and of the Son") in the creed that had been accepted at Constantinople in 381.

Sociological Differences. A contrast is said to exist between the speculative, philosophical attitude of the Eastern mind and the practical, legalistic attitude of the Western, between the Eastern "stationary tendency" and Western progressivism, between the "intellectual repose and apathy of Asia" and the "savage energy and freedom of Europe."

CHURCH ORGANIZATION

The Orthodox church started and proceeded on a road different from that taken by the Western church and helped to isolate Russia from the rest of Europe. Despite earnest endeavors from Rome during the times of Ivan the Great, Ivan the Terrible, Peter the Great, and Alexander I, no reunion was effected. The Orthodox church fused more thoroughly with the nation and its ambitions were closely linked with those of the people. Unlike the Roman church, the Orthodox church had few desires incompatible with those of Russia's rulers or of the nation; and it was the church which at many critical points in Russian history proved the rallying force for the people and which guided the nation.

Clergy. With the introduction of Christianity, the statues of the old gods were destroyed; and churches were built in Kiev, Suzdal, and other centers. A new clerical class arose, which soon gained secular wealth, lands, and other privileges, including jurisdiction in their own courts.

The earliest Orthodox priests in Russia seem to have come from the shores of the Black Sea and Tmutorokan, where Cyril had introduced Christianity. It is even possible that the first bishops were drawn from there after Vladimir's conversion. But eventually the majority of the clergy came from Bulgaria and Constantinople. They preached in the vernacular—an advantage inasmuch as many difficulties resulting from the impossibility of translating specific Greek terms into Latin could be avoided, but a disadvantage in that a lack of knowledge of Greek and Latin prevented the Orthodox clergy from participating in the intellectual work of the Catholic world.

In 992 the first bishopric was established. In 1037 a Greek bishop was consecrated as the first acknowledged metropolitan of Kiev. The appointment of a Greek, brought about by political circumstances and internal Russian feuds, had untoward consequences on the autonomy of the see at Kiev. When in 1051 Hilarion, a Russian, was created metropolitan without the assent of the Patriarch in Constantinople, he was forced out of office within two years.

Ritual. Religion was at first confined to outward forms. The ritual was carefully evolved, and it impressed the minds of the people—but only in a general and mystical way. The imprint of Christianity was not deep. Therefore, aside from a few attempts to better the conditions of slaves, a change in the spirit of the times did not follow, nor were learned works produced comparable with contemporary achievements of the Catholic world. The illiteracy of the Orthodox clergy and the lack of scriptural knowledge, as well as the emphasis on rites, remained a problem well into the eighteenth century.

Monasticism. Monasticism entered Russia at the time of Vladimir's son, Yaroslav, around 1015. The first famous monk was Anthony, a hermit, who lived in a subterranean cave not far from Kiev. After his death, a monastery was built around his cave, the *Pechersky* (Cave), which in time came to play a prominent role in the national and cultural life of early Russia. The ascetic ideal, a main feature of Oriental monasticism, was alien to the Russian mind. Although strong at the beginning, it was soon superseded by practical aspects. In times of national disaster the monasteries, being strongly built and well provided, constituted important centers of defense.

In the cultural field, the monks achieved as little as the secular clergy. Devoted to mysticism and contemplation, they possessed but small knowledge. No religious literature came into existence; even preaching the gospel did not fall to the task of the monks. They lived in a world of their own, trying to avoid the temptations to which, in the Russian mind, all ordinary men succumbed by virtue of the tasks of daily life. To a certain extent they promoted writing, philosophy, and craftsmanship, but dialectics and discussions of questions of form and of scriptural interpretation overshadowed the arts and sciences.

Worldliness soon entered monastic life. Laymen were admitted and whole families, men, wives, and children, retired with their servants and dogs into cloisters to escape the dangers of the outside world. Through them, all kinds of temptations began to besiege the brothers. Poverty, humility, and chastity were seldom found. Vast riches were amassed, so that in later centuries several monasteries controlled estates with tens of thousands, and even a hundred thousand serfs.

PROBLEMS

1. Discuss the introduction of Christianity into Kiev-Russia.
2. Discuss the main differences between Catholicism and Orthodoxy.
3. Discuss the early Christian organization in Russia.

MAP FOR HISTORY OF EARLY RUSSIA

CHAPTER IV

DECLINE OF KIEV-RUSSIA

PROBLEMS

Vladimir died in 1015, and Sviatopluk "the Accursed" succeeded him as grand prince of Kiev. With Sviatopluk began two centuries or more of grim struggle for power among the various members of the reigning family, a long and evil story interrupted by very few years of comparative quiet. The same question which Sir Bernard Pares in his *History of Russia* asked regarding the intrigues during the times of the successors of Peter the Great—"Who would take this miserable record as the history of a people?"—may be applied to the period of Vladimir's successors. However, the dynastic wars were but a small segment of the general picture; and, owing perhaps to the exclusive interest in it evinced by early chroniclers, the conflict of the princes is still overemphasized today. Behind the struggle loomed more important issues which account for the rivalries and for the ultimate disruption of Kiev-Russia: (1) divergent regional interests among the Baltic area (which includes Novgorod), the Black Sea area (which includes Kiev), the western regions (which include Galicia), and the slowly emerging northeastern region (which includes the upper Volga basin); (2) extraneous influences exercised from the south by Byzance, from the west by Poles, and from the north by Scandinavians; (3) religious questions, e.g., the struggle of Constantinople to secure and maintain supremacy over the Orthodox church in Russia; and (4) economic and social issues resulting from rivalry between, on the one hand, the trade interests of towns with oligarchic municipal governments and, on the other, the autocratic ideas of princes together with the agricultural perspective of landowners and peasants.

THE PRINCES

These problems formed the background for, and gave direction to, the rivalry among the members of the ruling house. The strife of the princes, enhanced by the absence of the concept of primogeniture and by the custom of dividing the land of a deceased ruling prince among all his brothers and their children, mirrored the great economic and geopolitical questions. It was a fearful struggle. Each generation and each line of the ruling house laid claim to its own territory. Patrimonies of all the various princes had to be exchanged in a definite order of precedence upon the death of one member, creating instability and disorder. Ceaseless divisions and subdivisions among the numerous princely offspring rendered impossible fair and efficient government. Breaches of treaties, fratricidal wars, and civil disruption mark the political history of Russia from the eleventh to the thirteenth century. No more than two rulers of Kiev stand out as builders of the empire during the first century after Vladimir's death and personify the growth of the country—Yaroslav the Wise and Vladimir II Monomachus.

Yaroslav the Wise. Yaroslav (1019–54) was a scholar. In 1036 after the death of his brother Mstislav, he reunited Novgorod, Kiev, and Tmutorokan. He founded schools and libraries, had Greek books translated, and was a patron of art and music. He beautified Kiev by building a palace and churches, such as St. George, St. Catherine, and the magnificent St. Sophia. His chief contribution consisted in his furthering of the great codification of Russian law (*Russkaya Pravda*). Customary law was compiled by members of the church and definite rules were introduced regarding slavery, theft, murder, inheritance, usury, and judicial procedure. Execution of the law became largely the task of the church, which found in Yaroslav a loyal protector anxious to promote its prestige.

With his external policies Yaroslav was successful only in some respects. In the south, his expedition against the Greek emperor in

Constantinople failed, but it at least put an end to Russia's constant warfare against Byzance. In the east, the Pechenegs, persistent disturbers of trade and peace, were routed; but they were replaced by other eastern tribes, among whom the Polovtzy, who conquered Tmutorokan around 1100, were to prove no less dangerous than the Pechenegs. In the west, Yaroslav regained Galicia, but stirred up additional strife with the expanding Poles. Nevertheless, so great was Yaroslav's eventual prestige that he was able to conclude marriage alliances for his relatives with the proudest ruling families of Western Europe, namely those of Norway, Sweden, France, various German duchies, and Hungary, and even with the Byzantine emperor.

Vladimir II. Vladimir Monomachus (1113–25), who more than half a century later—after a period of brutal, gruesome feuds and disrupting civil wars—succeeded in reuniting the country, followed Yaroslav's example. He reduced interest rates, furthered trade, and kept peace, except for a number of "crusades" after the European pattern.

DISSOLUTION AND MIGRATION

Renewal of Disorder. After the rule of Vladimir II's insignificant, peaceful son Mstislav I, internal strife revived and again the country was pulled to pieces, each sector gaining a vast amount of independence to the detriment of the whole. Conflicts for predominance among the various princely lines increased once more, and a precarious and unstable system of "balance of power" resulted, by no means serving the cause of peace and order. Byzance, watching events carefully, furthered the dissolution of the potential enemy to the north and with the help of the Patriarch residing at Byzance, who also established a separate archbishopric in Novgorod, not infrequently exercised a powerful adverse influence in internal Russian affairs. The tasks for which the Slavic tribes had once "called in" Rurik, namely defense of the trade routes, negotiations of trade treaties with foreign powers, and composition of internal discord, were thus no longer fulfilled by the later rulers. Disunion resulted, and every section was compelled to seek its own protection and advantage.

Formation of Classes. Changes in Russian society paralleled the decline of political consolidation. Classes developed. An entire caste was formed of the numerous descendants of the ruling houses; another of their guardsmen who, first employed as bodyguards, were to become eventually the formidable "boyar" class. A lesser nobility was recruited from small landowners, and a fourth stratum was formed by the burghers of the towns. The peasants themselves divided into classes, some free, some half free or indentured, and many slaves—the last in steadily increasing numbers. Small farms disappeared, giving room to princely estates.

Importance of Towns. Under the prevailing conditions, towns alone preserved order. Through their general assemblies of all freemen, the *vieche,* they contributed what progress Russia achieved in the twelfth, thirteenth, and fourteenth centuries. Pereslavl, Novgorod, Polotsk, Pskov, Smolensk, Rostov, and Suzdal gained steadily in importance as trading and cultural centers. They came to form the backbone of the country, imposing their will upon princes and counteracting the disruptive trends. The city of Kiev, however, was gradually reduced to the position of but one of many important places, and after three hundred years of predominance even this position was lost in the thirteenth century.

Decline of Kiev. This decline of Kiev, and with it of the Russian empire which had centered around it, became a determining issue in Russian history. A new empire had to be built, far from the fertile southern Russian region and the Dnieper basin. It was the advantageous location of Kiev at the crossroads of the waterways and on the fringe of the black-soil district which had brought her wealth and position; these same factors, inciting the jealousy of others, were also those to bring ruin. The causes for Kiev's fall may be summarized as follows: (1) the inroads of covetous foreigners on this richest region of Russia, mainly of the Polovtzy, who preyed upon the Kiev traders; (2) internal warfare involving Kiev as the disputed object of rival princes, which led to destruction, famine, and in two instances the sack of the city; (3) depopulation as a result of war and lowered prosperity; (4) deforestation, depriving Kiev of protection as well as of wealth; and (5) reorientation of trade as a result of the decline of Kiev's principal trade partner and cultural support, Constantinople, and the rise of Western trade centers.

Emigration. In view of these circumstances, emigration took place, partly in a westwardly and partly in a northeastwardly direction. In the west it led to Galicia, in the northeast to the region of the upper course of the Volga and its tributaries. It was in this latter area that the foundation for a new commonwealth was laid; it was there that the towns of Suzdal, Vladimir, and finally Moscow (first mentioned in 1147) were to assume the role once played by Kiev.

Suzdal was the first to gain the place of capital after the grand princes moved from Kiev. Vladimir near the Volga was the second, when energetic and autocratic Andrew Bogolubsky, resenting the tutelage of Suzdal's powerful and ambitious *vieche,* moved the political capital there in 1157.

EFFECTS OF NORTHEASTWARD MIGRATION

Territorial Losses.   Both Suzdal and Vladimir were less favorably located than Kiev had been. The princes here were far from the center of Russian realms and were unable to circumvent the secession of various provinces. Within two centuries, almost all the western parts of Russia were lost. Galicia gained autonomy only to be divided in due time, in the period from 1339 to 1352, between neighboring Poland and Hungary. Chernigov and Pereslavl followed; and finally Volhynia was lost and incorporated by its neighbor, Lithuania. About 1400, "Russia" comprised no more than the land within a radius of roughly two hundred and fifty miles around Suzdal, and was called "Muscovy" after the princely residence of Moscow.

Economic Disadvantages.   Yet, loss of territory was but one result of the shift northeastward. The country suffered also economically, because the forest-belted upper course of the Volga offered no economic opportunities equal to those on the lower Dnieper. The soil yielded less, and the people lived more primitively. They were poorer and consequently unable to help create by taxes a strong and healthy community. With the exception of Novgorod and Pskov, hardly any town of importance could be supported in a region where trade was reduced and where difficulties in agriculture caused scarcity of foodstuffs. But Novgorod and Pskov were difficult for the rulers of Suzdal or of Vladimir and Moscow to control. Their pride in their oligarchic republican constitutions, combined with their spirit of independence and their relations with the Swedes and Germans, removed them from effective Muscovite government. Their *vieche,* well suited to a progressive urban society, formed a bulwark against the autocratic tendencies of Muscovite princes.

Cultural Decline.   Culturally, the change was accentuated by the severance of the direct lines of communication with Constantinople and the rich Mediterranean basin. The long routes thither were cut by nomadic tribes roaming over southern Russia, and connections with the Baltic countries via Novgorod were insufficient and could not compensate for the loss in the south. Artisanship, highly developed in jewelry, carving, needlework, and many other trades, began to deteriorate, as the long winters in the northern regions afforded the peasants enough time to manufacture their simple household goods and so deprived the skilled artisans in the towns of their markets. The "land of the towns," harboring science, arts, and crafts, was transformed into a primitive "land of villages."

Racial and Social Changes. The Russian people themselves were transformed. When moving northeastward, they invaded territory largely settled by Finns, with whom they intermixed, forming the "Great Russian" type as opposed to the "Little Russian" in the Ukraine. Later, immigrants arrived from Germany, Hungary, and Poland, who erected villages of their own and brought fresh blood and different ideas and institutions. Though feudalism in its Western sense was never fully developed in Russia and though the feudal concepts of personal relationship and honor were nowhere introduced, many feudal institutions found entrance, and the landowning aristocracy increased its independence. The poor people had, perforce, to appeal to the strong for protection and to offer their work in exchange. The strengthened nobles, the boyars, formed their own councils, the "Duma of Boyars," which supplemented the council of the church hierarchy. Thus, a first and a second estate came clearly into being; but in Russia they were to pave the way for autocracy rather than for Western diets or popular representations.

External Dangers. Andrew Bogolubsky, grand duke of Suzdal and Vladimir, who profited from the new trends and established an autocratic government, was murdered in 1174. He had accomplished little, but his reign stood out as an indication of a different development that was to take shape in the northeast. His successors devoted themselves once more to feuds and rivalries, heedless of the growing menace from without. Indeed, in the west, enemies were rising in the persons of the Poles and the Teutonic Knights, who began to settle the Baltic seashore, and—far more ominous—in the east the Tartar empire of Genghis Khan emerged as a new and rapidly expanding power.

PROBLEMS

1. Discuss the importance of Yaroslav the Wise and the *Russkaya Pravda*.
2. Discuss the causes and effects of the decline of Kiev.
3. Compare the upper Volga basin and Kiev Russia as to their geographical and political advantages.

CHAPTER V

RUSSIA UNDER TARTAR DOMINATION

COMING OF THE TARTARS

Tartar Invasion. In 1223 the Tartars, who had extended their rule over much of Asia, began to expand farther westward, entering what is called Europe but what in reality is only a part of the Eurasian plains. They menaced first the Polovtzy, who, despite their own frequent penetrations into Russia, had formed a valuable buffer state against Asiatic nomads and who therefore received Russian support against the Tartars. In the Battle of the River Kalka, north of the Sea of Azov, the combined armies were routed (1223 or 1224). Although in spite of their victory the Tartars retreated, the peril for Russia remained ever present and in vain did the church plead for preparedness and internal unity.

Tartar Conquest. The feared resumption of Tartar invasions occurred about twelve years later when, after the death of Genghis Khan, the Russian lands were granted by his successor to Batu Khan, a grandson of Genghis. Vladimir, Pereslavl, and Chernigov were captured in 1238, and Kiev in 1240. Galicia was taken, and the Tartars entered Poland and ultimately invaded Germany by way of Silesia.

Of all the important Russian centers, Novgorod alone was temporarily spared, for the vast forests and swamps in the north hindered the advance of the equestrian invader. But as Novgorod was being simultaneously menaced from the west, she could not long escape Tartar domination. In 1240 it was the Swedes who attacked from the west and who were barely turned back on the Neva by the hard-won victory of Alexander, Duke of Novgorod. Two years later it was an army of Teutonic Knights (who had settled in Livonia and wished to extend their rule) that attacked and was beaten back on the ice of Lake Peipus by the same Alexander—now surnamed "Nevsky." Again, from 1243 to 1245 it was the Lithuanians who relentlessly sent invading armies into Novgorod's territory. Consequently, the resources of the city were so exhausted that, to avoid further warfare, Tartar sovereignty had to be recognized.

TARTAR RULE

Tartar Administration. Batu established himself on the steppes between the Aral Sea and the Black Sea, with his capital Sarai on the lower part of the Volga. In the name of the Khan in Central Asia, yet in reality semi-independently, Batu, as ruler of the "Golden Horde," exercised sovereign rights over Russia. To show his power, he marched his troops through the country from time to time, allowing them to commit every kind of atrocity. All Russians were compelled to register, in order to fulfill the two chief purposes of Tartar sovereignty: (1) to collect in tribute a heavy poll tax, and (2) to raise recruits for the Tartar army. In addition, the Tartars reserved for themselves the right to confirm the various Russian rulers, particularly the grand prince. As a rule, Russian princes were made to appear in person before the Khan to receive their appointments.

Significance of Tartar Invasion. The Tartars maintained sovereignty in Russia for almost two hundred and fifty years. Their hold was based on the efficiency of their financial administration, and their system of assessment and finance was hard. Themselves influenced by Chinese civilization, they introduced Eastern bureaucratic methods, with Armenians, Jews, and Chinese monopolizing the offices of tax collectors. The political, cultural, and economic history of this period is full of complexities. It does not break with the past, nor does it consist of elements wholly alien to Russian needs; yet it accentuates certain trends in Russian history which otherwise might have been submerged. From a present-day point of view, the significance of Tartar domination may be considered as fivefold:

CONTACT WITH THE EAST. Influences from the East increased. Tartar words and ideology found entrance into the Russian language. Asiastic customs were imitated—as, for example, regarding the position of women. Cruelty towards slaves and the conquered increased. Bureaucratic ideas and the Eastern financial system were eagerly and permanently adopted.

LOSSES IN THE WEST. Western kingdoms began to absorb Russian lands. Some inroads into Russian territory came from the Poles and the Lithuanians. The Poles expanded further into Galicia and Volhynia, where their ruthless aristocracy and haughty clergy uprooted Russian customs and religion and enslaved the population. The Lithuanians spread their rule southeastward, conquering during the fourteenth century Polotsk, Kiev, and in 1395 even Smolensk. Under their capable ruler Olgerd they penetrated along the Dnieper to the Black Sea, which they reached in 1363, thus overpowering much of Little Russia. Again, their roving expeditions led them almost to the gates of Novgorod and Moscow. Their conquest might have led (since they were heathen) to their adoption of the Orthodox faith, to the Russianizing of Lithuania, and to a healthy union of the two countries. Unfortunately, however, the extinction of the royal line in Poland led in 1386 to a different merger: that of Lithuania and Catholic Poland; thus, the Russian parts of Lithuania were combined with Poland and shared the fate of Galicia and Volhynia.

Other inroads came from the side of the Swedes, the Danes, and the Germans. In 1240, under Birger Jarl, the Swedes not only undertook the crusade against schismatic Novgorod which ended in their defeat on the Neva, but also invaded and subjected Finland and Karelia. The Danes conquered Estonia, west of Novgorod. The Germans—led by merchants, by priests, and finally by the Teutonic Knights—established themselves in Livonia on the shores of the Baltic, where they founded Riga, one of the great medieval ports, and gained control of the Duena River, one of the two great Russian waterways that connected northern Europe with the Black and Caspian seas. In 1348 the Teutonic Knights bought Estonia from the Danes, and for centuries thereafter they controlled Russia's only direct outlet to the sea.

Germans, mainly through commercial connections of the great Hanseatic League, also secured a dominating position in Novgorod, where their merchants built factories and staple places. Their presence emphasized the special character of Novgorod and partly removed it from the Russian orbit. Typical Russian art, which had flourished, deteriorated; but the political and economic life rapidly progressed along Western lines. A constitution, not unlike those of the free German Hanseatic towns, established equality of all freemen before the law, guaranteed fundamental rights within the hierarchy of classes, maintained the *vieche,* and raised standards through merchant and artisan guilds. Commerce flourished, and the town's wealth, power, and prosperity were unequaled in all Russia.

ASCENDANCY OF THE CHURCH. Not only was the position of the church maintained, its national prestige was immensely enhanced. The Orthodox Christian faith remained the strongest uniting tie among the Russian people. Despite its initial opposition to the Tartars, the church soon submitted and began to co-operate with them, making use of their religious tolerance. The Tartars in turn recognized the value of the church and granted it exemption from taxes. The metropolitan see was permanently removed from Kiev in 1299; Galicia—then independent—formed a separate diocese; and the metropolitan moved to Tartar-dominated Russia, choosing Moscow as his permanent abode in 1325. Although the schism resulting from Galicia's separation weakened the church and necessitated internal reforms, the church proved an effective influence in holding the country together and in nurturing the hope for independence. New cloisters were founded, among them the Trinity (*Troitsa*) monastery north of Moscow, which fell heir to the Pechersky tradition and prestige.

The position of the Orthodox church was threatened during the later part of Tartar domination, not by the victors, but rather from within. In 1438 a council convened at Florence at the direction of the Roman Pope and was attended by the Patriarch and other Orthodox bishops. Without special authorization they proposed the re-establishment of Christian unity and, accepting Cardinals' hats, acknowledged the supremacy of the Pope. Their action was disavowed by the majority of the Orthodox; and upon their return, after celebrating mass according to the Latin version, they were punished and banned. The cause of Christianity thus suffered, but the national aspirations of the Russians were furthered through the maintenance of the national character of their church. Soon thereafter, in 1453, the fall of Constantinople isolated the Russian church almost completely. Subsequently, it was to play a prime role in the liberation of Russia from the Tartar yoke.

RISE OF MOSCOW. Moscow gradually increased its prestige as Russia's leading city. With the loss of the western provinces, the eastern regions and their trade routes—for which Moscow was the natural terminus—assumed greater importance, and a unification process took shape around Moscow. The city, besides gaining economic position, strengthened itself as a strategic center through the construction of the Kremlin, Russia's strongest fortress of the period. Moscow's dominance was consolidated at the expense of the west, which was left to itself. Authority over Russia's political institutions —which the people of Kiev had once controlled but which, oppressed and dissatisfied, they no longer had an interest in maintaining— passed into the hands of Moscow. The transfer of the metropolitan see to Moscow added immensely to the prestige of the city. Surrounding territories were absorbed: first Pereslavl, then Nizhnii Novgorod, temporarily Tver in 1368, and even Novgorod in 1385.

RISE OF THE GRAND DUKES. Not only Moscow itself, but also its ruling house, emerged as a potent force for the future. Alexander Nevsky (1252–63) had recognized the necessity of co-operating with the Tartars and had gone to the Golden Horde and offered his submission. His successors imitated him and gained vast concessions in exchange, the most important of which was the right to collect in their own realms the taxes for themselves and for the Golden Horde. They also contrived to avoid Tartar interference in their political schemes and they largely suppressed the system of appanages. Under this system, each younger member of a princely house would claim a vast amount of autonomy for himself in his personal domains, and after his death every one of his heirs would claim the same autonomy over his share of the inheritance. For the sake of greater unity, this procedure was now suppressed. Furthermore, the grand dukes of Moscow, imitating the example of other provinces, subdued the minor nobility and then annexed the surrounding territories, securing for themselves a place more firmly entrenched than any Kievan grand prince had ever enjoyed. Although the Tartars, who cherished the principle of *divide et impera,* were not interested in this unification process, they did not dare oppose it owing to the diligence and punctuality of the grand dukes in collecting and paying taxes.

DECLINE OF THE TARTARS

Role of the Muscovite Rulers. Two rulers of Muscovy stand out for their achievements: Ivan I (Ivan Kalita, 1325–41), thrifty, industrious, just, and peaceful, whose diplomacy and wealth combined stimulated the willingness of other Russian princes to submit to him; and Dimitri (1359–89), who successfully defended the country against the Lithuanians and increased Moscow's prestige. It was Dimitri who made the first effective attempt to throw off the Tartar yoke—after a series of earlier attempts had failed between 1262 and 1327—and secured a politically promising (though militarily useless) victory over the Tartars on the Don in 1380. Tartar dominance was not broken, because of the rise of another great conqueror, the famous Tamerlane; nevertheless, Tartar prestige suffered materially, for Russia acquired practical advantages through reduction of the tribute. Dimitri, called "Donskoy" for his victory on the Don, further promoted the growth of Muscovy by abandoning the system of dividing the country between the heirs and by introducing for his dynasty the law of primogeniture.

Role of the City of Moscow. The personal shrewdness of Moscow's rulers furnishes only an incomplete explanation of that city's persistent rise to power. The true and fundamental causes were economic and political, resulting from the position of Moscow on the Volga highway, from the collection of dues for use of the waterways, from trade in corn, honey, and wax, from the increase of a taxable population, and from the support of the Khans with the co-operation of the church. Moreover, Moscow benefited by her strategic location in the heart of a region yet to be cultivated and organized. Even independent Novgorod could be dominated as a consequence of Moscow's control over the city's hinterland and sources of supply. Finally, an accidental element should be mentioned —longevity in the house of the princes of Muscovy. From 1389 on, a rare stability of government was achieved; and the bane of earlier times, devastating feuds among the princes, was eliminated. Over a period of practically two hundred years, until 1584, Moscow was ruled by only five princes, who gave a previously unknown continuity to governmental affairs.

Twilight of Tartar Rule. In the meantime, owing to disorders and disunion, the Tartars' might waned. The Battle of the Don was but one evidence of their weakened state. By the middle of the fifteenth century, Moscow, which had been besieged several times but only once taken and sacked, could look forward to the moment when she might hopefully defy Tartar rule. The introduction of latest artillery, ever since considered a weapon of prime importance to the Russian army, did much to move the balance in Moscow's favor. Had it not been for Tamerlane, the Tartar yoke might have been shaken off in the fourteenth century. As it happened, final victory was delayed until the times of Ivan III, later called "the Great," who ascended the grand ducal throne in 1462.

PROBLEMS

1. Discuss Tartar influences in Russia.
2. Trace the territorial changes of Russia under Tartar Rule.
3. Discuss the rise of Moscow as the leading Russian center.

CHAPTER VI

THE ERA OF IVAN THE GREAT

SIGNIFICANCE OF IVAN'S RULE

Breakdown of Medieval System. The reign of Ivan the Great (1462–1505) was a period of fulfillment rather than of inception or transition. His times saw the independence of the many small principalities under the appanage system terminated; they witnessed local self-government, as exemplified by the *vieche* system, reduced to complete submission. In his reign towns and trade, the pride of old Russia, gave way to a primitive agricultural society which, in turn, led to a social revolution in reverse: the peasant, free in early Russia, now became a sharecropper and a serf. The peasant who wished to be free had now to leave the land, abandon cultivation of the soil, and make his way to frontier regions; there, after Tartar example, he might devote himself as a "Cossack" to hunting, fishing, and the less selfish activity of defending the country. Muscovy emerged triumphant from her long and relentless struggle for leadership among the Russian people. Tartar rule collapsed, but recovery of the western parts of the country had to be renounced at least temporarily. The history of these parts was not to merge with that of the rest of the country until the seventeenth century. And so, a development extending over more than a century closes with Ivan III.

Personal Influence of Ivan. The grand duke himself was an able tool of the times. Son of Basil II, who had emerged victorious —though with the loss of his eyesight—from the last vicious family struggle over the throne, Ivan had learned patience and prudence. Slow in his decisions to the extent of inviting suspicion of cowardice, he moved stealthily and doggedly, while his thriftiness provided him with the necessary means to attain his ends. Nevertheless, his personal influence on internal affairs of Russia was limited, as greater forces than those let loose by a grand duke were at work. Only upon external changes did he exercise a substantial—and in many respects an unfortunate—influence.

INTERNAL CHANGES

Reduction of Nobility. Domestically, the most important issue consisted in the final metamorphosis of the upper class. The grand duke of Muscovy succeeded in establishing his hegemony. The power of the independent princes was broken; they had to recognize his leadership and obey him. Together with the boyars and a number of Tartar rulers who came to serve under the Muscovite grand duke, they began to form a new upper class, whose privilege was land-ownership and whose duty was military service. Their lands were granted them by the ruler and their rights did not include that of inheritance, except when coupled with the heir's obligation of continued service to the grand duke. This combination of ownership and service persisted as a characteristic of the Russian upper class well into the eighteenth century. It had considerable advantages, but it also brought grave dangers. Care of the land suffered because of the duties connected with its possession. Jurisdictional and administrative functions passed from the hands of ruling princes into those of landowners. In addition, land grants created a shortage of land and forced grand dukes who wanted to remunerate warriors onto the road of war and conquest.

New Law Code. These changes in the class structure found their reflection in a revised law code, the *Sudebnik,* which was based on Yaroslav the Wise's *Russkaya Pravda*. It embodied the principles of recently developed customary law and provided both criminal and civil codes.

Growth of Serfdom. As a result of the decline of the independent princes and the rise of the boyar class with its privileges, the position of the free peasant was undermined. Though he had never "owned" his lands, the *usus fructi* had been his; but now this right was curtailed—following the example of feudal Europe—by the new landowning class. Part of the crops and part of the labor were claimed by them. There was no other way for the peasant to escape the new burden than to move away into uninhabited regions. Legally, he still had the right to do so; but the exercise of his right became difficult. Colonization of the northeastern region, which had attracted the people from the Ukraine and had offered them a haven of freedom, was over and land had become scarce. Furthermore, landowners, alleging neglect of their estates, could put every obstacle into the way of a peasant's departure. In addition, financial burdens began to impede the movements of the peasant; in order to settle in the few fertile regions left unclaimed, he needed funds which he had to borrow at the risk of debt servitude.

Other factors, too, hindered his movements. Ivan had adopted from the Tartars an efficient system of collecting taxes and insisted on joint tax liability of each village community (*mir*); the community, therefore, was interested in keeping the services of each individual tax-paying member. The taxes, imposed according to the productivity of the soil, were heavy; in lean years they surpassed the peasant's ability to pay and necessitated seasonal loans which endangered freedom. Moreover, peasants were obliged to provide a specified number of recruits for the army. All these burdens were doubly heavy because of the lack of legal machinery to protect the individual against excessive requirements.

Thus—at a time when in Western Europe towns were multiplying, a modern financial system was taking shape, and serfdom was waning—bondage, primarily intended to make the peasant repay voluntarily or involuntarily contracted debts, was gaining a hold in Russia. Sometimes the burdens imposed by one landowner were so unbearable that the peasant resorted to selling himself in bondage to another from whom he expected better treatment. In each case, he began to work for his creditor under one of two plans: the *obrok* system, which implied the payment of a fixed sum in kind or money, or the *barchina* system, which meant the rendering of services (*corvée*) as demanded by the landowner. In this manner serfdom grew, although the final step, compulsory return and punishment of fugitives, was not taken until almost a century later.

Reform of Clergy. Simultaneously with the changes affecting the nobility and the peasants, a serious crisis confronted the clergy.

Having resisted the attempts at union made at the Council of Florence, the church was threatened by new dangers over the question of secularization of church lands. This measure (wholeheartedly wel comed by the grand duke, who needed land for distribution among his service-nobility) was proposed by reformers within the church who feared the evil influence of worldly possessions upon the spiritual level of the whole institution. The bitterly debated question affected political matters, as it was tied up with Ivan's succession plans, but eventually the clergy succeeded in having the whole problem postponed.

Establishment of Sovereignty.

END OF TARTAR RULE. The formal political sovereignty of the Tartars was ended in 1480. Accounts mention a battle on the River Oka, where the cowardly grand duke, pressed by the clergy whose bishops offered to lead the troops themselves, finally shook off the Tartar yoke. As a matter of fact, through negotiations with unruly elements within the Golden Horde and with neighbors surrounding the Tartar state, Ivan had long since undermined its power; and although armies confronted each other on the Oka, no battle was fought. Winter benefited the Russians and the Tartars retreated, many of them deserting to the Russian side. No longer was tribute paid to the Golden Horde. The Turks seized the opportunity and subjected the Crimea. Within less than twenty years, the Golden Horde disappeared. The pressure of Tartar people, however, constituted a danger and an annoyance for another three centuries.

RISE OF TSARISM. In his work and ambitions, Ivan III was supported by his second wife, Sophia, niece of the last Byzantine emperor. She was married to him by the Pope in Rome—where, after the fall of Constantinople in 1453, she had spent her youth. The Pope hoped, though in vain, that her marriage would contribute to a reunion of the Catholic and Orthodox churches. As a descendant of the great East Roman imperial family, Sophia was the driving power behind Ivan's rise to supremacy and behind Russia's claim to Constantinople's heritage. It was she who most violently opposed recognition of suzerainty and the payment of tribute to barbarians. Likewise, it was she who enticed her husband to shake off the tutelage of the haughty nobility. Since Constantinople had fallen to the Turks, she also led him to lay claim to the title of "Tsar" (believed to be derived from *Caesar*), which implied supreme worldly and spiritual power. She made him assert supreme rights over the Russian church, independent now from Byzance and separated from Kiev, which in 1358 had received a metropolitan of its own. Sophia also introduced Italian artists and tried to spread to Russia the glory of the Italian Renaissance which she had witnessed in Rome; but in this endeavor she failed, largely for lack of an educated nobility and middle class which in other countries proved the chief benefactors of artists and appreciators of their work.

EXTERNAL POLICIES

Poland.   In his external policies, Ivan's attention centered on the west. In the east, he confined himself to the addition of Perm on the road to the Urals; in the south, to a vague suzerainty over the Tartar state of Kazan; in the north, to the incorporation of the valuable and strategically important province of Tver. But his main objective was in the west: the curbing of Polish ambitions.

Ivan clearly recognized in Poland the implacable foe of Russia and he realized the impossibility of reconciling her aggressive policies with the growth of Muscovy. It was Poland which rendered hopeless the reunion of the lost western Orthodox provinces with Russia, which blocked a durable peace, and which by her ambitions forced a series of wars upon the Tsar, involving at the same time Swedes, Teutonic Knights, and Lithuanians. This multilateral struggle against Poland became the key to Ivan's foreign relations as well as to those of his successors. It was also Poland which caused Russia's attack on her neighbor, wealthy and powerful Novgorod—an attack that was to lead to the acquisition and unwise destruction of the most important Russian outlet to the Baltic Sea.

Novgorod.   Novgorod had not shared in the Russian trend toward an agricultural society, neofeudalism, and serfdom. Because of her advantageous location, the town had developed a special character strongly influenced by the West. All her inhabitants were free, and classes of their own had arisen: the boyars; the rich merchants, among whom there were the great Hanseatic exporters and importers with their manifold monopolies and privileges; a middle class of merchants with their guilds; the small tradesmen; the laborers; the free peasants; and the sharecroppers. The institution of the *vieche* still flourished, although dominated by boyars and the wealthy.

Naturally, there was considerable disunion within the town. The Orthodox opposed the Catholics; the moneyed aristocracy, the artisans; various parties of the nobility were pitted against one another; and the class struggle between rich and poor was pronounced. But the struggle for power between those favoring Catholicism and Poland and those adhering to Orthodoxy and Muscovy was the most ominous, as it involved the larger issues at stake between the two great neighbors. Moscow's ascendancy had been noticeable for several decades. Governors sent by the grand dukes to Novgorod had exercised increasing control, and through Moscow's dominance over the city's hinterland Novgorod had sunk economically into considerable dependence. The advantage would be lost to Russia, were the Poles, and with them Catholicism, to win in the internal struggle of Novgorod.

It was therefore strategic necessity in the campaign against Poland, and not only economic issues or desire for aggrandizement, which prompted Ivan's decision to incorporate the town. The true significance of Novgorod was unfortunately misunderstood by him, as he failed to see the commercial advantages which he could derive from it as a flourishing city with an exit to the Baltic Sea.

In view of the political split within the city, the conquest itself involved no military feat. In 1471, following the first attack, the city submitted to jurisdiction, taxation, payment of a war contribution, and recognition of tsarist sovereignty. From 1476 to 1477, when the assault on the city was renewed under pretext of revenge for its neglect to style the Tsar in the correct way, complete subjection took place. The people were evacuated by the thousands, deported to central Russia, and replaced by settlers from Muscovy. Trade was ruined to the extent that fifteen years later, in 1492, a new trading place had to be founded at Ivangorod, opposite Narva. In 1496, Ivan made his crowning mistake—the Hansa merchants were treacherously seized in Novgorod, their factories closed, their commerce ruined. Thus, much to the detriment of the whole country, its finest harbor was wrecked.

BASIL III

The war with Poland which had brought about the fate of Novgorod was continued after Ivan's death by his son Basil III (1505–33). Despite setbacks such as the defeat at Orsha in 1514, he pursued the path taken by his father. In 1510, without resorting to military measures, he put an end to Pskov's independence. In 1514, he regained Smolensk from the Poles, and three years later incorporated Ryazan. In the south, he protected his lands by strengthening the frontier fortifications against pressure from the remaining Tartars. Thus he consolidated the work of his father, adding new territory to Moscow. Internally, he continued the reduction of princes and boyars, a task which under his son Ivan IV led to the establishment of complete autocracy.

PROBLEMS

1. Discuss the changes in Russian social structure during Ivan the Great's rule.
2. Discuss the expansion of Russia under Ivan the Great.

CHAPTER VII

EMERGENCE OF MODERN RUSSIA

IVAN THE TERRIBLE

Personal Character. The evaluation of Ivan IV's importance and of his place in history has undergone many changes. At the present time, historians, particularly those of Russia, seem inclined to assign him a most prominent role in Russia's past. In view of the multiplicity of his achievements and of the directions of his endeavors, which anticipated future Russian development, research confirms such interpretation.

Ivan's personality is intriguing, and could have been a challenge to the dramatic powers of a Shakespeare or Schiller. As with other great Russian rulers, particularly Peter I and Alexander I, two natures struggled in him for dominance. The resulting contradictions made his own life as miserable as that of his subjects. Ivan was a curious combination of arrogance and humility, of brutality and mercy, of ignorance and scholarship. Lack of discipline or self-control (a result of neglect during his youth) and an animal spirit and craftiness on the one hand, coupled with great intellect and tenderness on the other, made him a barbarian, but a barbarian with admirable qualities. Throughout his life, one or the other side of his nature ruled him; and

39

this duality characterizes his personal development as well as his political career.

Opening of Reign. In 1533, at the age of three, Ivan succeeded his father on the throne. The regency was first in the hands of his mother, then in those of the two princely families Shuisky and Belsky. Unloved, Ivan spent an unhappy youth until he reached the age of thirteen; then the Shuisky regency was overthrown. At sixteen he had himself crowned "Tsar," thus laying claim to all the myth, glory, and privileges which that title implied but which neither his grandfather nor his father had been successful in maintaining. Ivan, "the Terrible," was to succeed. At seventeen, he married and took the government into his own hands. During the sixteenth century, when youth ruled everywhere, opened all doors, and was recognized by all, Ivan's youthfulness implied neither lack of maturity nor lack of respect from others.

As his chief advisers, Ivan appointed two men of comparatively humble origin: Daniel Sylvester, a priest and confessor of the Tsar, and Alexis Adashev. Their influence, though overweening, was fortunate for Ivan and the country. The period of their administration— i.e., until about 1560—was the most fruitful of Ivan's reign.

INTERNAL ACCOMPLISHMENTS

Establishment of Autocracy. Ivan accomplished the reduction of the power of the nobility and boyars, bringing them under the law as represented by the will of the sovereign. On the Continent, this task was not accomplished until the times of the absolutism of Louis XIV. Ivan's autocracy meant protection of the weak against the nobles. Unlike the policies of later French kings, it gained popular support, which found expression through popular assemblies, the *Zemsky Sobor*. A Zemsky Sobor was not a constitutional assembly but an advisory body, composed of military men, landlords, officials, and traders nominated by the government, and of delegates chosen at random from the provinces and Moscow and vicinity. The Zemsky Sobor was not a democratic assembly in the modern sense, and since there was no recognized Third Estate it could not develop into one; nevertheless it somehow reflected the will of the people, proved a support of the autocrat, and shared in the responsibility for the execution of orders.

Formation of Service-Nobility. The nobility was made part of the new autocratic system by the method of land grants, which created a large and wealthy military caste dependent upon the Tsar. The nobles enjoyed their possessions (*pomestie*) as long as they served the ruler. Private landholdings (*vochina*) whose possession was not coupled to service but constituted outright property of the holder became rare, and likewise the remnants of the petty princes with their small independent domains were reduced to insignificance. Several times, once during an illness of the Tsar, another time when one of the highest noblemen, Prince Kurbsky, deserted to Poland, the princes and boyars tried to escape their fate. But Ivan outplayed them. In 1564, in a daring countermove, he quit his palace in Moscow and retired to the monastery of Alexandrovsk, which he had founded and which he loved as a special place of refuge from his daily tasks. The people promptly clamored for their "indispensable" Tsar and recalled him—a summons not obeyed until his conditions were fulfilled and the subjection of the nobility could proceed without further hindrance.

Extension of Serfdom. In line with the compulsion of the nobility under a service system, the social status of the peasant was reduced. It is true that land was given to him at the expense of the aristocracy; but he, like the nobleman, had first of all to serve the state. Therefore, his attachment to the soil was strengthened, and his movements were restricted by regulations regarding his recovery if he became a fugitive.

New Law Code. In 1550, a revision of the law code was ordered. The work was entrusted to the supervision of Alexis Adashev, who was also made director of a "Ministry for Receiving Petitions." In the code, provisions were made to check corruption, particularly in the law courts, by introducing a jury system. Although the work was not wholly satisfactory, a sounder basis for administrative duties was laid through modernizing the laws and providing the people with a voice against injustice.

A number of other ministries and departments were created, but because of their overlapping functions, their dilatory work, and the unreliability of their officials, they proved of but little service to the people.

New Church System. At the same time, the work on revision of church practices was continued. In an attempt at reform parallel to that in the rest of Europe, church councils were convened between 1547 and 1554. These dealt with questions of ritual, morals, jurisdiction, and social institutions; but in the religious field no more was accomplished than the establishment of a printing shop for clerical books (the first of its kind in Russia). The needed inner moral and spiritual change was not achieved. Emphasis was placed on the national duties of the church. New measures were taken against further accumulation of wealth by the church and particularly by the monasteries. Ivan's personal reverence for the church, which led him to public confession of his sins, days devoted to prayer, self-flagellation, and other acts of devotion, probably interfered with the work of thoroughgoing reform.

In Ivan's time one of the few martyrdoms in the Russian church occurred when the metropolitan Philip himself was burned at the stake. Like Sylvester before him, but with less success, he had asked the Tsar to mend his ways and to show his people greater mercy. Philip's death increased the dependence of the church on the Tsar. It was also in Ivan's time that the Roman Catholic church made renewed efforts to bring about a reunion of the two Christian worlds. The Pope hoped to profit from Russia's political weakness in 1581, but his efforts came to naught.

Reform of Local Administration. Local administration was reformed and expanded. Each district elected members for its own administration. Their task was to collect taxes, to administer justice, and to be jointly responsible to the central government for their work. This local administration, which proved effective and promising and which might have led ultimately to a national assembly, was unfortunately discontinued under later regents.

Establishment of the Oprichnina. An important and peculiar institution was created: the Oprichnina. This was a separate, a parallel institution, "apart" from that of the state itself. It consisted of a complete administrative system, and its advantages for the Tsar were manifold: it was responsible to him alone, received orders from him only, checked on the activities of the regular administration, and supplanted or duplicated the latter whenever so desired. It undertook punishments ordered by Ivan, and thus combined the functions of a special, private police force with those of a superior political authority. It was identified not with the state, but with the will of the sovereign. The nation was divided into two parts; the one reserved for administration by the Oprichnina was at first small, but it included all strategic points from the economic as well as the military point of view.

The Oprichnina thus became the chief tool of autocracy; its illegality, ruthlessness, and irresponsibility caused it to be feared and hated by the people as well as by the regular administration. It exercised its main influence in the central regions, where its brutality and inhuman ways of tax collection led to the flight of the inhabitants and to depopulation, and thus ruined any valuable roots for a better organization of the state that might have developed.

EXTERNAL ACCOMPLISHMENTS

In external affairs, the second half of the sixteenth century likewise witnessed great developments:

Northern Trade Route. In 1553 English seamen found a route from Scotland around the North Cape to Archangel on the White Sea. For centuries Russian rulers had struggled for a connection with the rest of the world which was not dependent upon the good will of neighbors. Such a route was not only to serve unhindered import of needed goods, but to make intercourse with other nations possible without permission from surrounding princes. Five years earlier, in 1548, Ivan had again been made to feel the disadvantage of Russia's geographical position when he had tried to secure doctors, scientists, and artisans from Germany and when the ill-will of his neighbors on the Baltic had prevented their coming. The route around the North Cape opened up free lanes to the West.

It is true that, because of navigational dangers, the trade in the north with England as well as other countries did not develop as had been anticipated. The English, who had hoped to reach China and Japan when they found Russia, were slow in recognizing the value of Russian trade and still persisted in searching for trade routes to the Far East. The Danish king, fearing the loss of dues which he collected in the Sound from all ships entering or leaving the Baltic Sea, did his utmost to hinder the trade in the north unless the same dues were paid him for permission to traverse the sea lanes situated between his two possessions of Norway and Iceland. Yet, the possibility of reaching Europe by any means meant an enormous advantage for Russia. Treaties were promptly negotiated, particularly with Denmark and England, monopolies were granted to traders of important commodities, foreign merchants were invited to establish themselves in Russia, artisans were imported without consent from neighbors, and personal relationships with rulers in the West were entered into.

The opportunities thus offered were made use of in order to strengthen autocracy. With no one class in Russia devoting itself to trade, but all sharing as they could, the Tsar appropriated trade monopolies for himself, and strengthened his financial position through these and through the duties he imposed.

Southward Expansion.   In the south, Ivan secured even greater advantages. Three remnants of the Tartar empire still existed in Russia: the Crimea, Astrakhan, and Kazan—all practically independent powers ruled by Tartar princes. They constituted a permanent menace to Russia, which they repeatedly invaded. After unsuccessful negotiations, Ivan's armies entered Kazan in 1552 and Astrakhan in 1554. Both countries were completely defeated and their territories incorporated into Russia. Ivan's empire was thus vastly increased, and a perpetual threat was eliminated. Only the Crimean Tartars remained outside the reach of the Russians. Supported by the Turks, they continued to make inroads into Russian territory and to block the way to the Black Sea. In vain did Adashev and Sylvester advocate their elimination. Ivan, with sound judgment, anticipated Turkish opposition if he tried to take the Crimea and he preferred to seek access to the Baltic Sea. While Ivan was engaged there in 1571, the Tartars burned Moscow and led away uncounted numbers of prisoners. However, they did not consolidate their conquest but, satisfied with vast booty, retreated.

Westward Advance.   As Ivan through his southward expansion prepared the way for Catherine the Great's policies, so he anticipated those of Peter the Great in his attempt to reach the Baltic Sea in the west. Realizing the inadequacy of the newly opened northern route, the Tsar endeavored to gain the great harbors of Livonia on the Baltic Sea. Unlike his grandfather, Ivan III, Ivan the Terrible was to recognize the economic importance of Livonia. Textiles, wines, metal objects, armor, and salt were exchanged there for Russian wheat, rye, timber, flax, hemp, pitch, and tar. Political reasons likewise compelled the Tsar to interfere in Livonia, inasmuch as the rule of the Germans, exercised through the Teutonic Knights and the Hansa merchants, was collapsing. Poland and Sweden, both traditional enemies of Russia, were likely to seize the Baltic ports.

Ivan's campaign to gain Livonia extended over a period of twenty-five years. During the first three years, from 1558 to 1560, military measures were taken. Most of the flat land was conquered, but the two important harbors of Riga and Reval could not be gained. Another ten years were spent in diplomatic negotiations. Then a Danish prince, Magnus of Holstein, was appointed by Ivan to be puppet king of Livonia; but he was as incapable a ruler as a general, and he failed to secure the desired ports. In the fourth and last stage, Ivan once more used military might, but his troops were repelled by the now combined forces of Poland and Sweden. The Peace of Yam Zapolie, concluded with Poland in 1582, deprived the Tsar not only of his conquests in Livonia, but also of many Russian possessions formerly gained in the Polish-Lithuanian realms. The peace with Sweden, a year later, cost Ivan the small yet growing port of Narva, his last anchor in Livonia—a devastating blow for the Tsar, since the final destruction of Novgorod, which he had ordered in 1570, had left him with no outlet on the Baltic except Narva. Yet, although Russia had thus temporarily to abandon her plans in the Baltic provinces, the direction of her growth was clearly conceived and definitely indicated as a future aim of Russian rulers.

Eastward Movement. Finally, the momentous movement eastward into Siberia was begun under Ivan's rule.

PROBLEMS

1. Discuss the position of the nobility and the peasantry under Ivan the Terrible.
2. Discuss the significance of the discovery of a sea route around the North Cape.
3. Discuss the importance of Ivan's attempt to conquer Livonia.

CHAPTER VIII

SIBERIA

GEOGRAPHICAL FACTORS

The vast plains of Siberia bear significant resemblance to those of European Russia. The same four belts are to be found: an Arctic tundra, a forest, steppe, and desert zone. Except to the south, mountains are altogether lacking; and the climate, though more extreme, parallels that of European Russia. Again, and more important, Siberia's rivers form as excellent a network of communication lines as do those of Russia proper. Although a casual look at the map reveals no more than three great rivers, the Ob, Yenisei, and Lena (all flowing far apart from south to north into the Arctic Ocean), closer scrutiny shows that their tributaries form a highway from west to east for thousands upon thousands of miles. The Cossacks who crossed Siberia, being as proficient inland navigators as horsemen, found a route from the Urals to the farthest of the great rivers, the Lena. This route, entirely by water with the exception of two short portages (one of five miles from the Ob to the Yenisei basin, the other of ten miles from the Yenisei to Lake Baikal and the Lena basin), proved of utmost importance for the occupation of the land.

EXPLORATION OF SIBERIA

Opening of Siberia. In the sixteenth century, Siberia was by no means unknown to the Russians. Traders from Novgorod had traversed it from the eleventh century on; missionaries to China had entered and reported about it; in 1499 an attempt to conquer the Ob region had been made; tributes were paid by Tartar chieftains there. Therefore, no "discovery" was needed, nor any "conquest" necessary. What happened may be called a "settlement" of Siberia; but as Russia at the end of the sixteenth century counted fewer than fifteen million inhabitants, the occupation was slow. Essentially, the settlement was a "penetration" for future political and economic use, and this penetration was carried on by incredibly small forces. Indeed, half a continent with five million square miles was brought under Russian suzerainty by bands made up at the largest of eight hundred and fifty men, and sometimes of as few as twenty-five. Adventurers, mainly Cossacks, opened the way. They were strong in body, were of Orthodox faith, belonged to the unsettled elements of the population in quest of freedom, and followed the age-old call of "gospel, gold, and glory."

Stroganov. The expansion into Siberia began with Grigory Stroganov, a rich merchant from Novgorod who in 1558 secured a land concession on the Kama River east of Moscow. The grant, unlike those in the United States during the nineteenth century, was secured only under strictest conditions: Stroganov was exempted from taxes for twenty years, but in return he was pledged to build and operate salt works, to break the soil for agriculture, to equip a small army for protection, and to renounce claims to any mines discovered in the land.

Exploration.

Yermak. Stroganov found his concession profitable and his family secured additional grants which extended beyond the Urals. For the protection of their possessions they hired Cossacks, among whom there was a former robber and pirate, Yermak (Ermak Timofeyev). An energetic man who had proved his abilities though in an unlawful way, he was charged in 1581 with leading an expedition into the region east of the Urals. Accompanied by priests and interpreters, he sailed up the rivers as far as possible toward the Urals, dragged his boats across the crest, and sailed down in the direction of the Ob. Being equipped with firearms, he readily defeated opposing Tartar armies and took the city of Sibir, which was later to give its name to the country. He was pardoned for his misdeeds, and for his exploits he received rich gifts from the Tsar. With undiminished energy, he proceeded to establish trade connections not only with the tribes in western Siberia, but also with the more civilized people in central Asia around Samarkand and Bokhara; and by having *ostrogs* or forts built and equipped with small guns, he provided for the defense of the newly acquired region.

SUCCEEDING EXPLORERS. In 1584, Yermak lost his life by drowning in a river during a battle. After a temporary halt, his work was continued by a succession of Cossacks and explorers. Outstanding among them were: Poiarkov, who reached the Amur River in 1644 and who also undertook to travel down the Lena; Khabarov—an able explorer but lacking in all understanding of the value of his explorations—whose misdeeds around 1650 in the region of the Amur and among the Chinese did untold damage to the Russian cause; Stepanov, who likewise devoted his attention to the Amur region and who died in 1658; and Atlasov—a colorful personality, corrupt in many instances but not entirely devoid of intelligence and feeling—who discovered Kamchatka in 1697.

Penetration. Progress through Siberia, considering its expanse, was remarkably fast. In 1587 Tobolsk on the Ob was founded. From there, the Russians always strove to push southward and eastward into more habitable regions, but were persistently forced off their course by hostile native tribes into an undesirable northeasterly direction. This fact is of far-reaching importance: had the Russians used their small forces against the resistance of the southern tribes, they might never have had the strength to continue the penetration of Asia to the Pacific. On the other hand, had they succeeded in pushing southward, their later difficulties there and their rivalry with England might have been avoided; and the fate of India would certainly have been different.

In 1618 the Russians reached the upper course of the Yenisei; ten years later, the Lena, where in 1632 they founded Iakutsk. Upon reaching the Amur River in 1644, they beheld a great and uniquely different civilization—that of the Chinese. It was also there that for the first time they encountered good conditions for agricultural work. But again their attention was diverted to the barren northern parts. In 1644 they reached the mouth of the Kolima River on the Arctic Ocean, and in 1648 founded Okhotsk on the Pacific Ocean.

In the following year, a voyage was undertaken by a man called Dezhnev, who is sometimes credited with having rounded the northeastern corner of Asia, finding the seaway from the Arctic to the Pacific Ocean, and anticipating Bering's and Nordenskjöld's feats; but proof is dubious.

In 1651 Irkutsk on Lake Baikal was founded and, finally, in 1697 Kamchatka was explored and the extreme Far East taken into possession.

GOVERNMENT OF SIBERIA

Administration. The Russian government had taken no part in these explorations. Its interests were confined to strategic considerations of security against new nomad invasions; consequently, the initiative remained in the hands of lawless bands who had little sense of honor, no love of country, and no respect for promises. Their exactions from the natives were generally excessive; and whenever one of their leaders, such as Atlasov, endeavored to safeguard the elementary rights of the inhabitants, he faced charges of conspiracy and heresy. The farther the conquerors were away from Europe, the greater their lawlessness. Torture, abduction, murder, and cannibalism were among their crimes; and at the cry "The Cossacks are coming," the natives were stricken with terror. However, as with contemporary Spanish explorers, so it was with the Russians: not only the soldiers were to be feared, but so also were the traders who arrived in their wake and who, through speculation in land, provisions, transportation, and mines (particularly salt works), contributed to the disorder.

Siberian Department. The government reacted feebly. In 1637 a Siberian Department was founded in Moscow, and various administrative units were established in Siberia. These were centralized in 1670 in Tobolsk. The officers, however, were corrupt, robbing not only the people but also the government they represented; and their harshness resulted in the flight of many natives to China. Their chief occupation and task consisted in collecting taxes, their main support being their superior arms. Thus, in many respects Russian aims and administration in Siberia at the beginning resembled Tartar rule in Russia two centuries earlier. If taxes were paid, the people were left alone; provided they had adopted the Christian faith, they were allowed to intermix with the newcomers and to enter government service.

Commerce. Trade developed but slowly. The climate in some regions offered too great an obstacle to normal life, silver was not found in quantities as expected, and furs alone could reward the exertions of the settlers. Only when contact was established with the mighty Chinese empire, at that time enjoying a period of great prosperity, did trade begin to show some promise. Textiles, silk, gold, and silverware from China were exchanged for hides, furs, and foodstuffs—the type of commodities offered by either side giving a significant picture of its respective civilization and living standards.

Relations with China. Attempts were also made to establish diplomatic relations, but the overbearing attitude of the Chinese rendered impossible any normal intercourse. It was only after the Russians began to penetrate along the Amur River and into Manchuria that real necessity for diplomatic relations arose. The Chinese were not directly interested in the Amur region, particularly not along the lower course of the river; and had the Cossacks settled quietly, they probably would have been left alone. But the disturbances resulting from their activities and the reports of fleeing Chinese made it impossible for the government in Peking to remain unconcerned. Several armies were therefore sent out to drive away the intruders and, though not always successful, they made the Russian position most precarious.

TREATY OF NERCHINSK. Finally, embassies were exchanged, and on August 27, 1689, after two weeks of negotiations, a treaty was signed at Nerchinsk. It was drafted in Latin by Jesuits living at the Chinese court, and the Jesuits were of course more proficient in Latin than their treaty partners. Not only this, but their knowledge of Russia was far greater than the Russian ambassador Golovine's knowledge of China. As a result, the treaty turned out to be very satisfactory for the Chinese. Both sides of the Amur River remained China's, and Mongolia was kept within her sphere. Russia was confined to the northern, less habitable regions; but these were vast enough to provide a task for colonization which strained all the resources in matériel and manpower at the disposal of the Russians, so that there was little interest in additional territory. The peace concluded at Nerchinsk was to endure for more than one hundred and fifty years.

TREATY OF KYAKHTA. In 1727 the political treaty was supplemented, at Kyakhta, by a convention which regulated Russo-Chinese trade relations and diplomatic intercourse.

PROBLEMS

1. Explain the geographical and geopolitical structure of Siberia.
2. Compare the settling of Siberia with the Western movement in America.
3. Discuss the early political activities of Russia in Siberia.

CHAPTER IX

TIME OF TROUBLES

THE COMING OF THE "TROUBLES"

Estimate of Ivan's Reign. Ivan the Terrible died in 1584. Chiefly owing to the Livonian war and the Oprichnina, his reign had seen political insecurity, loss of agricultural production, forfeiture of taxes, further human degradation, devastation of the western and northwestern parts of the empire, and an accelerated trend toward serfdom. On the other hand, it had checked the license of the nobility, brought improvements in the church and in the legislative process, accomplished consolidation of the realm, opened new trade prospects, and fostered territorial expansion outlining the future destiny of Russia. His was the first modern government in Russia, and it is said that it constituted an early part of the great revolution known as the "Time of Troubles." It must not be inferred that Ivan himself was the impetus behind the revolution; indeed, the work of a single man could hardly be expected to carry such weight. Ivan himself was merely a tool shaping what was to be. Although not recognizable at the beginning, an idea simple and clear, a new trend, and the Russian people's wholly new attitude towards life were at the basis of the upheaval. Once this is understood, the Time of Troubles (*Smuta*) loses its confused picture and the roles of the political

figures—of the Godunovs, false Dimitris, Shuiskys, and Romanovs—
are reduced to incidents. The classical pattern of revolution is revealed.

The revolution, then, began with Ivan's reign, that is, with a
period of stated grievances and attempted reforms; its one remarkable feature was that the ruler allied himself with the dissatisfied
classes against the privileged and the nobility.

Boris Godunov. The second stage was again a typical revolutionary step, a time of hesitation and deliberate delay in an effort to
avoid otherwise inevitable destruction, terror, and later reaction. It
is marked by the rule of Boris Godunov, dominant figure behind
Ivan's son, Tsar Feodor I (1584–98), who succeeded his father.
Feodor played no role; he was a pious, incompetent, perhaps even
weak-minded man—"a sacristan, not a tsarevitch," as his father said.
His demise in 1598 was of importance only inasmuch as with him the
family died out; and since autocracy had stifled the people's ability to
govern themselves, it cleared the way for full assumption of power
by Boris Godunov. Himself a boyar, he was proclaimed Tsar by a
Zemsky Sobor which was convoked and cleverly manipulated by
him for the purpose. Able, shrewd, rich, and also vain and insecure
in his actions, Boris Godunov (1598–1605) accomplished a by no
means negligible job, continuing Ivan's struggle against the privileged
nobility and ruthlessly suppressing their attempts to overthrow him
and regain power. It was he who began to use Siberia as a place
of banishment for political adversaries. The period of his rule brought
comparative peace and order. Moscow gained enormously by the
raising of the metropolitan see to a patriarchate, trade was encouraged, exports increased, building activities were revived, and
further fortifications against the Poles, Tartars, and Swedes were
erected.

Legalization of Serfdom. But all this could not stem the tide
of revolution. Towards the end of Feodor's reign, signs of the coming upheaval had become unmistakable. Unrest had grown when attacks from the outside necessitated military expansion and led to
wider recruiting and the imposition of higher taxes. In consequence,
more peasant flights occurred and many joined the ranks of the free
Cossacks on the frontiers. To halt the exodus of peasants, a law of
grave consequences was passed in 1597 that permitted the landowners a five-years' interval for reclaiming fugitive peasants and
forbade the kidnaping of peasants from one estate to another. Thus,

the full attachment of the peasant to the soil and the status of serf-dom were legalized. After Godunov ascended the throne, the roused lower classes found an additional cause for discontent when a terrible famine occurred in 1601–03. This famine was closely connected with the flight of peasants from the cultivated central regions, and led to starvation and death for tens or perhaps hundreds of thousands. The superstitious populace put the blame on the new Tsar—upon whom, because of his numerous misdeeds, they saw God's wrath descend. They also accused him—and justly, in the opinion of modern investigators—of having killed Ivan the Terrible's youngest son Dimitri in 1591, in order to secure the power for himself. The dissatisfaction was turned to use by the boyars, who hoped to settle accounts with the hated "usurper" risen from their own midst. Their party was joined by merchants and people of the middle class, who were losing by the disorder and whose trade and travel were being disrupted by roving brigands. The situation worsened for Godunov when in 1604 the crops improved and the landowners, on the basis of the law of 1597, began to ask for the return of their serfs after having willingly let them go free during the times of starvation.

CIVIL WAR

Appearance of False Dimitri. At this point, the next revolutionary step was taken—that of violence and civil war. In the Russia of 1604, it took the form of the emergence of a pretender to Godunov's throne, who naturally found support among the dissatisfied elements comprising more or less the whole population. He appeared as a "false Dimitri," impersonating Ivan's son, whose murderers were said to have taken by mistake the life of a substitute. Although historians generally concur nowadays that "Dimitri" was an impostor, he may have acted in good faith, as he is said to have been carefully trained for his role from earliest youth. He secured military help from the Poles, who took pleasure in the opportunity to disturb the peace of Russia and who extorted vast territorial, religious, and political promises in exchange for their unofficial support. "Dimitri" invaded Russia and was joined by thousands, including the Cossack legions, whereas Godunov was confined to fighting him with weak forces and with propaganda accusing him of fraud and subservience to the Catholic church. In the midst of war (1605) Godunov died, leaving his claims to the throne to a well-educated and able son. Shortly thereafter, "Dimitri" took Moscow and induced the real

Dimitri's mother, Ivan's widow, to "recognize" him; then, disposing of the Godunov family, he established himself on the throne.

Reaction. During his brief reign in 1605–06, "Dimitri" (Demetrius I) proved a capable administrator, conscientiously working on affairs of state, easing the status of the serfs, lowering taxes, and raising wages. But the boyars had no desire merely to exchange one usurper for another. Taking advantage of "Dimitri's" foreign leanings, his disdain for uncouth Russian customs and manners, and his insulting behavior towards the patriarch (whom he had the poor judgment to replace by a man of doubtful orthodoxy), the boyars raised from their midst a Prince Shuisky and with the help of a handsomely bribed Zemsky Sobor set him on the throne. Shuisky (Basil IV, 1606–10) was weak and unreliable; and though "Dimitri" was eliminated by murder in 1606, he failed to bring back the conditions for which his backers had hoped. His incompetence led to the final and bloodiest stage of the revolution—foreign war and civil terror.

Polish Invasion. The Cossacks and underprivileged, after the death of "Dimitri," endeavored to produce another pretender as standard-bearer—either a false Peter or a second false Dimitri—and it is significant that they spoke of their "legitimate" ruler before he even existed. Several men vied for the position, and in 1608 a "second false Dimitri" succeeded in establishing his claims and gaining the support of the Cossacks. He invaded Russia with another Polish army and was received by the "first false Dimitri's" wife (the adventurous Polish noblewoman Marina Mniszek) as her legal husband, although secretly, after sharing his bed, she had herself married to him by a Jesuit priest. The Polish danger prompted Shuisky to call in the Swedes, and a triangular war and civil strife ravaged the unhappy country. The "second false Dimitri" was unsuccessful in his attempt to take Moscow. In vain a supporting Polish army besieged the capital and also the famous Troitsa cloister, which withstood assault for a year and a half under the direction of a dauntless patriarch.

Realignment in Russia. The new pretender's abilities did not match those of his predecessor. His troops pillaged the country and discredited the revolution. In 1610 he was murdered in a private feud; and although worse suffering was still to come, this year brought a clarification of the issues at stake and the emergence of definite parties engaged in the struggle. On the one side were the Poles, murdering, raping, and destroying. Their king, Sigismund, wanted the Russian throne for himself or his son and he pursued the customary policy of territorial aggrandizement at Russia's expense; but he insisted also on reunion with Catholicism. He was supported first by the lower nobility and merchant class, later only by the high boyars, who expected to secure the same extravagant privileges which their Polish brethren had won. On the other side were two groups: (1) a national movement rallying around the church under the valiant leadership of the patriarch, stout defender of independence, and (2) a social movement supported by the Cossacks, who struggled for economic improvements. Shuisky had nothing to offer to either and therefore was deposed early in 1610 and banished to a cloister. The throne was left vacant.

Climax and End of "Troubles." During the ensuing interim, the Poles penetrated to Moscow, burned the suburbs, and established themselves in the Kremlin. This fearsome peril to the nation and to the Orthodox faith brought a fusion of the Russian forces through which, it is true, the social revolutionary aims were defeated; but the national cause was saved.

First a triumvirate was instituted, consisting of a boyar, a nobleman, and a Cossack hetman (the latter being also the third husband of Marina Mñiszek, who had not yet given up her hopes for the throne). This triumvirate failed to rally all national forces, for it lost the support of the radical elements by publishing a number of decrees which benefited essentially the service-nobility and which neglected the interests of those in favor of free land. It also was unable to stem the tide of foreign enemies—the Poles who conquered Smolensk and the Swedes who captured Novgorod. A new organization had to be created, and this was done in 1611 by leaders of the church and by volunteers from the more conservative strata of the population, among whom were such outstanding men as the Novgorod merchant, Kuzma Minin. With their help, a national army was called into being and organized in the unoccupied northeastern provinces. Then this army, more homogeneous than that of the triumvirate, marched against Moscow. It succeeded in engaging the support of the moderate elements among the triumvirate's forces, and the thereby-strengthened national army started the siege of the Kremlin. The Poles, who had committed the crime of starving the Russian patriarch to death, now suffered a like fate themselves, and at the end of 1612 Moscow and the Kremlin were retaken. In the meantime, the revolutionary Cossacks and their friends, weakened through defection, had to retire into Astrakhan, where their forces gradually dissolved. As the capture of Moscow and the expulsion of the Poles marked the end of the national struggle, so did the disintegration of the revolutionary Cossack forces terminate the civil war.

RECONSTRUCTION

Michael Romanov. The task now pressing was the choice of a new head of state. As generally following a revolution, the desire for order was paramount. The service-nobility, which had espoused the national cause and had shown its preponderance toward the end of the Time of Troubles, represented the class best fitted to fulfill this desire. Under their influence, a Zemsky Sobor which was called in 1613 and included also boyars, peasants, and Cossacks appointed the new Tsar. A compromise candidate, sixteen-year-old Michael Romanov, was chosen. He was a member of the high nobility and a relative of the first wife of Ivan the Terrible, yet he was also acceptable to the service-nobility and the peasants. With him in 1613 begins the reign of the dynasty which was to last until 1917, and with him order was re-established.

As a revolution, the "Troubles" had failed. Few social gains had been achieved; for autocracy and the service-nobility, as founded by Ivan the Terrible, triumphed. The social gains which were achieved had all been anticipated by Ivan the Terrible, and the behavior of the Cossacks themselves was to a large extent responsible for the failure of further reforms. Yet Russia survived. Poland, momentarily within grasp of uniting the Slavic world, had bungled the task; if Poland had succeeded, Siberian and eastern interests would certainly have been sacrificed to European schemes. As it was, Russia entered a new and definitely separate stage of her history, a period of enormous outward expansion and painful inner tension.

PROBLEMS

1. Discuss the social significance of the Time of Troubles.
2. Discuss the role of a "popular voice" (Zemsky Sobor) at the turn of the sixteenth century.
3. Discuss Russia's international position during the Time of Troubles.

CHAPTER X

CONSOLIDATION UNDER ROMANOV DYNASTY

CONDITIONS AT END OF THE "TROUBLES"

Social and Economic Conditions. The revolution encompassing the reign of Ivan the Terrible and the *Smuta* or "Troubles" consolidated the triumph of the service-nobility over the great hereditary nobility. It also confirmed the failure both of the peasantry, which had risen against the landholding classes, and of the middle class, which had been unsuccessful in gaining a political voice. Thus, the times ushering in the house of Romanov brought no social improvement.

Economically, Russia was largely ruined: the material damage, aggravated by the foreign wars which had accompanied the *Smuta,* called for extensive repair; money was needed for the treasury; foodstuffs were necessary for the stores; manpower—through exchange of prisoners—was required for work on the land. Trade revival was exigent and had to be bought at the price of vast privileges and monopolies in foreign commerce, which were accorded to the English and the Dutch, adversely affecting the future of the Russian merchant. Politically, peace had yet to be concluded with Poland and Sweden. With the former, no final settlement was possible; the latter, under its great king Gustavus Adolphus, agreed to the evacuation of Novgorod but held fast to the Baltic harbors in Livonia and Ingria.

The Tsars. The government itself needed reorganization. Michael (1613–45), the first Romanov, was a weakling Tsar, whose reign acquired color only through his father, Patriarch Philaret, who took the title of *"Veliki Gosudar"* and thus, as a second "Great Lord" or sovereign, exercised until his death in 1633 equal power with the Tsar in state and church. Michael was succeeded by Alexis (1645–76), a man of high principles, humanity, and ability, but likewise possessed of insufficient resolution. After the period of Alexis came the short reign of Feodor III (1676–82).

The rule of these first three Romanovs witnessed the gradual consolidation of the empire, the settlement with Poland, and widespread social changes.

REORGANIZATION

Finances. Consolidation of the country was carried out through centralization under autocracy. For the purpose of strengthening central authority, the taxation system was revised. The burdens on the taxpayers, having increased because of the revolution, were further aggravated through direct and indirect impositions. To a high sales tax were added scores of internal duties, salt taxes, and especially regular capital taxes which sometimes amounted to as much as 20 per cent. Strict edicts were issued against selling oneself into bondage in order to escape payment, and against various other stratagems resorted to for the same purpose. But despite all government laws, the inefficiency and corruption of the administration were too great to guarantee the correct use of taxes. As everywhere in Europe, a large share of these never reached the treasury; and, likewise as in other countries, good use was seldom made of those amounts which did come in. Instead of being applied to financing productive improvements, gold and jewels were stored and wealth was hoarded; in France or Spain these would have served at least to increase the credit of the nation, but in Russia they lay unused in palaces and churches.

Army. The autocracy naturally paid close attention to the army, and vast sums were expended for improving it. All the gentry were required to serve in the wars, and specific contingents of common soldiers were recruited forcibly from each estate—a measure hindering the rebuilding of the land. A nucleus was formed of *Streltsi* (archers) who furnished the professional part of the army and at the same time formed a praetorian guard for the ruler; many among them were mercenaries from France, Switzerland, Germany, Scotland, or other countries.

Trade. Foreigners also formed the backbone of the revived trade. Not only did the Dutch and English profit, but artisans were attracted from various other countries. They opened shops, produced goods, imported and exported. Their importance grew, particularly that of the Germans, who introduced not only their skills but also their ways and customs. Their cleanliness, order, and thrift were commonly appreciated; and the "German suburb" of Moscow, which housed other foreigners as well, became the most progressive part of the capital and an example to be imitated by all Russia. The Russians thus profited much from their guests; but they also suffered, for no strong merchant class of their own developed nor were native artisans trained. Most of the trade that existed among the Russians was not handled by established merchants but was shared by a motley crowd of boyars, soldiers, peasants, and artisans, every one of whom tried to gain some additional income through trade in the most varied commodities. The disadvantages of the situation were reflected in stagnation and emphasized by want of markets, as the rich would not buy Russian products and the poor—particularly the peasants—because of poverty produced their own most primitive tools.

Self-Government. Through centralization, taxation, and reliance on foreign help, the administration succeeded in reducing self-government and in emancipating itself from the Zemsky Sobors and other former popular institutions of the country. The first Romanov had owed his crown to a Zemsky Sobor, and at the beginning of his reign the assembly retained no inconsiderable amount of power. It sat virtually continuously from 1613 to 1622 and during this time not only enacted a number of important measures, such as those concerning taxation, but also showed its independence by boldly assuming questionable prerogatives—for example, in confirming the patriarch in 1619. But because of the general trends, the Zemsky Sobor began to recruit its members more and more exclusively from the service-nobility and no longer represented the Russian people as a whole. It thus forfeited the support of other classes, and ultimately relinquished all power to the growing autocracy. Until 1642, the Zemsky Sobor continued to influence domestic issues; and it was active upon at least one foreign question, that regarding the fortress of Azov conquered by Don Cossacks. As a matter of fact, the assembly advocated its return to the Turks lest war with them result. In 1649 the Zemsky Sobor was consulted in connection with the new law code of that year, but by then no peasant representative could be found among its members and its role had become entirely passive. After 1653, it convened no more.

Law. The reorganization of the country was confirmed through the law code of 1649. Although in many respects a retrogressive one, the code marked an important step in the development of the Russian nation. It constituted a revision of the code of 1550 adopted in Ivan the Terrible's time. But it went further, for it was a collection of customary procedures or a codification of existing legal concepts, and it introduced new precepts and methods derived from the study of the laws of Byzance as well as of those of the Lithuanian grand duchy. However, despite all endeavors, the code represented no truly scientific approach to the establishment of principles of justice, but remained a superficial work. Its adoption led to an intolerable chain of misdeeds.

PURPOSE OF THE CODE. The primary purpose of the new laws, as of most of the measures taken during the seventeenth century, consisted in the strengthening of central authority. All over Europe the trend was toward centralization and theories of the "divine right of kings," and Russia made no exception. In the code of 1649, not only was the taxing power of the state secured, but commerce was made dependent upon the state. The trading privileges of the foreigners were greatly restricted. The jurisdiction of the church was limited and so were its rights to the acquisition of property. Moreover, stipulations were made providing for a certain amount of state control over all private property.

DEFECT OF THE CODE. The chief shortcoming of the code consisted in its failure to define the legal position of the peasants, who actually found themselves outside the law. In 1646, they had been compelled to register at the places where they lived and worked and, this once done, they had been forced to remain there. In practically every respect the peasants became subjected to the landowners, who were made responsible for their work and taxes and who, from now on, could reclaim them, if fugitive, without time limit. Jurisdiction over them was granted the landowner, and thus the last stone was laid in the structure for enslaving the agricultural workers. A peasant became a mere piece of property, attached not only to the soil but also, as a personal belonging, to a master.

Defense.   Externally, the reign of the first three Romanovs saw a shift in the balance of power from Poland to Russia. This shift, again, was the work not of one man—although statesmen such as Ordyn Nashchokin and Artamon Matveyev distinguished themselves in diplomatic transactions—but rather of a negative force, consisting in the deterioration of everything Polish. Possessing men and institutions morally, as well as practically, unfit, Poland had to abandon ambitions for external greatness. Eight wars between 1615 and 1667 confirmed the rise of Russia, brought the return of the lost town of Smolensk, guaranteed greater future security, and established Russian supremacy even in the internal affairs of Poland.

The disintegration of Poland had far-reaching consequences. It led not only to a settlement between Russia and Poland, but also to a decision of the territorial issues between Russia and Sweden. From the time of Ivan the Terrible on, Sweden had increased her hold on the southern shores of the Baltic Sea. With the collapse of Poland, she tried to further increase her transmaritime possessions, and was brought once more into conflict with the Tsars. A long war (1656–61) was fought, but for the first time did not result in encroachments on the Russian sphere. Because of general exhaustion, peace was concluded at Cardis (1661) without gain to either side, thus bringing a stalemate which was to be followed in Peter the Great's time, less than half a century later, by a full reversal of previous power relationships.

PEASANT RISINGS

The direction of reconstruction and consolidation in the middle seventeenth century was challenged by the peasants, at whose expense it took place. However, the development of internal conditions in Russia is not traceable to the whim of any lawmaker, but stems directly from the rapid succession of social upheavals in the sixteenth and early seventeenth centuries. Chaos had led to a reduction of cultivated land, to depopulation, to appalling accumulations of private debt, to dangerously reduced armed strength, and to a vast decrease of state income. Recovery necessitated resettlement of free or abandoned land and the insertion of the individual into the whole for the benefit of the state. In its essence, the development may therefore be described as a natural and compulsory result of prevailing circumstances; but at the same time, it was destined to lead not only to graver complications in the future, but to violent opposition while in progress.

Revolts. The period of the first three Romanovs, and particularly that of the benevolent Alexis, is indeed marked by an almost uninterrupted chain of revolutionary outbreaks. Freedom prevailed only on the fringes of the empire, in the north, in Siberia, and in the territories of the Cossacks to the south. There the independent elements assembled, the fugitive peasants found haven, and from thence issued the spirit of liberty. Hundreds of small-scale revolts are traceable. By 1648 and 1650 the disturbances commenced to increase in violence. In 1662 a serious uprising occurred in connection with the depreciation of money, when the minting of valueless copper pieces in lieu of silver resulted in inflation and impoverishment.

Stenka Razin. These sporadic outbreaks finally touched off a revolt of great magnitude. It began in 1667 and reached its climax in 1670. Led by a Cossack, Stenka Razin, who promised liberation of the peasants, forces of from seven to ten thousand men succeeded in seizing thousands of square miles of Russian territory, and fleets of the revolutionaries sailed up and down the Volga River and on the Caspian Sea, plundering as great a harbor as Derbent. Important cities like Tsaritsyn and Astrakhan were seized. Razin's actions were directed against the rich landowners, and his fidelity to the Tsar or at least to the institution of Tsarism was frequently reiterated. However, as it generally happened, the behavior of the Cossacks themselves, their outrages and brutality, cost them the fruits of victory and alienated the sympathies even of those for whom they were said to be fighting. By 1671, the government had the situation in hand. Stenka Razin was betrayed, captured, and executed. More than one hundred years were to elapse before the forces for a new great uprising could be collected.

The suppression of the Cossack revolt of Stenka Razin was of fundamental importance for the success of one of the greatest tasks accomplished during the reign of the first three Romanovs, the reabsorption of the long-lost southern parts of the country, the Ukraine.

PROBLEMS

1. Discuss the rise of the service-nobility and the decline of popular representation.
2. Discuss the change of the balance of power in eastern Europe.
3. Summarize the causes of the discontent of peasants and Cossacks.

CHAPTER XI

THE UKRAINE

CONDITIONS UNDER LITHUANIAN RULE

Separation from Russia. The reabsorption of the southern parts of Russia into the commonwealth during the seventeenth century marked the end of a period which had brought misfortune to both sections. It had been in 1320, after continuous wars during which Lithuania and Poland had carved off vast regions of the Ukraine, that Kiev, the capital, had fallen under the rule of Lithuania. Thus, in the midst of the Tartar period, the old Russian center had been severed from the political body of Russia. Autonomous local Russian princes remained, nominally under Tartar suzerainty but in reality dependent upon Lithuania. But toward the end of the fourteenth century, three political events altered the situation: Tartar rule in western Russia ceased to function around 1375; in 1380 the last Ukrainian prince of Russian blood was deposed; and in 1386 a personal union was established between Lithuania and Poland, and the Poles established their supremacy in the united countries.

Desolation. The beginning fifteenth century showed the consequences of these changes. Externally, the country was exposed anew to invasions. The Tartars tried to reconquer their former possessions and, together with Turkish tribes, sent expeditions into the Ukraine

The eastern parts of the country were laid waste, settlers fled, and what once had been one of the most prosperous regions of Russia was abandoned to wild beasts. Internally, the Poles caused similar destruction. As long as the Lithuanians were dominant, the Ukrainians had peacefully practiced their Orthodox religion, hoping to spread it also among their conquerors. The union with Poland, however, drove a wedge between Lithuanians and Ukrainians; for the Poles were Catholic and introduced their own faith into Lithuania. The Orthodox creed lost its chance of serving the amalgamation of Lithuanians and Ukrainians, and found itself exposed to violent persecution. The Orthodox clergy was suppressed and public offices were filled by converts to Catholicism.

Uprisings. Against these injustices, revolts soon broke out; and, finding no other support in their struggle, the Ukrainians sought help from their Orthodox brethren in Muscovy. From that time on, a constant struggle between Poland and Russia raged over the possession of the Ukrainian lands, the religious issues emphasizing the irreconcilable aspirations of either side. In 1500 Tsar Ivan the Great seized the opportunity and proclaimed a protectorate over the Kievan region. To counter the blow, the Poles found themselves forced into concessions which culminated in 1539 in the establishment of an Orthodox bishopric in Lvov.

Flights and Resettlement. Caught between Russia and Poland, many Ukrainians decided to leave their homes. In their search for freedom and relative security, their attention was attracted by the deserted eastern parts of their country. The first to re-enter this region were typical frontiersmen. Hardy, brave, and adventurous, they organized themselves into armed bands and made the steppe their permanent home. Attracted by the plenitude of fish, buffalo, duck, and other game, they may have intended to live by hunting and trading. But being good horsemen and excellent sailors as well as hunters and traders, they undertook also to recognize the suzerainty of the Poles and to defend the land for them, in exchange for a guarantee of their personal and religious freedom and of political autonomy.

ZAPOROZHIE COSSACKS. Below the Dnieper rapids the frontiersmen erected forts and established themselves as a Cossack Union, famed under the name of "Zaporozhie Cossacks." Profiting by their power and independence, they soon began to attack and plunder

Tartars, Turks, and Muscovites alike. As long as their military might was needed, they were able to preserve the privileges granted them. During the times of King Stephan Báthory of Poland, they even secured the concession of a special governor for their region, whereby they were removed from the jurisdiction and supervision of the central authority. They elected their own officials, and among their commanders (hetmans) such able leaders are found as Vishnevetsky (c. 1550), Kishka (c. 1600), Sahaidachny (c. 1620), Khmelnitsky (c. 1640), Doroshenko (c. 1665), and finally Ivan Mazepa (c. 1700).

SETTLERS. The frontiersmen were followed by settlers. Peasants, attracted by the fertility of the soil, arrived to complete resettlement and to reclaim the soil. They hoped to find in the eastern Ukraine "a land without a landlord," to be free from exorbitant taxation and from toil for the nobles. At first they found what they sought; and, living among lowly and freedom-loving Cossacks, they enjoyed unaccustomed freedom. But their position was inconsistent with the trends of the time and was untenable in the face of a new influx of peasants. The vicious cycle of political encroachment and economic oppression started anew.

INCORPORATION OF EASTERN UKRAINE

Toward the end of the sixteenth century, the final stage of Polish domination in the eastern Ukraine began. It was introduced by threefold measures, pertaining to the enserfment of the peasant, the subjection of the Cossacks, and the extirpation of the Orthodox creed; and thereby the end of Ukrainian autonomy was envisaged.

Serfdom. The first steps toward the enserfment of the peasants were undertaken by Stephan Báthory, who granted estates in the eastern Ukraine to Polish noblemen in order to compensate adherents for their services during the war against Russia. The recipients promptly introduced the inhumane conditions of serfdom prevailing in Poland. During subsequent decades, they steadily increased their demands on the labor and production of the peasants; for now that many wars had destroyed crops in other regions, the high prices paid for wheat and other agricultural products offered opportunities for great profit.

Subjection of the Cossacks. Simultaneously, measures were taken to weaken the position of the Cossacks. The Cossacks derived their main strength and importance from their position as defenders of the realm. But after the wars with Russia were over, their services were no longer needed and consequently their influence was reduced. The Poles saw a chance not only to deprive them of the privileges granted under pressure of war, but also to punish them for pillaging and creating disturbances in times of peace. In 1596 a punitive expedition was sent against them which subdued the unruly elements and reduced their liberties.

Religious Oppression. Furthermore, the Poles undertook to settle the religious issues. Because of the inadequate support which Muscovy could offer its coreligionists at the end of the sixteenth century, the moment seemed favorable for severing the religious bonds which tied the Ukrainians with Russia and which constituted a threat to Poland's national unity. On Christmas Day, 1595, the Orthodox in the Ukraine and White Russia were compelled to submit to a Polish decree: although they were allowed to maintain their own discipline, they were enjoined to recognize the Pope and obey the Catholic church. The bishops acknowledging the new order were henceforth known as "Uniate" bishops.

This arrangement, however, did not turn out to Poland's advantage; for thousands of Orthodox refused to recognize the "union," and what had been intended to lead to a strengthening of the Polish state led in reality to a further split which, in due time, was to culminate in the disruption of the entire nation.

Resurgence of Independence Movement. Enserfment and political and religious oppression revived the national spirit in the eastern Ukraine. The Cossacks, favored by Polish embarrassments in new external and civil wars, took the lead. They succeeded in strengthening their own ranks and soon their fellowship numbered not fewer than twenty thousand men. They increased their financial resources through successful expeditions against Moscow (1604–12), the Turks (1606), and the Tartars (1608), which brought them rich booty. They furthered their own Ukrainian culture, which was preserved through excellent and growing educational centers at Kiev. Strong and independent, they also began to interest themselves anew in the fate of the peasants, many of whom were related to their own lower ranks. And most of all, they rebuilt among their people the Orthodox church. In 1620, against the stipulations of the "union," they had secretly chosen a new metropolitan and ordained five Orthodox bishops, and in this way strengthened their links with

Moscow, toward which the new clergy necessarily looked for support and inspiration.

Polish Countermeasures. The Poles watched the trends with grave premonition. In 1625, choosing a moment when no external enemy threatened them, they suddenly attacked the Cossacks, subdued them, and forced them to reduce their forces from 20,000 to 6,000 men. They required all members to register so as to prevent secret restoration of Cossack strength. Their measures proved inefficient; for several years later the Cossacks got help from their brothers of the Don region and took revenge, and from then on a bitter struggle raged, bringing alternating successes. In 1639 the Poles believed themselves to have gained the final victory, but a new Cossack uprising in 1647 reversed the situation. Once more the Cossak forces were raised to 40,000, the Uniate church was abolished in the eastern Ukraine, autonomous Cossack administration was reestablished, and in 1649 the Poles guaranteed the new status.

Transformation of Independence Struggle. However, as time had gone on, the social background of the Cossack state on the Dnieper had changed and directed the whole struggle into different channels. The interests of Cossacks and peasants drifted apart. The land became densely settled; Cossack officers seized large estates; and a caste of landed Cossack proprietors was built up, not less interested than the Polish gentry in attachment of the peasant to the soil and in compulsory labor. Serfdom as it existed in Poland and Russia became also an integral part of Ukrainian life. Hence, the "independence struggle" of the Dnieper Cossacks and the Ukraine, which had become a struggle of survival for Poland as well as for the Cossacks, could no longer be hailed by the peasant as a means of his own liberation. In the final analysis, it assumed the form of warfare between two governments or ruling classes in which the common man had scarcely a share.

Submission to Russia. In the light of these facts we must view the step which, after the Poles defaulted in their promises of 1649, was undertaken by the Cossack hetman Khmelnitsky, a gifted national leader but also a rich and greedy landowner. It was he who in 1654 determined to transfer the allegiance of the Cossack state from Poland to Russia. His action, undertaken for selfish reasons, reflected the redistribution of power between Russia and Poland; and the Tsar, after consulting the last Zemsky Sobor convened in 1653, did not hesitate to accept Khmelnitsky's submission and to declare war on Poland.

The transition from Polish to Russian suzerainty, accompanied by renewed warfare, failed, of course, to benefit the peasantry; but neither did it bring the expected fruits for the Cossacks. Although at first the Tsar treated them with consideration, he refused to make promises regarding Ukrainian autonomy. Moreover, he demanded the subordination of the metropolitan at Kiev to Moscow's patriarch. In fear lest his policy prove unworkable, Khmelnitsky began to look for allies and to conspire with Sweden. His death prevented the completion of his plans, but his actions served as a warning to the Russians. They profited by the existing rift between Cossack and peasant interests and by the resulting discord and weakness and, accusing the Cossacks of perfidy, tightened their hold. In vain did Khmelnitsky's successors try to gain the assistance first of Poland and later of Turkey and to play these two against Russia. The balance of power inclined to Moscow's side, and in 1667, in the Peace of Andrusovo between Poland and Russia, the fate of the Ukraine was settled. The country was divided, the eastern parts were annexed by Russia, and the west remained Polish. Kiev itself was temporarily handed over to Russia, and definitely incorporated in 1680.

Effects on Russia. Thus, after centuries of foreign domination, at least a part of the Ukraine, including the old capital of Kiev, returned into Russian hands. Politically, this was a great Russian success, for it so weakened Poland that she no longer could challenge Russian predominance. Economically, it was likewise a gain for Russia. Renewed migration from the right bank of the Dnieper to the left helped to re-establish the productivity of the region, and the wealth of the nation was proportionately increased. Strategically also it strengthened the position of Russia, particularly in relation to the Turks; and it increased Russian manpower. Only socially, the acquisition brought no advantage. The freedom formerly allowed in the Ukraine was not extended to the rest of the people, but the exact reverse. The concepts of serfdom and the policy of oppression, as existent in Russia, strengthened the conditions introduced in the Ukraine under hetman autocracy and precluded the social rejuvenation which a free Cossack state might have brought to the whole of Russia.

PROBLEMS

1. Discuss the growth of Cossack might in the Ukraine.
2. Trace the causes of tension between the Ukraine and Poland.
3. Discuss the effects of the reincorporation of the Ukraine into Russia.

CHAPTER XII

THE SCHISM

CHURCH AND STATE

During the reign of the first Romanov, Michael, the patriarch Philaret had played a dominant role. The spectacle of father and son ruling together ended with the death of Philaret; but there was to emerge in the times of Michael's son, Alexis, another patriarch, Nikon, destined to exercise still greater influence upon Russia's growth.

Position of Church. Nikon followed Philaret in his advocation of reform, just as Philaret had followed his predecessors. The desire for change in the church can be traced from the convening of the church councils during the early reign of Ivan the Terrible—a desire which increased as attempts at carrying out reforms were thwarted. It is true that, chiefly because of its role during the "Troubles," the church had gained enormously in prestige during the hundred years from 1550 to 1650; it had augmented its material wealth, the administration had been reorganized and extended to Siberia, and the clergy had successfully defended such privileges as exemption from taxes and from state jurisdiction. The church had also succeeded in maintaining satisfactory relations with the state without aspiring to dominate it, since not only religious but also political and economic

factors linked the two institutions and made each an indispensable
partner of the other.

Weaknesses. But in the spiritual field, no healthy growth had
been witnessed. Attempts at moral reform had miscarried; formalism
remained a characteristic preoccupation of the clergy, and national
piety was still coupled with forms and ceremonies. The education
of the clergy was unsatisfactory; books were unavailable for lack of
adequate printing presses, and scores of volumes published earlier had
been destroyed during the "Troubles."

NIKON'S PATRIARCHATE

Nikon. Nikon's patriarchate, beginning in 1652, marked a change.
Yet it would be as incorrect to infer that he endeavored to carry out
a thoroughgoing internal moral reform as it would be to assert that
he wanted to lay claim to leadership in the state and to raise the
church above the Tsar. Arrogant and arbitrary, but courageous,
noble, and devoted, he pursued no such remote aims. His work was
confined to a realignment of the Russian church, and the adoption
of the slightly different principles embodied in the contemporary
Greek branch of the Orthodox church. Politically, such a change
was necessary after the incorporation of the Ukraine, to allow for
the reabsorption of the Ukrainian church and the Academy of Kiev,
which showed definite leanings toward Greek teachings. Without
concessions to the Ukrainians a split might have resulted, endangering the authority of the Moscow patriarch over the whole of the
Russian church.

The Proposed Reforms. Theologically, a reform of the church
according to Greek precepts meant the introduction of some new
ceremonial details, which, to be sure, were closely connected with the
very dogma of the church. It involved the making of the sign of
the cross with three fingers instead of two, the eastward direction
of processional marches, the ban on beard shaving, a correction in
the Russian spelling of the name "Jesus," and the singing of the word
"Hallelujah." It also included correction of the theological books
and eradication of errors which had slipped into them in the course
of the centuries. However, unlike the reforms of the humanists of
western Europe during the sixteenth century, this correction was
based not on the original texts but on the traditions of the Greek
patriarchate. There were also certain changes proposed in connection with reforms of the church choirs and the introduction of ser-

mons, for which most of the ignorant clergy were unqualified. But what, in a practical sense, caused the greatest stir and most furious opposition was the fact that Nikon chose to surround himself with Greeks who favored his ideas, and appointed them to church offices coveted by the indigenous clergy.

Opposition. The result of the innovations was the formation of several factions. The archpriest Avvakum—a man in many ways similar in character to Nikon—was outstanding among the opposition. Alexis backed the patriarch, for whom he had love and respect; but exacerbated by Nikon's arrogance, he eventually withheld his support and in 1658 the angry patriarch laid down the insignia, confessed his sins, and retired to a monastery from which he continued the struggle. No new patriarch was named. After a number of years, Nikon tried to resume his functions, but he was condemned by the church hierarchy and ignored by his former friend, Tsar Alexis. In a moving scene he thereupon resigned his high office and, refusing all proffered gifts, went into exile, one of the most dramatic figures in Russian history. Only when near death was he permitted to return, but he was not to see the capital again. On the way to Moscow, he died and was buried with all the honors of a patriarch. Nikon's adversary Avvakum was to meet with a worse fate. Twice condemned and exiled, he persisted in the fight for his cause. With moving devotion, his wife supported him until the cruel end, when he was burned at the stake.

THE SPLIT

The Raskolníki. Although Nikon himself was deposed, his reforms were essentially upheld by the church council of 1666 to 1667. Being confined to forms, the innovations represented neither progress nor true contributions; but they led to most serious consequences. A schism arose within the church and promptly engulfed the state, endangering its existence. The separating party, known as *Raskolniki* (schismatics, "Old Believers," or "Old Ritualists"), clung to time-honored Russian traditions; they not only denounced Nikon as the Antichrist, but also broke out in open rebellion against the government which had accepted Nikon's reforms. They transferred their hatred from the dead patriarch to the Tsar; from the Tsar to his daughter Sophia, who followed her father's policies; and from her to her successor Peter the Great, who, by ordering men to shave their faces, incited them to commit a sin punishable by excommunication.

As a result of their stand, the Old Believers found themselves exposed to persecutions, to discrimination, and—in practical-minded Peter's times—to special taxation; and serious armed revolts occurred. The most famous incident happened in the far north, on the shores of the White Sea, to which many Raskolniki had fled. There, finding refuge with the monks of the Solovetsky monastery, they defended themselves successfully for seven years against the persecuting armies of the Tsar.

Split within the Raskol. From a religious point of view, the gravest difficulty confronting the Old Believers consisted in the problem of preserving the true church, because, after the introduction of the innovations, the reformed hierarchy was considered unqualified to duly appoint and anoint new members of the priesthood. Some of the Raskolniki solved the problem by dispensing entirely with priests —believing, as had Luther, that no clerical intermediary was necessary between God and the faithful. Others insisted on formally appointed priests, and secretly and precariously preserved a system in which each new priest was consecrated by a predecessor who had himself been anointed according to the true faith and who had not accepted the Nikonian innovations.

THE PRIESTLESS. The priestless (*Bespopovtsi*) were desperate enough to believe that with the Antichrist the end of the world had come. Thousands of them committed suicide; others migrated to the inhospitable north, where they settled in small communities and, incidentally, formed a rather useful and important economic force in the colonization of those regions. Some of them later made concessions to the government and, in exchange for an unmolested life, paid a double poll tax. Others refused any compromise, departed, and relinquishing all worldly possessions led the life of wanderers, with no home, no legal marriage, and no status within society.

THE PRIESTISTS. Of the priestists (*Popovtsi*), who adhered to the traditionally anointed clerics, many emigrated and for a hundred years lived abroad on the Danube, in the Hapsburg empire, and even beyond the seas. Under Catherine the Great, they were invited to return and were promised an undisturbed life. Scores did return and settled in regions beyond the Volga; but in the nineteenth century they were exposed to new persecutions. Both the priestists and the priestless were later to give rise to new sects, the Beguni, the Khlysti, the Dukhobors, and others. Of these, many were alternatingly persecuted, reconciled, accepted, or expelled.

Significance of Schism. Thus, the only advantage of Nikon's innovations and of the resulting schism was an increased religious consciousness among those within the official church as well as those without; but this was by far outweighed by the evil consequences generally accompanying religious persecution. A considerable part of the population found itself excluded from the life of the nation; bad instincts were evoked in the "righteous"; through emigration, able and devoted workers were lost for the country's economy; regard for law and internal unity was endangered.

The total of the Old Believers during the second half of the nineteenth century has been estimated at between ten and twenty millions. Such an enormous part of the population could not indefinitely remain under special laws. In the revolutionary years of 1903 to 1905, the schismatics were granted many rights; but full equality was not restored to them until the advent of the Provisional Government in 1917.

PROBLEMS

1. Discuss the significance of Nikon's attempts at reform.
2. Discuss the results of the schism.
3. Discuss the relationship of church and state.

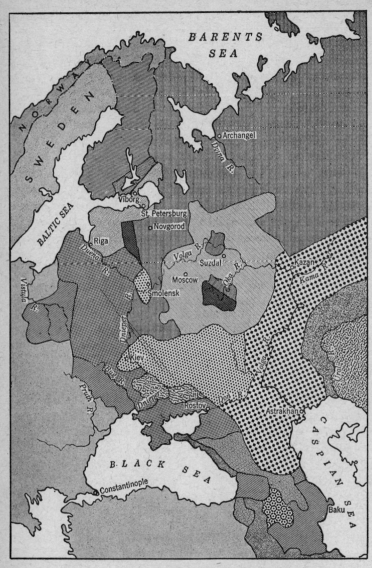

BARENTS SEA

NORWAY

SWEDEN

BALTIC SEA

Archangel

Dvina R.

Viborg

St. Petersburg

Novgorod

Riga

Dvina R.

Volga R.

Suzdal

Kazan

Kama R.

Moscow

Oka R.

Vistula

Smolensk

Dnieper R.

Kiev

Don R.

Ural R.

Pruth R.

Rostov

Volga R.

Astrakhan

CASPIAN SEA

BLACK SEA

Constantinople

Baku

EXPANSION IN EUROPE

MUSCOVY 1462

IVAN III d. 1505

VASILY III d. 1533

IVAN IV d. 1584

MICHAEL d. 1645

ALEXIS d. 1676

PETER I d. 1725

ANNA d. 1740

ELIZABETH d. 1761

CATHERINE II d. 1796

PAUL d. 1801

ALEXANDER I d. 1825

NICHOLAS I d. 1855

ALEXANDER II d. 1881

CHAPTER XIII

EMERGENCE OF RUSSIA AS A EUROPEAN POWER

The rule of the first three Romanovs had brought no social progress. Specifically, the well-being of the people had been neglected, whereas the needs of the army and the accumulation of gold in the Tsar's treasury had found paramount attention. Even so, the basis for future advancement had been laid; for the country was led along the road to reunion with the West through contact with Poland, through the reincorporation of parts of the Ukraine, through the coming of foreign scientists and merchants, through the first attempts to build seagoing ships, and through a sporadic struggle with Sweden for the possession of Livonia. The greatest step in this direction was, however, left to Peter I (1682–1725), later called "the Great."

EARLY PART OF PETER'S REIGN

Accession of Peter. Following a suggestion by the patriarch, Peter became Tsar at the age of ten upon the death of his stepbrother, Tsar Feodor III. The actual rule, however, was exercised by his older sister, Sophia, who had usurped the regency with the help of the archer guards, the Streltsi, and of her lover, Prince Golitsyn. Golitsyn was a well-meaning and enlightened administrator, but utopian in his aims with regard to emancipation of serfs,

77

rapid introduction of Western standards, and the creation of a powerful army. The over-all effect of his work was slight. An unsuccessful war in alliance with Poland against Turkey put an end to his plans and to the rule of Sophia. With the support of the Streltsi, whom Sophia had tried to suppress even though she owed them her regency, Peter made himself ruling Tsar in 1689. A weak-minded older brother, Ivan V, who had formally shared the throne from 1682 on, continued as co-Tsar until he died in 1696.

Peter I.   Peter's education had been neglected; but he was alert and thirsted for knowledge. In the "German suburb" of Moscow, he learned a variety of arts and skills and also a deep respect for foreign customs and accomplishments. He possessed inborn genius, intellectual curiosity, and an uncommon capacity for work; and it was his good luck subsequently to find capable tutors and advisers, such as Patrick Gordon, a Scotsman, and especially François Lefort, a Swiss. From early youth, Peter's attention to military affairs was keen (regiments formed of his playmates were to become later the famed Preobrazhensky and Semenovsky guards). Though he himself never lost his uncouth manners, he learned to appreciate Western culture, which he ardently hoped Russian accomplishments would one day "put to shame."

Conquest of Azov.   In 1694 Peter visited Archangel, where acquaintance with the sea stimulated his childhood interest in shipbuilding and a navy. Whether because of an understanding of the influence of sea power or because of love for military affairs in general, this preoccupation remained with the Tsar for the rest of his life. The need for a strong navy was soon to be demonstrated to him. To fulfill treaty obligations and to prevent recurrent invasions by Crimea Tartars, Peter was forced to declare war on Turkey in 1695, and a siege of the fortress of Azov was started. Despite all efforts, no gain could be made until after a navy had been hurriedly built during the winter. In the following year this proved its value; for by cutting off Azov's sea lanes to Constantinople, Peter forced the garrison of Azov to surrender.

Journey through Europe.   However, Turkey could not be induced to withdraw from the war, and in an effort to strengthen the coalition against her, Peter sent a "great embassy" composed of his principal advisers to various European powers. He himself joined them incognito as a minor official for the purpose of studying European ways and methods. During the journey he hired artisans and doctors whose services and knowledge were to be drawn upon to further Russia's progress along European lines. He negotiated with the Elector of Brandenburg, the Hanover family, the Dutch government, the English king, and the German emperor; he met one of the great thinkers of the century, Leibnitz, and the Dutch scientists Leeuwenhoek and Boerhaave; but he spent much of his time in manual work as a shipwright in Holland and England. He intended to visit also Turkey's most persistent enemy, the great commercial and maritime center of Venice, but his journey was interrupted by news of a rising of the Streltsi at home.

Suppression of the Streltsi. The rebellion of the Streltsi was due partly to mistreatment by their officers; but more important, with the advent of modern military methods, many of the Streltsi feared the loss of their places and privileged position; they disliked the Tsar's foreign leanings and were antagonized also by his harsh policies toward dissenters, many of whom they counted among their own ranks. Although the rising had been suppressed even before Peter reached home, the Tsar proceeded to brutally and mercilessly destroy the whole organization, thus abolishing in time a potentially dangerous praetorian guard and strengthening the freedom of action of the autocrat.

NORTHERN WAR

Baltic Plans. Having failed to bring about the desired anti-Turkish coalition, and faced with an English and Dutch conspiracy against Russia in Constantinople, Peter was compelled to abandon his plans for gaining a firm hold on the Black Sea coast and to content himself with the cession of the fortress of Azov. Peace on this basis was concluded with Turkey in 1700. To make up for the failure to reach the sea, it was planned to annex the Baltic Sea coast instead. Following ideas proposed by Ordyn Nashchokin three decades earlier, an alliance was made with Poland—and also with Denmark—in order to detach some of the Baltic ports from Sweden. But the Swedish king, Charles XII, anticipated the attack. He resolutely invaded Denmark and in a lightning war crushed her completely. Then, in November, 1700, he turned quickly against Russia, and, despite numerical inferiority, won a smashing victory at Narva.

War with Sweden. Historians have speculated as to the possible course of events had Charles pursued the victory and marched on Moscow instead of turning, as he did, against Poland and reducing that country. Perhaps he could have taken Russia's capital; but it is unthinkable that little Sweden could have dominated Peter's growing empire for any length of time or that Charles could have changed the course of history. In any case, while Charles was occupied in Poland, Peter had time to reorganize his forces, and from 1701 his armies were generally successful against Sweden. Slowly all of Livonia and Ingria were conquered and successfully defended, even after Poland had been forced to make a separate peace in 1706, leaving Russia alone to face Charles's might. In 1709 the decisive battle was fought at Poltava in southern Russia. The Swedish king was enticed there by strategic and economic considerations as well as by the hope of finding a powerful ally in the Cossack hetman Ivan Mazepa, famous for his philanthropic work—the remodeling of the Pechersky monastery and the protection of the Kiev Academy of Sciences—but also for his autocratic character and his faithlessness. But the expected support was only partially forthcoming. The Swedish army was beaten, the country's power broken, and Charles XII obliged to flee to Turkey.

Significance of Victory at Poltava.

WITHIN THE RUSSIAN REALMS. The Russian victory had significant consequences. Not only did it raise the international prestige of Russia as the first nation able to cope with the famous conqueror, but also it strengthened the Tsar's position at home. It enabled Peter to hold on to the Swedish possessions in Livonia and thus to accomplish an old Russian ambition by gaining free access to the sea. It precipitated the full incorporation of the eastern Ukraine. Although most of the Ukrainians had remained faithful to Russia, the Cossack state was dissolved and the hetmanship abolished and never—except nominally—revived. Russian commanders and judges as well as tax collectors were imposed on the Ukraine; Cossack detachments were made to serve in Peter's wars regardless of the regions in which they were fought; laborers were drafted for the building of canals and roads or any other task, wherever it might arise. Great areas of Cossack land were granted to Russian noblemen replacing Cossack officers; forced labor, existing *de facto* since the middle seventeenth century and legalized by the Cossacks themselves during Mazepa's hetmanship in 1701, was expanded. Serfdom proper, however, was not recognized by law until the second half of the eighteenth century.

In European Relations. The most important result of Peter's reign was Russia's entry into European affairs and participation in Continental diplomacy. After the Battle of Poltava, the seat of war did not long remain in the south. Brought about by the fugitive Charles's intrigues, a short new struggle with Turkey ensued which led to disastrous results for Peter. It had to be concluded in 1711 at the price of the recently won fortress of Azov, which was returned to the Sultan. From then on, attention was once more focused on the Baltic region. Not only did Peter gain there the provinces adjoining Russia, but by forming marriage alliances with other Baltic countries, by moving his capital to St. Petersburg in 1713, and by building and maintaining a navy on the Baltic Sea, he soon came to exercise dominating influence on the entire sea and began to formulate plans for securing its outlet. It was even rumored that while starting an invasion of southern Sweden Peter went so far as to consider also the conquest of Denmark. Such ambitions were viewed with great alarm by most European powers, notably England, which now had to allow for Russia's place in the European balance-of-power system. To underscore his new position and to conclude trade treaties and further his Swedish invasion plans, Peter undertook a second trip through the Continent in 1716 and 1717, and this time included France in his itinerary. Together with Prussia, France was induced to acknowledge the changes in northern Europe and to guarantee their permanence.

Peace of Nystad. With Russia thus strengthened against English ambitions, negotiations were started to bring an end to the Northern War. Begun in 1718, they were concluded at Nystad in 1721. Russia's incorporation of Livonia, Ingria, and parts of Finnish Karelia were confirmed.

War against Persia. Despite English misgivings, another triumph was secured during the following two years when an expedition against declining Persia led to the acquisition of a large part of the west coast of the Caspian Sea, including the towns of Derbent and Baku with their naphtha and petroleum resources.

SUMMARY

Viewed as a whole, Peter's times witnessed an enormous strengthening of Russia. Excellent ports were acquired on the Baltic and in the Caspian area, though not on the Black Sea; free intercourse with the West was established; Poland and Sweden were both definitely eliminated as powerful enemies; and, entering the political scene of Europe as an important factor, Russia secured contact with progressive nations which was to stimulate the political and intellectual life within the empire.

Spectacular as Russia's international progress during Peter's reign thus proved to be, it was matched by the importance of the changes introduced in the interior (see Chapter XIV).

PROBLEMS

1. Discuss the training of Peter the Great.
2. Explain the issues of the Great Northern War.
3. Compare the international position of Russia at the beginning and at the end of Peter's reign.

CHAPTER XIV

DOMESTIC REFORM WORK

BASIC FACTORS

The list of Peter's achievements in domestic affairs is truly impressive. A concerted program of reform, however, cannot be traced; for the work of Peter was dominated by needs of the moment. Mercantilist ideas prevailed regarding the exploitation of mineral wealth, reforestation policies, and establishment of an active trade balance. Their exponents demanded restrictions on raw-material exports. Protection through tariffs was granted domestic industries, monopolies were accorded for tobacco trade and many minor commodities (up to Peter's time tobacco had been forbidden in Russia), and subsidies were freely given to weak industries. Socially, corruption of judges and administrative officers, criminality, lethargy, and lack of cleanliness were fought; but little was done about such evils as tyranny, flogging, serfdom, and the prevailing disregard for human dignity. Essentially, military and fiscal considerations rather than humanitarian ideals dictated Peter's actions.

SOCIAL REORGANIZATION

Nobility. The council of the boyars was abolished. Nobility was subject to service, a *noblesse de robe* was put on equal footing with the hereditary nobility, and the noble service class became the leading element within the state. It was rewarded by land grants, and land possession was made hereditary.

Military Class. The army, navy, and entire military class were reformed. The Streltsi were abolished and recruits were drawn from all classes and all regions of the empire. Promotion was based on ability; the abolition of tables of rank for the nobility—put into practice by Prince Golitsyn in 1682—served toward the streamlining of the entire military system. Soldiers were used for police as well as for military service.

Clergy. The church and clergy were completely identified with the state. This arrangement was accomplished with little difficulty because of the pre-existing close relationship. In 1721, the patriarchate, unfilled for twenty-one years, was entirely abolished and replaced by a council, the "Synod," which was less likely ever to exercise immoderate political influence. The administration of church wealth was put under state supervision, the training of the clergy was improved, the growth of monasteries was restricted and discipline restored. Tolerance was extended to several non-Orthodox religious groups, but not to Jews or dissenters.

Merchant Class. The growth of a merchant and artisan class was encouraged. The social status of the commercial class was raised and brought into integration with other classes. Guilds were re-established to give the merchant standing, to control his activities, and to form a link between him and the state, which he was to serve in his field. Foreigners were invited into the country for the purpose of increasing production and developing material resources.

Peasantry. As the noble service class worked for the state, so was the peasantry made accountable to this service class. Bondage was extended to hitherto free territories, and strict fugitive serf laws were enforced; all proposals for the abolition of serfdom were categorically rejected by Peter. Additional burdens were imposed on the peasant by a new recruiting system for the army and by a poll tax levied on every male peasant ("soul") regardless of age or ability to work. Although tens of thousands of peasants were thereby driven into unsettled regions or Cossack territories, the area under cultivation was vastly increased.

Factory Workers. The laboring class was expanded. Bonded peasants could be bought by factory owners and put to work in mines and other industries. Unoccupied sons of priests, vagabonds, and criminals were recruited for useful service in state and private enterprise.

Women. Special attention was paid to a change in the status of women. On his trips through Europe, Peter had witnessed the freedom and activities of women abroad; and despite his own shameful relationships with women and his promiscuity, he contributed to a thorough improvement. The *terem* was abolished; women were partially emancipated; and the female sex was invited to court functions, receptions, and balls, thus setting an example for social life in all spheres.

ADMINISTRATIVE CHANGES

Government. The country was divided into provinces and districts and, notwithstanding the principle of absolutism and autocracy, a certain amount of decentralization was brought about. Through a very complicated administrative system eight, and later eleven, districts were created, each with a governor and a judicial and a financial officer; and a number of "colleges" (departments) for finance, commerce, justice, manufacturing, and the like were organized. Owing to overlapping functions of central and local authorities, the new system never worked satisfactorily. A special order for townships was instituted also; this, however, proved equally unsuccessful. Above the districts and municipalities was created a Senate, which was to advise the Tsar and to govern the country in his absence. It was also invested with judicial functions.

FOUNDING OF ST. PETERSBURG. A new capital, St. Petersburg, was founded near the Baltic shores and designed to serve as a connecting link with the West, to emphasize Russia's international position, and to strengthen the European character of Russian court life and manners. Because of its location in unhealthful and unfavorable surroundings, the city has been called "an outrage to common sense"; its construction alone cost the lives of more than twenty thousand workmen. Eventually, however, it was to serve well the purpose for which it was developed.

Educational Measures. Schools were founded and attendance was made compulsory for the children of the noble service class; but they gave only the rudiments of learning and necessitated supplementary training abroad.

THE ACADEMY OF SCIENCES. A new calendar was introduced, beginning the year on January 1 instead of in September, counting the years from the birth of Christ rather than from the Creation, and eliminating a difference of eight years between Russian and Western chronology; on the whole, however, this innovation was unsatisfactory inasmuch as the Julian calendar was adopted instead of the Gregorian one used in most European countries. A simplified alphabet likewise was worked out and put into practice. Moreover, an Academy (founded by Peter the Great, but not established until after his death) was created after European models. It greatly promoted the study of geography and exploration. Although all these activities have been termed "a lisping of barbarians striving to spell out European civilization," the Academy of Sciences was to become in due time an important cultural factor.

MANNERS. For the improvement of manners, special institutions were founded, and various enactments put into effect. The long dresses of the peasants, despite their obvious advantage during the rigors of the winter, were forbidden so that the peasants would be unencumbered while at work. The beards of men, except of clergy and peasants, were ordered shaved as a sanitary measure—although some hold that this decree was a result of the Tsar's drunkenness and the shortcomings of his own beard. This decree was a challenge to the church, which demanded unshaven faces, and it led to grave new difficulties with the Old Believers. Eventually beards were allowed provided that a special tax was paid.

Economic Measures.

FINANCES. The enormous burdens shouldered by the state in carrying out reforms could not be met without a parallel increase in the budget. The military in particular expended heretofore unheard-of sums, absorbing from one-half to three-quarters of the total revenue. In consequence, all means had to be strained to provide the necessary income. Church lands were confiscated whenever possible, trade monopolies were sold to the highest bidder, state industries were endowed with special rights which would make them profitable, and the customary and worst expedient of all was also resorted to: adulteration of coin.

TAXATION. In addition, greatly augmented taxes were levied. The poll tax was the most important item. Unfortunately, it brought terrible injustices; it implied, for example, that a wealthy peasant with three daughters capable of work would have to pay less than any poor peasant with two male babies and an aged father to support, since only male persons were counted as taxable "souls." Furthermore, owing to corruption and the system of farming out taxes (in use also in contemporary France and elsewhere), not more than one-third or one-half of the collected sums reached the treasury.

INDUSTRIES. Factories were built. Many remained in government hands, particularly those in the Ural mining district. Others, which were allowed to pass into private hands, were subjected to state supervision. State assistance was granted if needed, although this policy often served to increase corruption and waste. Fiscal needs and military considerations essentially governed decisions concerning the foundation of new factories. All plants suffered from a scant labor supply and from want of competent directors. The century-long neglected bourgeoisie were unable to provide the necessary men for the organization and management of efficient industries.

Building. Roads, bridges, and canals were constructed. Inspired by the Dutch example and following the old Russian tradition, the Tsar exerted his utmost energy in the direction of increasing and bettering existing waterways. Many important constructions were undertaken and plans were laid for a Don-Volga and for a Ladoga canal; both were completed after Peter's death.

SIGNIFICANCE OF PETER'S REFORM WORK

Criticism. The list of Peter's personal activities is imposing; his unflagging energy and detailed advice stand behind many of the achievements of the time. But historians, and foremost those of Russia, do not agree as to his usefulness. Peter is given credit for having gained for Russia access to one sea, but he is accused of destroying the Russian way of life, of introducing lax morals through the example of his own dissolute living, his coarseness, and the vulgarity of his amusements—jesters, dwarfs, and their kind. Furthermore, his reforms are said to have been too speedily adopted, and thus to have been lacking in depth. Yet he encouraged activity, and "finding little, he left much." The charge that his influence sufficed to lead Russia on a road not in line with the country's natural development is untenable, because such is beyond the power of one human being. But it may be true that the abruptness and speed of his reforms damaged existing constructive institutions, and exercised an unwholesome influence on the civilization of the people. And it may also be argued that "the technique of Western peoples" was "reproduceable only within the framework of their whole style of living."

Reaction.   Reaction against Peter's work was strong and, as so often in Russian history, it was supported peculiarly enough not by the older but by the younger generation. This characteristic trait was mirrored in the opposition of Peter's son Alexis to his father. The drunkard weakling Alexis, devoted to narrow ideas and conspicuous for bad manners, is no attractive personality; but his struggle against his father, his flight to Italy, return, and gruesome end by torture (consumption would have ended his life soon enough) do not lack the elements of great tragedy. Had Alexis succeeded his father on the throne, opposition to the innovations might have retarded the Westernization of Russia. But lack of decision in the actual successors made impossible the formation of an influential opposition, and Peter's death left the way free for his most trusted ministers, Menshikov and Ostermann, to consolidate, if not carry further, the work of their master.

PROBLEMS

1. Discuss the main causes for Peter's reform work.
2. Discuss the social changes brought about by the "Westernization" efforts.
3. Discuss the justification for criticisms of Peter's reform work.

CHAPTER XV

POLITICAL TRENDS AND SOCIAL PROGRESS IN THE MIDDLE EIGHTEENTH CENTURY

The period between the death of Peter the Great and the accession of Catherine the Great, 1725 to 1762, has been considered by some historians as an era of shallowness, confusion, and decay, whereas others attribute to it much of Russia's spiritual growth and political advancement. The truth seems to lie on both sides. Rapid and violent changes, as under Peter, were discontinued, but slowly the process of Westernization went on, gaining in depth and leading to a better proportion between the ambitions and the actual potentialities of the country.

RULERS

Peter's Successors. During the middle of the eighteenth century few contributions to the rise of Russia were made by her rulers. Most of Peter's successors owed their thrones to usurpation and to the support of court cliques and factions which they dared not antagonize even after gaining autocratic power. Peter himself had laid the basis for these conditions when he altered the succession law and left to each ruling prince the choice of his successor; however, he had died before so appointing his own successor and straightway the intrigues had begun. They led first to the accession of Peter's wife, Catherine I (1725–27). Her elevation, a "triumph over prejudice," for she was a woman and she came from the lowest stratum of society, she owed to her former lover, Menshikov. At the time of her death, two years later, the succession law was again altered, and she was followed by a boy, Peter II (1727–30); after his short reign came another woman, Anna I (1730–40); then an infant, Ivan VI (1740–41), who was promptly dethroned; then a third woman, Elizabeth (1741–62); and finally, for a few months, Peter III (1762). None of these rulers possessed sufficient character and ability to give direction to Russian growth; by sheer inertia, the work of Peter the Great was followed through and his ideas, unchallenged, gradually entrenched themselves as a part of Russian life. The next self-willed ruler, Catherine II, was not to mount the throne until almost forty years after his death.

STATESMEN.　The main agent directing the continued Westernization and integration of the country according to Peter's aims was Menshikov, who was dismissed and banished in 1727 because of his arrogance, vanity, and ruthlessness. After him came the so-called "German" party. Its strongest exponent was Baron Ostermann, an excellent and honest administrator and a capable foreign minister, to whom the Russia of Peter's immediate three successors owes much of its stability. Men like Münnich, builder of the Ladoga Canal and successful general, contributed their share; but many of the Germans were too ambitious and too selfishly engaged in connections alien to Russian interests; others, such as Tsarina Anna's infamous favorite Biron, pursued no other aim than that of personal aggrandizement. Political mistakes, combined with the fact that they were of foreign origin and that their positions were coveted by native Russians, accounted for the small favor the German party found with the service-nobility. Their domination was ended in 1740. Succeeding them were less progressive men, mostly Russians, and of less than mediocre stature with the possible exception of Alexis Bestuzhev-Ryumin, foreign minister under Elizabeth.

THE OPPOSITION.　All statesmen during this period had to fight the conservative opposition which, under the leadership of the old noble families, repeatedly came to the fore. Upon the accession of Anna in 1730, the aristocracy saw themselves within reach of their aims. They succeeded in returning the court and the "colleges" from St. Petersburg to Moscow; they renounced Peter's maritime plans; and they managed to impose on the new ruler, Anna, a constitution modeled after Sweden's, which restored their lost privileges and freed them of compulsory service. But Anna, once secure on the throne, recognized that in a struggle with the court aristocracy she would be able to enlist sufficient support from their opponents, and she subsequently abrogated all prior concessions.

Anna. As a matter of fact, Anna became the most autocratic of Peter's successors. She reduced the powers of the Senate and subordinated the whole body to a "cabinet" which, however, was not to remain long in existence. The decay of the administration was halted; with utmost cruelty, order was reintroduced and rebellious elements were punished with torture, death, and exile. While giving little attention to the navy, Anna saw to the rejuvenation of the army and the establishment of a cadet corps.

Elizabeth. Elizabeth, who succeeded Anna except for the brief intermezzo of the baby Ivan VI, is generally credited with having restored "Russian" ways. Indeed, the capable and devoted Ostermann, together with General Münnich and the worthless Biron, was tortured and exiled. But the overthrow of the German court officials increased the scope of other alien influences and intrigues, particularly French ones, and strengthened the power of the landholding nobility, which was freed of many service obligations and received special rights to army posts. The nobles also gained a monopoly on ownership of serfs and so extended jurisdiction over them that the position of the peasants became almost indistinguishable from that of slaves. As was to be expected, Elizabeth, ignorant, dissolute, bigoted, and lazy, was incapable of improving the state of the country; and, though she sometimes showed a kindly disposition and a flair for meeting popular needs and demands, the vaunted "Russification" meant no essential change for the better.

Peter III. In 1762 Elizabeth died, leaving the throne to her nephew Peter III. It is not easy to speculate as to which road Russia would have taken had he kept the throne for a number of years. In the memory of the people, particularly of the lower classes, he lived on as a reformer, sympathetic to their desires. Their hopes were derived from Peter's various edicts regarding a general amnesty, dissolution of the secret police, toleration of sects, secularization of church property, reduction of salt prices, and freeing of the gentry from obligatory service (an edict believed to promise parallel action for enserfed peasants). Yet, despite the remarkable and numerous liberal edicts of the few months of his reign, Peter's character was not such as to warrant the expectation of a steady progressive course. His injudicial, blind imitation of foreign manners and alien spirit, his extraneous interests, his insistence on Prussian military drill, his arrogance and recurrent seizures of insanity made him unfit to rule, and he was forthwith overthrown by the court nobility in a *coup d'état* supported by his wife Catherine, who thereupon seized the throne (1762–96). A few days thereafter, Peter was murdered by one of the accomplices.

SOCIAL PROGRESS

Culture. Culturally, little was accomplished during the period from 1725 to 1762 that may properly be called of Russian origin. French ideas found entrance, and the manners and customs as well as the philosophy of France began to exercise a powerful influence at least among part of the ruling caste. Some new schools were founded, yet education continued to encompass but a limited number of fields and benefited only the privileged few. The Academy of Sciences was enlarged and the first great Russian scholar, Lomonosov, made his appearance. In 1755 the University of Moscow was founded. But the cultural centers in the Ukraine continued to decline; Kiev lost its long-held reputation for scholarship, and Great Russian dialect and customs supplanted the indigenous civilization there.

Commerce. Trade was encouraged and increased when, due to Ostermann's foresight, tariff barriers were lowered in 1728 and 1729; but his judicious policy was not persistently carried out. England remained the best customer of Russia. In Siberia, commerce developed slowly. Settlements there remained scarce, though some were established in the western parts. To protect them against nomad invasions, it was necessary to erect a fortification line extending from the Caspian Sea to Orenburg (founded in 1760) and thence to the upper Irtish region. The parts inhabited by Kirghiz tribes and consisting chiefly of barren steppe were incorporated in 1740; but essentially, Russian activities in Asia were limited to the task of exploration.

Discoveries. Exploration was carried on under the auspices of the Academy of Sciences. The Transcaspian region was explored and the direct way to India opened, but the major part of the operations centered around the task of establishing the confines of Siberia. Five separate expeditions were charged with circumnavigating and mapping the north coast, each being assigned to a different sector. Because of a mild season in the summer of 1737, they were successful. The rounding of the corner farthest east remained unaccomplished, but a land expedition did manage to reach the limits of Asia in the northeast. Finally, in 1741 Vitus Bering, a cautious and conscientious Danish explorer but one who lacked true genius, succeeded in reaching the American shore and, through the work of his companion, the German botanist Steller, established the fact that the two continents were separated by water. Thus, after having tried for thirteen years, during which he had travelled as far north as $67\frac{1}{4}°$ and, without realizing it, had actually sighted America in 1732, Bering solved the long-perplexing question whether or not a land bridge connected the old and the new world.

FOREIGN POLICIES

In external affairs, considerable progress was made, though it may be said that it happened despite, rather than because of, the work of the administration, and was achieved by sheer weight rather than through wisdom and skillful diplomacy. Russia's role was strengthened; in matters of Continental importance, her consent was sought and her might appreciated. But only towards her neighbors—Sweden, Poland, and Turkey—was an active and conscious policy followed. Toward the Western powers, Russia had no policy of her own, but remained their tool in various commercial and political schemes and in the system of balance of power.

PROBLEMS

1. Discuss the persistence of Western influences in Russia after Peter I's death.
2. Discuss the exploration and expansion in Asia in the middle of the eighteenth century.

Significant Dates

Nobility Freed from Obligation of
    Service 1762

Secularization of Church Lands 1764

CHAPTER XVI

LIFE AND ACTIVITIES IN THE EIGHTEENTH CENTURY

Military achievements, foreign policies, personalities of rulers, and court intrigues mirror eighteenth-century civilization and hold a significant place in the development of human society. But even when these represent the key for an understanding of a nation's growth and the direction of its evolution, the picture must be supplemented by an analysis of the social currents and the economic status of the people as a whole.

COURT AND TOWN LIFE

The Court Nobility. In eighteenth-century Russia, the governing class was made up of the court nobility, and in Russia even more than elsewhere it was separated as by an abyss from the mass of the people. It enjoyed the comforts of life, partook in the intellectual achievements of the era, and preserved the privileges of times gone by in a form perhaps less refined than that of the *ancien régime* in France, but essentially identical with it. Politically it was interested chiefly in court intrigues, in struggle for power, and in foreign affairs.

The Service-Nobility.   Apart from the court, dominating influence was exercised by the service-nobility. This class had begun its rise under Ivan the Terrible; during the Time of Troubles it had gained pre-eminence, and under the first three Romanovs it had entrenched itself. In exchange, it was sworn to perform continued service in the armed forces or in the administration. During the eighteenth century, it tried to rid itself of as many of these obligations as possible. Some of the gentry secured in 1730 the right to escape military service on condition that they withdraw from the capital and reside on their estates. This was the first break in the system of service, and it was carried to its logical conclusion under Peter III when in 1762 the gentry were freed from all obligation of service and thus became a leisure class. As in France, the very existence of this class undermined the welfare of the state.

The Bourgeoisie.   The bourgeoisie remained without influence in the eighteenth century. Peter's attempts at raising the standing of the merchants and artisans had borne some fruits, but so long as the gentry retained the exclusive political power and the peasantry was held to a status of want and serfdom small progress could be made. Towns stagnated; even by the end of the century out of a population of about forty million, less than 5 per cent lived in towns, and only part of these belonged to the bourgeoisie. Professions and commerce found little attention.

Trade.   Trade was increasing somewhat; indeed, exports were more than ten times as great by 1800 as in 1725. But the figures give a deceptive picture, for the raw materials as well as the man-hours invested were woefully undervalued in Russia, and thus increased exports meant an actual loss for the nation. Imports, consisting largely of luxury articles, were generally overpriced and only satisfied the vanity of a small upper class instead of benefiting the national economy. Their true extent cannot be ascertained, because smuggling and corruption among customs officials permitted imports not to be found in official statistics. Internal trade was still more inadequate. Industries grew, but only the nobility (by shifting serfs from their lands to the factories) could secure the necessary laborers, and in consequence they almost monopolized a field which might have prospered better under bourgeois direction.

INDUSTRIAL LIFE

The Industrialists. The industrialists found themselves in a difficult position. Many had acquired their factories, particularly during the times of Elizabeth, as compensation for meritorious service, just as in former times faithful servants had been awarded landed estates. In such cases, state supervision and interference persisted. The owners had few outlets for their products: most of their goods had to be produced for the government; some was for export; only a little could be sold on the free market and even then to the gentry only. The bulk of the population had to rely essentially upon the products of their own home industries.

The Proletariat. In Western countries industrial workmen began to make themselves felt, but in Russia they remained without importance. No common interests of the industrial workers could lead to the formation of a specific class for the reason that industrial labor was recruited partly from among peasant-serfs. These were forcibly "ascribed" to factories, from which during certain seasons they regularly returned to resume their agricultural duties. A great many worked in mines owned by the state, but the more unfortunate were ascribed to private enterprises.

Factories. In the factories the workmen were ill-treated and overworked. Their fundamental grievances were long hours, enforced transfer from their lands to factories, long journeys between their homes and the mines with consequent loss of pay, and irregularities in the payment of wages. Innumerable complaints poured in at St. Petersburg; but neither investigations and regulation of wages by state officials nor the occasional confiscation and transfer of ownership of whole factories remedied the evils. Furthermore, redress was generally delayed, sometimes even beyond the lifetime of the claimant. In desperation, many workers sacrificed their small earnings and tried to buy themselves free by hiring still more wretched persons who would be willing to take their places. Others—and there were thousands of these—fled to Siberia and other possible havens of freedom.

Shirking and drunkenness among workers added another problem to industrial life. Poor helpers, like everyone else, had to be cared for in times of depression and in the event of accident and sickness. The entire system of forced labor was burdensome, and free labor and competition would have been more productive and profitable. The more industrialization advanced, the more the factory owners suffered from labor shortages. Labor shortage came to a peak at the end of the century, when the industrialists were forbidden to buy peasants and separate them from their land for employment in mines and factories.

AGRICULTURAL LIFE

The Peasants. Approximately sixteen million peasant men and women who made up the peasantry in the middle of the eighteenth century found themselves in a sphere altogether unique. Few of them were free except younger sons of noblemen who had found no other occupation, sharecroppers who had no permanent residence, and peasants in outlying or recently acquired parts of the empire.

Serfdom.

On State Lands. A part of the serf population lived and worked on estates owned by the state or by the Tsars personally. These were comparatively better off than those subject to private masters. The laws of the land, instead of the arbitrary will of a profit-seeking owner, were applied to them. But they, too, were bound to the land whose *usus fructi* they enjoyed; and at all times they faced the unwelcome prospect of being ascribed to factories.

On Private Estates. On the other hand, the private and hereditary serfs, who formed the majority of all peasants, found themselves in a desperate position. It was up to the landowner to regulate their lives, to arrange their marriages, to exercise jurisdiction over them, to punish and banish them, and to keep control of their personal belongings. Government regulations for the betterment of their condition remained ineffectual, for a peasant could not bring suit against his master, and was exposed to merciless punishments. To be sure, there were many humane members among the landholding class; but in a general atmosphere such as existed during the eighteenth century even their humanity was but relative, and when an owner went so far as to free his serfs from servitude he often gained for them no more than the status of agricultural wage-slavery.

Obrok. As hereditary serfs, the peasants were subdivided into two principal groups: the *obrok*-paying and the *barchina*-rendering serfs. During the eighteenth century, those on *obrok* (i.e., those paying a fixed sum) lived to a large extent in the less fertile northern regions where the landowners found it more profitable to ask for money than for labor. Often the results in crop raising and cattle breeding were poor, especially because peasant skill and industry were inferior to those in other parts of Europe, where crops of two or three times the value were harvested with the same size and type of land. Furthermore, the peasant's plot of land was sometimes too small to make its cultivation adequate for the maintenance of a family and the payment of dues. To provide the necessary sums, the land was therefore not infrequently left to the care of women while the men tried to earn the *obrok* through work in a factory. While they thus served to supply labor for industry, agriculture suffered, and the extension of the *obrok* system was therefore opposed by the government.

Barchina. The *barchina* peasants were still worse off. They were not even free to go into factories and augment their incomes, since their labor was demanded by the masters approximately three days a week. During harvest season they were often compelled to give even more time to their masters and to neglect their own urgently needed crops.

The Mir. To avert the disastrous consequences of such a system, co-operation was emphasized and peasant holdings were treated as the common property of a whole village community (*mir*) so that they could be looked after by all those not engaged in work for the squires. This, naturally, strengthened social consciousness among the peasants. The common land was distributed by the *mir* and at intervals redistributed among the individual members, the state taxes and often the *obrok* being handled by the *mir*. Care was given to the aged, the sick, and the orphaned. Education was likewise under the auspices of the *mir;* but it was very meagre except in the Baltic provinces, which after Peter's conquest remained socially under domination of the Baltic Germans with their higher standards. Unfortunately, the *mir* was frequently under the influence of an indolent priest or a rich peasant (*kulak*) who, unmindful of his own earlier sufferings, exploited the work of his fellow men or oppressed them through loans at usurious rates. Under such circumstances, even the *mir* did not gain as much for the individual peasant as should have been possible; and the serf became so fearful and despondent that any innovation, even if it held definite promise for his betterment, was denounced lest it somehow be so interpreted as to heighten his distress.

IN HOUSEHOLDS. It is to be noted that in the eighteenth century another class came into being—the household serf—which was developed by ascribing children of peasants to the household of the owner. Here they received special training and later served as domestic help, being employed for spinning and weaving and other household duties, and occasionally as musicians and teachers. From this group arose distinguished writers, artists, and scientists, some of whom received additional training in special public institutions or abroad.

CLERICAL LIFE

The Upper Clergy. The top hierarchy enjoyed the favor of the government and were honored with rank and distinction. They formed one of the most important pillars of the state and were to a large extent dependent upon it. Under Peter the Great, they were relieved of much of the administration of worldly church affairs, which had passed into the hands of the Synod. In 1762 church property was entirely confiscated; disposal of it by the church had been curtailed in Ivan the Terrible's time. Now it was ordered secularized; and in 1764, under Catherine, the order was executed. A state budget was introduced which provided for the maintenance of the clergy; although it served to link the church entirely with the state and subject the hierarchy to government direction, it was possible for the hierarchy to draw substantial incomes and lead a life of luxury as well as of influence.

The Lower Clergy. The position of the village clergy was in sharp contrast to that of the higher ranks. Though free, they formed in some respect the lowest of all classes, despised by nobility and peasantry alike. Before the eighteenth century the position of priest or "pope" had been often elective; those who bid for the lowest salaries had been not infrequently chosen. Therefore, the least qualified had monopolized many of the positions. Education among the clergy was scanty; they had to guarantee, but not to prove, that they could read and write and they were expected to pass a perfunctory examination in religion, but not until Napoleonic times was serious theological training prescribed. Their moral standards were equally low; many were equipped neither to teach the gospel, to preach, nor to enlighten. Their own lives set no example, and their work consisted largely in serving as useful tools of the state (sometimes in police matters) rather than in the propagation of the faith.

In Peter I's time, elections to parsonages were gradually discontinued. Instead, either popes were nominated by the diocese or, more frequently, the office of priest passed from father to son. This led to the establishment of a hereditary clerical class, which from time to time had to be purged of superfluous members; the unhappy victims were sent to factories or estates. The only advantage the village priest enjoyed, from 1738 on, consisted in being exempted from the poll tax. Otherwise he belonged to the lowest strata of the population, and until 1796 he could be subjected to corporal punishment and flogging. The wives of the popes continued to be subjected to such indignities for some additional forty years.

SYSTEM OF AUTOCRACY

As a whole, Russia in the eighteenth century presented the picture of a country where the concept of service to the state was paramount. Nobleman, merchant, peasant, and clergyman alike had to correlate their lives and activities with the needs of a state which was autocratically governed by the ruler. Yet, the ruler himself was not free in his decisions, for he was subject to custom and dependent upon the continued support of the most essential class, the service-nobility. In the hands of an efficient and farsighted monarch the system might have worked to common benefit; under incompetent men and women, it led to grievous and often ineradicable injustices, to social rifts, to economic insecurity, and worst of all to destruction of human dignity which for centuries was to leave its scars on the nation.

PROBLEMS

1. Discuss the stratification of Russian society in the eighteenth century.
2. Discuss the service obligations for nobility and peasantry.
3. Discuss the economic significance of serfdom.

CHAPTER XVII

INTERNAL CONDITIONS IN CATHERINE'S TIMES

CATHERINE II

Catherine, a German princess, was thirty-three years old when she ascended the throne in 1762. To all appearances she had accepted the Orthodox faith with much sincerity, which—to the mind of her Russian supporters—contrasted favorably with the agnosticism of her husband. Her marriage had been a failure, and after a few years she took a lover, who in due time was succeeded by eight or nine others by whom she had several children. But her love affairs and dissipations, which mirrored the concepts of the times and resembled conditions at the French court, were not to interfere with her devotion to duty as a ruler. She was an indefatigable worker, an interested student of political affairs, a diplomat, a linguist, a sculptress, painter, reader, and correspondent. Under the influence of the writings of Montesquieu, Beccaria, and Voltaire, she herself showed certain traits of an "enlightened, benevolent despot." But her actions hardly justify her claim to practical enlightenment. Internal improvements during her reign were limited in scope and served her personal vanity and desire for applause more than the needs of the people.

Perhaps the disposal and subsequent murder of her husband and later the murder of the one other claimant to the throne, the former baby-Tsar Ivan VI, who had by now grown to manhood, left her with an uneasy conscience, made her dependent upon those who had elevated her, and prevented her from insisting on innovations lest she risk her crown.

CATHERINE'S RULE

Attempts at Reform. In 1767 Catherine set out to achieve administrative reorganization and improvement in municipal and economic institutions, and to better agricultural conditions. Accordingly she convened a commission of more than five hundred members, elected by all classes except the serfs, to deliberate the contemplated great reform. She herself wrote a rather general directive, which was applauded throughout the Continent for its liberal spirit; but it was stripped of many of its generous suggestions on being submitted to the commission. Deliberations took more than a year. No progress was made, and in 1774 the whole work was abandoned.

Failures and Achievements. Institutional changes were limited to the administrative system; the powers of the Senate were reduced and the land was redistributed into fifty-one districts. Both measures served to enlarge the autocratic powers of the ruler and those of the gentry. Corruption in the administration continued to flourish as Catherine had found it. As before, the inhabitants of the country were excluded by edict from participation in public affairs. Serfdom was not only preserved, but it was vastly expanded by enormous grants of public land to the gentry and by its extension to the Ukraine, where all remnants of autonomy were abolished. Capital punishment and torture were seldom resorted to, but the first had already been officially abolished by Elizabeth and the latter by Peter III; asylums and hospitals were founded, but in this case again Peter has to be credited for the initial measure. Vaccination was introduced and was propagandized. Education was extended to women, but only to those of the upper class. Schools were founded in agricultural districts and even among some of the most backward Asiatic tribes, but instruction was insufficient and the lack of understanding of local conditions sometimes led to preposterous contradictions. Only in the complete emancipation of the merchant class in 1785 and in a liberal attitude towards the Old Believers, some of whom were encouraged to return to Russia, could signs of true enlightenment be found; yet even these faded during the era of the great French Revolution (1789–95), when the privileged classes, fearing a similar upheaval in Russia, supported the passage of reactionary measures.

Court Life. The court at St. Petersburg during Catherine's reign was fashioned along French patterns. It was a late blossoming of the pseudo-culture of a Louis XIV. Art treasures were brought from abroad at the expense of toiling workers; French actors and dancers and also physicians were hired at great cost, and, besides Western philosophical ideas, they introduced stilted manners little in harmony with the crude pleasures enjoyed by Catherine and her court. From Germany, teachers and artisans were introduced. The foreigners eventually spread the liberal concepts of their home countries and found disciples in men like Novikov, scientist, author, and editor of a paper, *The Drone,* and Radishchev, famed for his realistic and accusatory description of social conditions in his *Journey from Petersburg to Moscow*. Both were bitterly persecuted by Catherine and exiled, but nevertheless a liberal movement took firm root in Russian Society.

PUGACHEV REVOLT

Preliminary Uprisings. Since Catherine's lengthy rule of nearly thirty-five years thus marked no true progress in the social development of a country urgently in need of reform, general unrest increased. Numerous minor outbreaks occurred and a serious rising followed the pestilence which swept the country in 1770, but none brought amelioration of conditions. Eventually, a revolt broke out which surpassed in size and violence that led by Stenka Razin one hundred years earlier, and darkly foreshadowed the collapse of the autocratic system that was to occur in the early twentieth century.

Grievances. As in the times of Razin, the revolution was directed not against the institution of Tsardom, but against the nobility. The tsarist idea was firmly maintained, because only from a supreme autocratic ruler could relief be expected from the oppressions of a small gentry and of the landowners. And if such relief had not been forthcoming in the past, that was seldom blamed on the inefficiency or unconcern of the Tsars, but rather on the malevolence of the court nobility, who were accused of preventing the complaints of the poor from reaching the throne and of falsifying ukases of the Tsars. As a matter of fact, peasant delegations sent to submit petitions had frequently been waylaid en route to the capital or, if they finally did arrive, had been imprisoned and flogged.

Pugachev. The revolution broke out in 1772. In contrast to the Razin rising and despite all oppression, not the peasantry but the Cossacks (those from the Ural) acted as the driving force behind the upheaval. They had their own grievances with regard to military service imposed upon them, corruption of their officers, persecution of the numerous dissenters among them, and an edict of the government ending their right to choose their own superiors. They seized upon the occasion of a war between Russia and Turkey, and provided a legitimate basis for their rising by spreading rumors that Peter III had not died but had reappeared. Peter was vested with all manner of liberal ideas which, it is very likely, he had never cherished. He was credited with special sympathy for Old Believers, although in reality indifference in religious matters had accounted for his tolerance towards them. Once these rumors were given credence, several impersonators of the dead ruler appeared. It was a Cossack, Pugachev, who, despite difference in both appearance and age, finally emerged as the "true" Peter and was acknowledged leader of the revolution. Though less a pilot than a tool, he showed enough independence and shrewdness to engage the help and co-operation of the peasants by promising them emancipation from serfdom, religious freedom, and abolishment of military service.

Revolution. Although the interests of the peasants were no longer identical with those of the Cossacks and although many of them stood in fear of Cossack outrages, a large number thereupon joined with Pugachev, and soon the rising spread to the European part of the empire as well as into western Siberia. Had Pugachev been as able in strategic planning as in evoking the enthusiasm of the impoverished masses rebelling against their masters, the revolution might have been successful. But despite an army of more than fifteen thousand men, his siege of the fortress of Orenburg, crucial link in the defense system of the government, miscarried after exhausting attempts. In March, 1774, reaction set in accompanied by defeats. It was only by the greatest exertion that Pugachev was still able to enlist the help of new recruits, to seize the town of Kazan, and to threaten Moscow. The government answered by putting an end to the war with Turkey and, with the freeing of sufficient troops, countered the menace. Betrayed by personal enemies among the Cossacks, Pugachev was captured in August, 1774, and executed in January, 1775.

Results. As had many premature revolutions, the Pugachev revolt showed the urgent need for reforms, yet by its very lack of success defeated any chance for improvement. The charter issued by Catherine in 1785 strengthened serfdom by placing additional burdens on the peasants, and historians have justly argued that the work of social reform was thrown back by half a century.

CATHERINE "THE GREAT"

If Catherine in her internal policies showed herself hardly worthy of the surname "the Great," wisdom and steadfastness in external affairs should explain the attribute accorded her. Yet, success rather than ability and perseverance account for the title; and success was essentially achieved by a combination of favorable circumstances, able help, and weight of Russian power, while Catherine herself contributed but little. As a whole, the policies pursued under previous reigns were carried on by her. No clear pattern emerged with regard to Western European powers, and only in connection with Russia's immediate neighbors can a consistent policy be witnessed.

PROBLEMS

1. Discuss Catherine's claims to the title "the Great."
2. Trace the conditions leading to the Pugachev revolt.
3. Discuss the effect of the revolt.

CHAPTER XVIII

GROWTH OF RUSSIA'S INTERNATIONAL ROLE

The era from Peter the Great to the death of Catherine the Great in 1796—the latter date marking the year when Napoleon appeared on the international scene—constituted a transition period in Russia's role in the European community. Before Peter, the country was a practically unknown barbarian empire beyond the pale of European concern; after Catherine, it was an integral part of Europe, a full and independent partner in the system of Continental politics.

The transition period itself was characterized by the spirit of the time according to which foreign affairs were conducted as a private art—the art of diplomacy—practiced by rulers or ministers according to certain rules and standards of a very distinguished guild; opportunistic motives and personal inclinations furnish a better key to an understanding of this period than any attempt to trace trends or plans.

RELATIONS WITH CENTRAL AND WESTERN EUROPE

Alliances. After Peter's death, Russia for a time continued the policy of friendship with Prussia and France laid down by the great Tsar. But in 1733 France tried to place on the Polish throne the father-in-law of Louis XV, Stanisław Leszczyński, whereas Austria and Russia herself supported the candidature of August of Saxony. From that time on, a strong movement was felt in Russia to abandon the Franco-Prussian side and to support Austria, which was allied with England. This had its advantages; for Austria was a traditional and permanent ally in the struggle with Russia's most dangerous enemy, Turkey, and also the court at Vienna shared Russian interests in Poland. Conversely, the change had the disadvantage of necessitating a readjustment of relations with the English, who had proved jealous and aggressive ever since the creation of a Russian navy and the progress of Russia towards the Baltic Sea ports, and whose co-operation could be counted upon only as long as a need existed for Russian timber, tar, cordage, and other commodities, such as grain for the British navy and home economy.

Seven Years' War. It was the chancellor Bestuzhev-Ryumin who most strongly advocated this Anglo-Austrian course, the course that was pursued until in 1756 the entire policy suddenly collapsed because of a reversal of the European alliance system which reflected complete disregard and neglect of possible Russian interests. England changed sides and joined Prussia; and, in exchange, France reconciled herself with Austria. Prussia's king, Frederick the Great, had inspired this reversal of alliances, because he hoped to recover through England the old friendship with Russia or at least to secure her neutrality in the coming struggle with Austria. However, Frederick's cynical remarks about the dissolute Tsarina Elizabeth precluded such realignment, and Russia found herself on the newly created Franco-Austrian side and involved in a war that was to last in Europe for seven years. In the campaigns, defeats and victories alternated. During a few days of the year 1760, Berlin was occupied by Russian troops, but indifference on the Russian side and inertia of the generals rendered useless all efforts. In 1762, Elizabeth died and her successor, Peter III, who adored the Prussian king, put a prompt end to the superfluous bloodshed; thus he renounced, and gained nothing from, a war which had little relation to the true interests of the country and which probably could not have ended with different results for Russia even with "victory."

New Diplomacy.

FRANCE. After the war was over and Prussia and Austria had composed their differences, Russia followed a policy of amity with both those countries which it continued until the end of the century. As to the Western nations, France vied alternatingly with England for Catherine's favor. Up to the outbreak of the French Revolution in 1789, Catherine, with her predilection for French *esprit* and cultural exchange, would have preferred to secure also a political bond with France; however, when the storm broke, co-operation between the revolutionary Western nation and the autocrat of the East came to nothing.

ENGLAND. Relations with England after the Seven Years' War remained vacillating. As at the time of Bestuzhev, a faction at court—now under the leadership of Potëmkin, a remarkable, capable man and one of Catherine's favorites—worked for an English alliance. During the seventies, British offers were considered according to which, in exchange for naval support against the revolting colonies in North America, a colony in America or on Minorca in the Mediterranean was to be ceded to Russia. The French, supported at the court by the party of Count Panin, did their best to circumvent the scheme, which eventually collapsed because of its own impracticability. The British resumed their infringements on Russian as on other nations' neutral rights on the seas; their actions led to a dangerous rift enhanced by Catherine's promotion of co-operation among all northern powers against the island kingdom. However, England's final defeat in 1783 cleared the way for the resumption of normal relations. With Britain's increasing need for Russian grain during the period of industrialization and urbanization, the connection soon became comparatively close. But political collaboration remained sporadic until the Napoleonic invasion of central Europe.

RELATIONS WITH NEIGHBORING COUNTRIES

Basic Aims. In contrast with her policies towards the Western powers, whose course was dominated by Western interests, Russia pursued determined self-centered aims with regard to her three neighbors Sweden, Poland, and Turkey. Seeing them weakened in their structure by the transition from absolutism to bourgeois rule or by outmoded despotism and dated feudalism, Russia consistently encouraged their internal disorders and opposed reforms in order to bring about their disintegration and absorption into the Russian commonwealth.

Sweden. With regard to Sweden, ill-feeling persisted after the conclusion of the Great Northern War in 1721, and in 1740

Sweden tried to profit from the succession disputes after the death of Tsarina Anna by making war, ostensibly for the purpose of helping Elizabeth to the throne. Elizabeth showed little gratitude. When the Swedish armies were beaten, she imposed a harsh peace which deprived Sweden of parts of Finland including the great harbor of Viborg. Later, relations improved and in several instances co-operation was achieved, such as in the northern alliance against England; but at no time were plans for the ultimate partition of Sweden lost sight of, and internal opposition to the Swedish government was regularly encouraged in order to further them. Not until 1787 was a temporary end put to Russian schemes, when Gustavus III of Sweden profited from Russia's engagements in the south and undertook a war.

Turkey.

TREATY OF BELGRADE. Russia consistently followed the fundamental principle of her policy regarding Turkey—namely, to gain access to the open sea in the south. With this objective in mind and at the same time with the aim of putting an end to the invasion of Turkish-ruled Tartars of the Crimea, the peace concluded by Peter in 1711 was broken in 1735. Persian support was bought at the cost of Baku and Derbent on the Caspian Sea, both previously conquered by Peter and now voluntarily relinquished because there was no material profit to be derived from their possession. The Russians were victorious; and had it not been for the desertion of Russia's other ally, Austria, the whole northern coast of the Black Sea might have been taken. As it was, the Turks secured a comparatively favorable peace (Belgrade) in 1739, dismantled the fortress of Azov, and ceded the Black Sea coast from the mouth of the Don to the Bug River—but only under the condition that Russia would neither erect military installations nor maintain a navy on the Black Sea.

TREATY OF KUCHUK KAINARDJI. The struggle was resumed in 1768, when Turkey intervened in the Polish turmoil to strengthen her northern borders, thus threatening the success of Russian domination over all Poland. Notable victories were won by the Russian army under the generals Rumiantsev, Golitsyn, Panin, and Suvorov, and this time not only the rest of the northern Black Sea coast but also the Crimea was conquered. A Russian fleet, which had left the Baltic Sea to stir risings against the Turks in Greece, sailed around Europe and succeeded in defeating the Turkish navy. Peace was finally concluded at Kuchuk Kainardji in 1774, marking the overwhelming ascendancy of Russia and carrying the tradition of Peter a step farther. The fortress of Azov passed conclusively into Russian hands and most of the Black Sea coast from the River Bug to the foothills of the Caucasus range was incorporated. The Crimea itself was constituted as an autonomous Tartar state—naturally promising little stability—and nine years later was dissolved and absorbed by Russia. The conquered territory was reorganized by Catherine's lover Potëmkin, towns and harbors were erected, schools and factories founded, and people settled; and, although many of Potëmkin's new institutions were staged rather than real, eventually the region began to prosper. In 1796, the harbor of Odessa was founded, and it developed into the greatest market for grain exports from southern Russia.

TREATY OF JASSY. The Treaty of Kuchuk Kainardji provided also for a protectorate of Russia over Moldavia and for her right to interfere in internal Turkish affairs, should the interests of the Christians living in the Sultan's empire seem to be threatened. It was in order to throw off these stifling conditions that the Turks availed themselves of Russia's illegal acts of annexing the Crimea in 1783 and of constructing a large Black Sea fleet. They resorted to arms in order to free the Balkans from Russian political penetration and to free themselves from economic competition. Again, however, fate was against them; this time Russian forces, led by Suvorov, succeeded—though only after enormous losses—in taking the Turkish key fortress of Ismail on the Danube. In the meantime, Russia's ally Austria pushed from the northwest into the Turkish empire. But again she prematurely dropped out of the war, so that the subsequent Russo-Turkish Peace of Jassy of 1792 added little to the gains of Kuchuk Kainardji. The *de facto* annexation of the Crimea was recognized *de jure,* and territorial gains were made extending to the Dniester. However, after Russia had thus moved closer to the heart of the Turkish empire and to the Straits leading into the Mediterranean, her penetration into Turkey began to assume international ramifications and importance.

Poland.

DISINTEGRATION. Sweden and Turkey both possessed sufficient inner strength and international importance to preserve their independence; but Poland fell victim to Russian pressure and diplomacy.

It is incorrect, though it has often been done, to view Poland's collapse as a result of the "greed" of her neighbors, particularly Russia. In reality, century-old oppression of the great bulk of the Polish population, oligarchic and anarchic rule, persecution of dissenting religious groups, license and arrogance on the part of a small, uneducated lower gentry, chauvinistic and aggressive policies not in line with the strength and value of existing institutions—these and resulting disintegration necessitated a radical change. The logic of events was on Russia's side.

CIVIL WARS.   The beginning of the final chapter in Polish history was marked by a renewed succession struggle in 1733, when a national reform party elected Stanislaw Leszczyński as king against Russian will and Leszczyński attempted to ally himself with Sweden. Russia expelled the candidate by armed force and saw to the continuation of previous conditions through the choice of August of Saxony. After an uneventful reign, August died in 1763 and again Russia interfered in the election, using as pretexts political complications in the Polish province of Courland and the old religious differences over the position of the Orthodox within the kingdom. Eventually Catherine succeeded in having one of her former lovers, Prince Stanislaw Poniatowski, elected king. The troops which had helped him remained in Poland, and soon the Russian ambassador in Warsaw exercised greater power than the king. Thereupon, in order to recover freedom of action, new internal reforms were introduced by Poniatowski and some of the powerful noble families. These reforms were actively opposed by Catherine in order to prevent recuperation of Polish strength, and the blind Polish lower gentry joined the opposition through fear of losing their privileges. Civil war broke out, in which the peasant saw his chance and also took up arms. A triangular struggle ensued between a reform-minded upper nobility, a foreign-supported gentry, and a desperate peasantry. Under pressure from abroad the struggle ended in cancellation of the intended reforms, except for those referring to religious tolerance; Russia reserved, as in Turkey, her right to interfere in Polish internal affairs if the interests of the Orthodox Christians demanded it.

FIRST PARTITION.   Catherine intended to use this privilege as a steppingstone to complete domination; but Frederick the Great, anxious to connect his outlying Prussian possessions with Brandenburg, from which they were separated by Polish western Prussia, made use of the Tsarina's simultaneous preoccupation in the Turkish war and in the Pugachev revolt, and proposed instead annexation of parts of Poland by the three neighbors Russia, Austria, and Prussia. Russia had to consent and in the Treaty of 1772 secured most of former White Russia, which in the late Middle Ages had been annexed by Poland's partner, Lithuania. A properly bribed Polish diet confirmed the cession.

SECOND PARTITION. Poland, largely confined through this first "partition" treaty to her ethnographic frontiers and relieved of most of the vexing religious problem, endeavored to rebuild on a sounder basis during the following twenty years. The elective monarchy was abolished, majority rule instead of unlimited veto power was introduced, and peasant reforms were prepared. In 1791, a new constitution was adopted which satisfied Prussian and Austrian designs, but which seemed to Russia to lay the foundation for future resurgence of the Polish threat. Again Catherine decided to interfere, and once more she was afforded the opportunity by the reactionaries within Poland. At their request, Russian soldiers were sent anew into the country and under pressure the constitution was abrogated and the old state of disorder re-established. Then a second treaty was imposed by Catherine in 1793, which provided for further cession of land, including most of ancient Lithuania in addition to the rest of White Russia. Moreover, Poland subordinated her external policies to those of Russia and combined her military forces with those of Catherine.

THIRD PARTITION. The stipulations—unlike those of 1792—left no room for future free development of Polish life, and necessarily led to a revolt by freedom-loving elements within the country. Inspired by the successful defense of the newly founded French Republic against the apparently overwhelming power of monarchies encircling it, the Poles, led by Thaddeus Kosciusko, rose in armed resistance to Russian dominance. But they had to pay the penalty for their misdeeds. Unlike the French, among whom the liberal Republic could inspire devotion to a great cause, the oppressed people of Poland felt little inclined to preserve with their blood the domination of their abusive ruling class—notwithstanding the promised reforms and the admission of peasants to the army for the first time. The uprising of 1794 failed; Kosciusko was taken prisoner. Warsaw surrendered to Suvorov, and the remnants of the country were divided among the three neighboring powers. Once more Russia took the largest slice, helping herself to the Baltic coast with strategic Courland.

The acquisition of two-thirds of former Poland by Russia marked the greatest territorial gain in Catherine's time, but not an unequivocally secure or profitable one. Two years following the last partition, Catherine "the Great" died.

PROBLEMS

1. Summarize the chief objectives of Russian foreign policies in the eighteenth century.
2. Describe the territorial changes of Russia from 1725 to 1796.
3. Discuss the role of Russia in the Seven Years' War.

CHAPTER XIX

THE TURN OF THE CENTURY

PAUL I

Catherine was succeeded by her son Paul (1796–1801), whose parentage remained unclear—perhaps even to Paul and Catherine themselves. Paul has been called "an idealist in pursuit of the Absolute"; and this description does him better justice than do many of the adverse judgments of romantic and nationalistic historians within and without Russia. Certainly he was mentally ill, as violent changes of temper and erratic orders indicate; but he was no more mad perhaps than Ivan the Terrible or possibly Peter the Great. It merely happened that the age in which he lived, unlike earlier periods, offered no scope for the display of such personalities as he represented. Generosity and sincerity were by no means absent from his make-up; and the tyranny of his actions was mitigated by a thwarted yet strong sense of duty that was manifest throughout his reign. But Paul was afraid. This is not to say that he, like many other Russian rulers, was wanting in personal courage, but that he feared the evil court intrigues about him—he feared that these could put a premature end to the reign which he had so eagerly awaited since the murder of his father through the thirty-four years of his mother's usurped rule. His own murder in 1801 demonstrated the justification of his fears.

THE DOMESTIC SCENE

Rise of New Concepts. Paul's rule introduced the "Modern Age" into Russia. To trace to Catherine's time the background for modern concepts of state is not difficult, but it was the end of the century which actually ushered in visible changes. "Ruling" in the old sense—in the sense of exercising absolute privilege, of pursuing private pleasure, of practicing good administration as one would in his own large household—had to make room for different standards which involved duty and responsibility. Territorial gains became identified with ideas of national will and, perhaps, of geopolitics; they were no longer exclusively linked with the personal grandeur of the ruler. Morality at the court, though not much better in Paul's time than in Catherine's, now had to live up to triumphant bourgeois standards, at least ostensibly. It was also under Paul, and not under his mother, that the first effective step was taken to solve Russia's knottiest problem, that of serfdom.

Bureaucracy and Autocracy. The Tsar's activities brought many arbitrary and useless measures: censorship was strictly enforced to keep out the liberal ideas of the French Revolutionists; books of scientific and literary value were indiscriminately banned; details of dress were regulated (i.e., laced shoes and round hats like those preferred by the Parisian mob were proscribed, *sans-culotte* costume was not suffered) and tight, unhealthful, and impractical uniforms were introduced for the army. Through inflexible regulations, progress was stifled and imagination among officials suppressed. Arbitrary appointments and dismissals poisoned the atmosphere, and exaggerated severity hit those guilty of the slightest default in the prescribed duties; a punctilious and stifling court ceremonial undermined independent thought and action.

Military Affairs. But the short reign of less than five years brought astounding changes. With his intense interest in military affairs, Paul's first move was to remodel army and navy. Warships were reconditioned, and the army was provided with adequate and modern artillery. Training of sailors and soldiers was raised to meet the high standards, if not of Napoleon, then at least of Frederick the Great. Superfluous charges were abolished and posts of command were reserved for trained officers in place of idle nobles.

Government.   The administration was put on a sounder basis.
The instability in the highest position, the throne—a result of the
succession law established under Peter the Great and Catherine I—
was abolished upon adoption of the law of primogeniture. The
highest administrative units, the "colleges," made room for appointed
advisers of the Tsar, who now were obliged to shoulder personal
responsibility.

Education and Commerce.   Catherine's hesitant proposals in
the educational and commercial field were translated into practice.
The University of Dorpat, great seat of learning for German scholars,
was reopened. Although commercial activities suffered from Paul's
veering policies in international relations, trade was encouraged. With
government support, the Russian-American Company was founded
and set to the task of exploring and colonizing Arctic America. Russian rights in America were reserved north of latitude 54°40′, and
guaranteed by treaties with Spain, England, and the United States.
Tolerance was maintained toward adherents of the non-Orthodox
faiths as well as toward dissenters.

System of Service.   The principle of compulsory service to the
state, abolished unilaterally for the gentry by Peter III in 1762, was
revived—although the Tsar's assassination precluded its legal reintroduction. On the other hand, the burdens of the peasants were for
the first time, if not eased, then at least defined; and this limitation
by law of the rights of the landowners meant more than any wholesale attack on the institution of serfdom itself. It is true, under Paul
as under his predecessors, hundreds of thousands of peasants were still
"given away" to small landowners; but at least a peasant could no
longer be separated from his land like a slave, nor was the amount
of his *corvée* or *barchina* any longer left to the arbitrariness of his
master.

RUSSIA'S INTERNATIONAL ROLE

Opposition to Revolutionary France.   In Paul's reign external affairs were conducted in an abrupt, moody manner; yet the
historian cannot fail to recognize that the fundamentals of Russian
foreign interests were at no time overlooked. At the time of Paul's
accession, the basic struggle of autocracy against the Revolutionary
French Republic was in the foreground. Opposition to the Republic,
inherited from Catherine's reign, accounts for the outbreak of war
between the two countries in 1799. French annexation of Malta, then

under Tsar Paul's protectorate, and renewed disturbances in Poland, the result of French Revolutionary doctrines, were but secondary causes.

Coalition against France. The war, undertaken in alliance with England, Austria, and Holland, showed the solidly good condition of the Russian armies. They fought in various theaters of war; foremost was the army under General Suvorov, who had been in retirement as a result of one of Paul's evil whims but who was recalled and generously accorded full and unconstrained power. Under him, a Russian army crossed half of Europe and recaptured northern Italy from the French in a campaign as brilliant as that which Napoleon had conducted three years earlier when winning the Po valley. The very success of Russia, however, stirred up jealousy among the Austrians; and subsequently Suvorov was deserted by his allies, his plans for invading France were overthrown, and nothing was left for him but to retreat via Switzerland. Despite heroic efforts and excellent leadership, the difficulties of terrain, the resumed attacks by the French, and the lack of support by Austria brought enormous losses; and a woefully decimated army returned to Russia. Suvorov himself died shortly thereafter, and the coalition with the Hapsburgs against France ended abruptly.

Reconciliation with Napoleonic France. What followed was not so much a "reversal" of the existing system of alliances occasioned by Paul's disappointment, as it was the logical outcome of changed circumstances. Napoleon's actions in 1799 and 1800, particularly his internal policies, revealed him to Paul as no longer the heir of the Revolution, but the liquidator. Such about-face tactics coincided with the autocratic principles on which the Russian state system was built, and consequently a rapprochement took place which opened the way to Russian politics for the pursuance of the unremitting task of opposition to England. The latter country, growingly alarmed at Russia's interference in its European systems of balance, began to fear Paul's accelerated naval construction and his expansion in Asia. For during Paul's reign not only did armies participate in the Western European scene and effective fleets threaten in the Baltic and Black Seas, but also troops marched in the direction of what Britain considered her "life lines," namely the Mediterranean, Turkey, and Persia. In 1801 the territory of Georgia submitted formally to Russia and brought her within a short distance of English supply routes. The hazard to England was increased when, incited by France, Paul ordered Cossack regiments to assemble in southwestern Siberia for an invasion of India itself. The importance of the undertaking and the effect it might have had on all future times cannot be minimized—although the preparations were so incomplete and the losses so great, even before the expedition started, that success should scarcely have been expected.

THE MURDER OF PAUL

Before the rupture with England became definite, Paul fell victim to the hatred and fears of a disappointed and enraged—and possibly Anglo-supported—nobility. His political measures (designed to reduce the nobles to their previous status of servants of the state), his lack of tact in personal relations, and his insane decisions had provoked their resolution to do away with him. With the connivance of Paul's oldest son, Alexander, conspirators fortified by alcohol—men whom Paul regarded as his friends and guardians—broke into his bedroom on the night of March 23, 1801, and butchered him in the cruelest manner.

Thus ended an unhappy and in many respects evil, yet important, rule that did not lack in progressive elements. Alexander, avowing his complicity in the deposal plans, denied any foreknowledge of the murder, but failed to prosecute the perpetrators of the act. Some of them mounted to high posts under him, and only after many years was the last one of them dismissed from office.

PROBLEMS

1. Discuss the change in the spirit of the age after the French Revolution.
2. Comment on the chief reforms of Paul I.
3. Describe the international position of Russia as seen by Paul I.

CHAPTER XX

RUSSIA AND FRANCE

ALEXANDER I

The first decade and a half of the nineteenth century is overshadowed by the political events stimulated by Napoleon's activities. Internal planning in Russia had to be subordinated to external needs, and little was accomplished. Alexander (1801–25), whose initiative was needed for domestic adjustments, disappointed the expectations of the progressives. Though trained in liberal ideas by his tutor, the Swiss La Harpe, and though gifted with imagination, personal charm, intellectual curiosity, and perseverance, he was superficial, lazy, unstable, and given to dissimulation. He revoked many of the abortive orders of his father, yet his insincerity caused the work of reform to be neglected. He surrounded himself with capable men (Speransky, Nesselrode, the Pole Czartoryski, the German vom Stein, the Corsican Pozzo di Borgo, the Greek Capodistrias) but gave little heed to their advice.

NAPOLEON'S ASCENDANCY

Alignment with England. Inheriting from his father an alliance with France and an expedition against India, Alexander immediately reversed the course. He called back the troops en route for

119

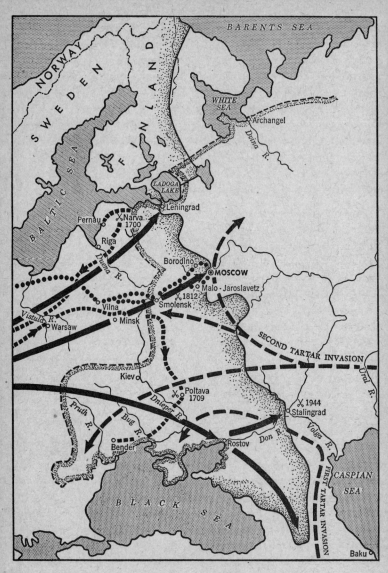

INVASIONS OF RUSSIA

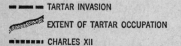
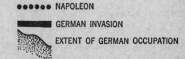

- - - TARTAR INVASION

EXTENT OF TARTAR OCCUPATION

- - - CHARLES XII

•••••• NAPOLEON

▬▬▬ GERMAN INVASION

EXTENT OF GERMAN OCCUPATION

India, and sought a rapprochement with England. The greater Napoleon's ambitions, the more decidedly did Alexander pursue a pro-English policy; and when Napoleon committed the outrage of executing the Duc d'Enghien and had himself crowned emperor, an alliance with Britain was made. At first envisaging only peace and arbitration, it soon led to war with France; and in 1805, after the Austrians had joined the Allies, an army was dispatched to central Europe. Under Alexander's command the famous battle of Austerlitz was fought—against the counsel of General Kutuzov; and the complete rout of the Russo-Austrian forces put an end to Alexander's plans. Austria was obliged to sue for peace, and only distance saved Russia.

French Alliance. The state of war continued, but little action was taken until Napoleon had attacked Prussia and conquered Berlin. Then Russian troops joined with the Prussians and, after two indecisive engagements, were again beaten in the battle of Friedland in 1807. With Napoleon master of the Continent, Alexander, flattered by the victor's magnanimous treatment, concluded peace at Tilsit. Though Russian generals considered such a peace inopportune and unnecessary, Alexander expanded it into an alliance with the erstwhile enemy. He agreed to the restitution of a Poland to be formed of parts which Prussia had secured in the treaties of 1772 to 1795 and of which she was now deprived; and he joined in Napoleon's economic war against England. He closed all ports to British and, under the "Continental System," stopped all direct Great Britain.

DISADVANTAGES OF FRENCH ALLIANCE. F the treaty providing for the resurgence of C great discontent in Russia. Politically, it lik ing, for Napoleon refused to concede in e Constantinople, which Russia hoped to ac waged against Turkey. Equally disadva consequences of the stipulations provid Trade with Britain in timber, flax, iro factor in Russian economy, and Franc England. France neither needed the c bulk of Russian exports to England n intercourse, for the British fleet domina est and most influential class in Russi the exchange rate of the ruble sank

"Continental System" undermined prosperity and respect for law. The English, experienced in piracy and smuggling, profited from the corruption among Russian custom officials and found leakages enough, and the Franco-Russian alliance was subjected to serious strains.

DECLINE OF FRENCH ALLIANCE. A new meeting of Alexander and Napoleon was therefore arranged in 1808 in Erfurt; but Franco-Russian relations, governed by economic needs and political trends and not by dynastic and personal arrangements, were not improved. The French minister, Talleyrand himself, secretly advised the Tsar against concessions and called attention to the deterioration of Napoleon's position in France, to his lack of success in rebellious Spain, and his renewed incurrence of Catholic resistance which followed his highhanded policies towards the Pope and the Papal states. The French emperor thus failed to engage more vigorous Russian support in his persistent struggle with England; likewise, Alexander's aid to his French ally was only very inadequately forthcoming when war was renewed between France and Austria in 1809. Alleging the need of his forces for the continuation of a campaign against Turkey and a war against Sweden, in which he had been engaged since 1808, the Tsar ordered his troops to avoid serious action against Austria.

NAPOLEON'S INVASION OF RUSSIA

By 1811, Europe began to speak of an impending war
ce and Russia. People became increasingly aware of
of French political ambitions with Russia's se-
ntally opposed economic interests of the two
ianism of a Continental rule divided between
r. In view of these basic differences, minor
great issues constituted insurmountable ob-
of peace on the Continent. Thus severe
ilure of a plan suggested at Erfurt ac-
between Russia and France was to be
riage between Napoleon and one of
support against Austria in 1809 and
grés in Russia added to French mis-
ded French trade in wine and other
ntal System" was circumvented, with
can and other neutral ships. Con-
ed by Napoleon's annexation of the

German principality of Oldenburg (whose hereditary prince was Alexander's brother-in-law), by the re-establishment of Poland, which was contrary to Russian plans, and by French support of Turkey in defending the Straits.

Preparations. Napoleon carefully evaluated his chances in a war against Russia and judged them favorable. He withdrew troops from Spain and secured contingents for his army from Prussia, Austria, and other satellites. Russia answered these preparations by composing her differences with Sweden and Turkey. The Swedish campaign of 1808 and 1809 had led to brilliant results. Russian soldiers had conquered Finland, crossed the frozen Gulf of Bothnia, and invaded Sweden proper, and in the Peace of Frederikshavn (1809) the whole of Finland had been ceded to Russia; now the Swedes—under their new crown prince, Bernadotte—were pledged to the promise of military aid against Napoleon. Likewise, Alexander succeeded in protecting Russia's southern flank; peace with Turkey was concluded at Bucharest (1812), and although Russia failed to gain her main objective, the Straits, she advanced her borders to the Pruth River (Bessarabia) and was confirmed in her protectorate over Turkey's Orthodox subjects.

Attack. With preparations completed on both the French and the Russian sides, war broke out in June, 1812. French armies of 650,000 men, half of them foreigners, crossed the Russian border at various points, the main assault being launched in the center along the Vilna-Smolensk-Moscow line. Bad weather, lack of discipline, desertions, and particularly the early breakdown of the supply system made enormous difficulties for the French. Nevertheless, the Russians were forced to retreat. Several generals had recommended retreat from the beginning, anticipating that Russia's wide expanse would lead to Napoleon's destruction; but their counsel went unheeded, and necessity alone accounted for Russian movements. In vain was the supreme command of the army transferred from Alexander himself to the able Barclay de Tolly, a Baltic baron of Scottish descent, and later, for nationalistic reasons, to Kutuzov. The latter endeavored to halt Napoleon's advance; but even the bloody Battle of Borodino failed to stop the French, and in September, 1812, Moscow fell to the enemy.

Moscow. Napoleon had intended to smash Russian resistance through a single mighty stroke but had been denied the opportunity by the Russian retreat. By occupying the heart of the country, he now sought to end the struggle. But again he was disappointed. Russia's scorched-earth policy had greatly weakened his position; and the masses, who might have been won by the promise of emancipation, failed to support him because he hesitated to release the revolutionary forces in Russia for fear of the reaction on Europe. His offers to Alexander for peace negotiations went unanswered. Instead, the Russians redeployed their armies, and their church called upon all to support the national movement and to show utmost perseverance in the holy war against this pillaging, desecrating enemy.

RETREAT. In the middle of October, Napoleon was forced to withdraw from Moscow. A devastating fire, in part the result of Russian orders but in part the consequence of neglect, had destroyed stores and quarters, rendering it impossible for the French to pass the winter there. To avoid the rigors of the weather and to reach Europe through not yet scorched territory, Napoleon led his loot-laden army—now reduced by battle, disease, and desertion to 100,000 men—in a southerly direction. At Maloyaroslavets he was stopped by Kutuzov and forced onto the old Smolensk road. Overcautiousness cost Kutuzov the opportunity to destroy the enemy. He refrained from attacking in force and instead, marching parallel to Napoleon's army, harassed and whittled away at the half-starved, demoralized, weary French by costly yet successful rear-guard and guerrilla action.

BEREZINA. After Napoleon had passed Smolensk, where contrary to plan he could not spend the winter for lack of supplies, the cold intensified and added to the sufferings of the struggling army. Yet the temperature was not low enough to freeze streams and swamps. Therefore, when the small Berezina River was reached, the progress of Napoleon's army was halted, and two improvised bridges had to be thrown across to allow passage. This moment was seized upon by the Russians, who attacked in force; and the frenzied crossing in icy weather, under enemy fire, over burning and breaking planks, became one of the great military catastrophes of all ages. The ensuing gruesome march from the Berezina to Vilna virtually destroyed the decimated force which thus far had saved itself from disaster. By the end of the year, the last of Russian territory was freed.

Triumph over Napoleon. Incited by England, Alexander elected to continue the war until the destruction of Napoleon was complete. On December 30, 1812, a Convention was concluded at Tauroggen with the Prussian General York, and treaties with Sweden and Austria followed in 1813. Reluctantly the country followed a policy which favored essentially non-Russian interests. Napoleon was pursued through Germany; the Allies won the decisive Battle of Leipzig; and in 1814 France was invaded. In July, Alexander and the Prussian king made their triumphant entry into Paris, and Napoleon was forced from his throne.

Congress of Vienna. Peace was concluded at Paris and supplemented by the Congress of Vienna. The question whether or not all of Poland should be ceded to Russia, and whether Prussia should be compensated for her share of Poland by parts of Saxony, very nearly led to rupture among the victors; and only the new peril arising with the reappearance of Napoleon saved the wartime alliance. While Prussian and English forces rushed to defeat Napoleon once more (Waterloo, 1815), negotiations came to a successful close. Russia received the disputed territory, and she granted a certain amount of autonomy and a constitution to Poland as well as to Finland. A special covenant, the "Holy Alliance," supplemented the political settlement. It was inspired by Alexander himself, who had fallen under the spell of mystical religious groups and "evangelists," such as the Baroness Krüdener represented. The Holy Alliance stipulated that internal as well as international relations should be based on Christian ethics, and it provided for co-operation in the preservation of peace on the basis of the Viennese arrangements.

Russia thus emerged from the Napoleonic era secure in her realms, greatly enlarged, and with increased international prestige. She had acquired additional Polish territory through the Congress of Vienna; she had gained Finland in the Peace of Frederikshavn and Bessarabia by the Treaty of Bucharest; and in 1813 she had also succeeded in forcing Persia to cede Baku. In international affairs Russia held a first place, and the stipulations of Vienna combined with those of the Holy Alliance seemed to give permanence to this position.

PROBLEMS

1. Discuss the difficulties of Franco-Russian co-operation in Napoleonic times.
2. Discuss Napoleon's failure in Russia.
3. Discuss the territorial aggrandizement of Russia, 1800–25.

Significant Dates

Period of Congresses . . . 1818–1822

Emancipation of Peasants in
    Baltic Provinces 1816–1819

Beginning of Greek War of
    Independence 1821

CHAPTER XXI

THE POST-NAPOLEONIC PERIOD

FAILURE OF LIBERALISM

International Congresses. The effect of the Napoleonic Wars on Russian internal conditions necessarily differed from that on other European countries. In most of Europe the ideas of liberty released by the French Revolution spread swiftly, but in Russia the broad masses remained untouched by the new liberal trend. Its influence was correspondingly small, being limited to the narrow upper layer of society. Unlike governments of other countries, the Russian autocracy therefore refrained from introducing reforms during the war, and after peace was concluded Alexander continued to disappoint the liberals. A victim of obscurantism and reactionary mystical and pseudo-religious ideas, he neglected internal improvements; and, his vanity flattered by his international role, he kept his attention focused on external policies. He participated in a number of congresses called to maintain the wartime alliance through which, under the Austrian chancellor Metternich's influence, the *status quo* was to be preserved. Progressive movements in Germany, Italy, and Spain were suppressed; even in Greece, which waged a desperate war of independence against Turkey, Alexander found himself in the paradoxical position of having to support the "legitimate" rule of the Sultan although Russia's interests lay in the opposite direction—in the success of the Greek revolt, the disintegration of Turkey, and the acquisition of Constantinople and the Straits.

Polish Constitution. In newly acquired Poland, Alexander granted a constitution. It was more liberal than that imposed on France; but it was of a definitely aristocratic character because a middle class was wanting and the peasants were neither freed nor represented. Alexander himself became king, his brother Constantine commander of the army; and, to the disappointment of all, not even the governorship was placed in the hands of Alexander's Polish friend Czartoryski. The constitution itself was repeatedly violated in budget and other matters, and the diet was not regularly convened as stipulated. Thus Alexander's liberalism was limited abroad as well as at home.

Ministers. In Russia, the Tsar left most of the work to "ministers," whom he had created after foreign models. Among them, two "favorites" and virtual "vice emperors" were outstanding: Speransky, who personified the liberal beginnings of Alexander's reign, and Arakcheyev, who dominated the later reactionary course.

SPERANSKY. Mikhail Speransky (1771–1839) was the son of a village priest. Educated first at a seminary, then at a university, he subsequently became a professor in St. Petersburg and after a short army career was appointed to the Ministry of the Interior. At the age of twenty-two, he found himself ennobled and, a few years later, in the special graces of the Tsar. In 1809, he was appointed Secretary of State, but was dismissed in 1812 and exiled because of his arrogance, his pro-French leanings, and the intrigues of jealous courtiers. Only in 1814 was he recalled and, having lost many of his liberal ideas, he then served again under Alexander and later under Nicholas I.

SPERANSKY'S REFORM PLANS. Under the influence of the West, and particularly of French ideas, for which he was bitterly attacked by the famous historian Karamzin and other Slavophils, Speransky worked out projects of fundamental importance for the future development of Russia. He advocated a constitution, retaining different class rights, however, and also serfdom for the time being. He proposed a modern administrative system through separation of the judicial from the administrative department, and he planned popular representative bodies in the form of legislatures. They were to be elected by nobles and free peasants, and each community, district, and province was to have its own legislature; another was to be established on a national level. In cases of disagreement, each could appeal to the next higher body. At the top of the structure was to be a Council of State working directly under the autocratic ruler, whose voice was final except when infringing upon "fundamental laws." Speransky also drafted municipal reforms and church statutes; and, as governor of Siberia from 1819 to 1821, he worked on the reorganization of Siberia, which was to be divided into two governor-generalships. Under Alexander's successor Nicholas, from 1826 to 1833, Speransky made perhaps his most definite contribution by directing a new and long-overdue compilation and codification of Russian law, embracing principles of private property as well as civil rights.

ARAKCHEYEV AND REACTION. Most of Speransky's far-sighted projects remained unfulfilled for many years; instead, after the War of 1812, reaction triumphed, as everywhere in Europe. Not Speransky with his progressive ideas, but Arakcheyev, an honest but brutal and subservient man who lacked Speransky's vision and ability, was called upon to direct the path of Russian policies. Mysticism and religious bigotry prevailed, while liberal ideas were confined to secret societies (Freemasons, Northern Order, Sons of the Fatherland). Universities, whose number increased, were put under strict supervision. The teaching of natural sciences was limited out of dogmatic considerations, and theological studies were made compulsory. To prevent popularization of "atheistic, enlightened" science, many lectures were given in non-Russian languages, and half of the professors were foreigners. Primary and particularly secondary schools fared better; although few new ones were founded, their quality was improved.

Military Colonies. A notable innovation of the period was the "military colonies," which Alexander created in the special interest of his beloved army and which Arakcheyev, noted also for his improvements in the artillery, was charged to administer. Certain territories were set aside for military administration. Whereas the rest of the country was freed of compulsory service, everyone in the special areas was brought automatically into the armed forces. Every peasant in the military colonies was at the same time a soldier, free from taxation, looked after for life, but also subject for life to military rule. He was always in uniform; every step was supervised; his private life, including his marriage, was regulated; and his children were brought up as soldiers. By 1825, about one million men and women lived in such military colonies. Alexander had envisaged economic as well as humanitarian advantages for the soldiers by combining military service with agriculture and freeing most of the rest of the country of the financial and personal burden; but the idea as carried out proved unworkable. Soon the colonies, even those with trustworthy officers and good order, resembled prison camps; and desperate revolts, brutally suppressed, only served to aggravate conditions.

ECONOMIC CONDITIONS

Reconstruction. Economic conditions in the post-Napoleonic period were naturally poor, but reconstruction proceeded at a quicker pace than had been expected—even in the face of prevailing corruption. Cotton, flax, grain, coal, oil, and copper production was raised; closer economic ties were secured with China and central Asia; expeditions were sent out to explore Russian America and other regions; and the resources of European Russia and the newly acquired territories were developed. Exports in 1814 amounted to forty-five million silver rubles (as against imports valued at about twenty-eight) and they rose steadily. However, because of undervaluation of the products of Russian soil and Russian labor, the trade balance still worked to the disadvantage of the national economy, and the government itself was close to bankruptcy.

Industries. As in other countries, factories increased speedily in size and number. Steam power came into use in larger plants and enabled them to compete successfully with home industries. Lower cotton prices led to the establishment of scores of textile mills. This general trend was furthered by government measures; the ban on free-market selling was partly revoked, the currency was stabilized, more appropriate credit institutions were founded, and tariffs were introduced to protect infant industries. Although the system of *vochinal* workers (who were heritable property and subject to the jurisdiction of the owner) and of possessional serfs (who were granted and ascribed to industries from agricultural districts) was preserved, a change came also in labor conditions. Factory owners benefited from whatever number of serfs were set free and, instead of employing unsatisfactory forced help for which they had social responsibilities, they could draw upon an increasing reservoir of a freely shifting industrial proletariat.

Agriculture. The advance of industries, a result of economic pressure and world-wide trends and not of conscientious planning, was bought at the expense of agriculture. Following his grandmother's example, Alexander had convened at the beginning of his reign a committee to investigate and reform agricultural conditions, but it had achieved as little as Catherine's. Emancipation of the serfs was again postponed; only some forty thousand were voluntarily freed by progressive landowners during Alexander's reign, and many of them benefited but little, for they slid into economic bondage created by the factory system. Even the landowners were unable to free themselves of the great debts incurred through the wars, and agricultural prices declined steadily.

Serfdom. Noticeable progress was traceable in only two fields: the discontinuation of the practice of "giving away" additional peasants into serfdom, and the emancipation of serfs in the Baltic provinces. There, in Estonia, Latvia, and Courland, the German barons anticipated future needs and unanimously freed their peasants from personal servitude (1816–19), though without allocation of land. It was an important and progressive measure, although unsatisfactory to the extent that no secure foundation was laid for the life of the peasant under the new conditions and that most of the freed serfs came to fill the ranks of an uprooted proletariat.

DEATH OF ALEXANDER I

In 1825, when none of the high hopes which the world had placed in the genius and liberalism of Alexander I were as yet fulfilled, the Tsar suddenly died on a trip to the south. Few witnesses being present, rumors were spread that his death had been staged and that in reality, in order to atone for the murder of his father and other unchristian deeds, Alexander had retired into a monastery in Siberia. The legend has never been conclusively disproved; but to the world, in any case, Alexander was dead.

PROBLEMS

1. Discuss the scope and significance of Speransky's reform plans.
2. Discuss the extent of the liberalism put into practice by Alexander I.
3. Discuss the economic conditions in Russia after the Napoleonic Wars.

Significant Dates		
Reign of Nicholas I . . .	1825–1855
Dekabrist Rising	1825
Russo-Turkish War . . .	1828–1829
Crimean War	1854–1856

Chapter XXII

ERA OF SUSPENSE

Alexander I has received considerable attention from historians. The promise of the young Tsar and the failure of the man, his curiously dual nature, and the fortuitous fact that he lived in an era of decision account for this preoccupation with him. But his lifework was indifferent, and his death more important than his life. To be sure, the death in itself made no incision, but it was taken as the signal for a revolution which—although of small scale, and unsuccessful at that—gained great significance in Russian history.

THE DEKABRIST RISING

Alexander's Succession.   Alexander had no children, and the throne should have fallen to his eldest brother, Constantine. But because of private affairs and his dislike for reigning, Constantine had waived succession rights; yet neither the next presumptive heir, Constantine's younger brother Nicholas, nor the government and people were informed. When news of Alexander's sudden death reached St. Petersburg, Nicholas therefore took an oath recognizing Constantine as Tsar, while Constantine, residing in Warsaw, did likewise in favor of Nicholas.

The Revolutionaries. The uncertainty which resulted from the confusion and, owing to distance, from the delay in proclaiming a new Tsar was seized upon by a group of revolutionaries, whose hopes for the redress of existing wrongs had been deceived by Alexander. Many of them were members of romantic secret societies which, as in other parts of Europe, were formed by students, professors, poets, idealistic officers, and members of the nobility inspired by a sense of their responsibilities toward the people. They were embittered by persistent corruption, faulty jurisdiction, police tyranny, censorship, degradation of human beings through serfdom and corporal punishment, and suppression of free thought in universities. They resented the fact that neither the new spirit which had swept Europe nor the devotion shown by all the Russian people in the defense of their country had helped to improve the lot of the common man. Using the American constitution, the French constitution of 1791, and the Spanish constitution of 1812 as their models, they accordingly worked out plans for radical changes. Abolition of monarchy and of military dictatorship, emancipation of serfs, communal possession of land, and reduction of the clergy were among the aims advocated by them. Some proposed abolition of a standing army, free access for all citizens to any trade or profession, and autonomy for subjugated nations within their ethnical borders. Others, on the contrary, demanded of these nations the sacrifice of their "national rights to political utility"; in this sense, they advocated the resettlement of Jews, who formed a state within the state, in Palestine, and they envisaged a class struggle which was to lead to state socialism and to the Russification of the empire.

The Dekabrist Revolt. Two groups were outstanding among the revolutionaries, the "Northern Society" and the "Southern Society," which counted among their leading members the guard officers Pestel and Bestuzhev-Ryumin and the poet Ryleyev. Believing the confusion after Alexander's death opportune for pressing their aims, these men, although unprepared, started a revolution in December, 1825 (Decembrist or—in Russian—Dekabrist rising). Just when accord between Alexander's two brothers was reached and Nicholas was proclaimed rightful Tsar and autocrat, they incited the soldiers of some imperial guards to keep their sworn allegiance to Constantine (an object hardly worthy of the devotion of a revolutionary) and to demand a constitution. The rising was essentially confined to St. Petersburg and two places in the south; it was vigorously suppressed, and five hundred soldiers paid the extreme penalty for their undertaking. Outrages were committed by the Tsar's troops, and finally many of the revolutionary leaders were caught. Pestel, Ryleyev, Bestuzhev, and two others were hanged, thirty-one imprisoned or exiled for life; and ·the revolutionaries, deprived of their leaders, were for many years unable to recover.

STRUGGLE AGAINST REVOLUTION

Autocracy. Nicholas I (1825–55) took the Dekabrist rising as a warning. As a dutiful guardian of Russian tradition he held down any liberal trend with an iron hand, and "Autocracy, Orthodoxy, and Nationalism" became the watchwords of his reign. During the thirty years of his rule none of the great problems facing the country were solved. Notwithstanding humanitarian principles typical of nineteenth-century liberalism, emancipation was again postponed. The government confined itself to convening new commissions which, after prolonged sessions during the years 1826 to 1830, 1835, 1839 to 1842, and 1844, recommended only minor changes in the existing status. Not even voluntary emancipation and the granting of small acreage to the liberated serfs was permitted the landowner, although in view of a rapidly increasing population and oversupply of laborers serfdom came to mean a grave economic burden for him. Only in cases of mutual consent by owner and serf was complete liberation allowed, provided the peasant, though freed, continued to render some state service. A special law stipulated that whole villages (but no individual peasant) might gain the right to purchase their freedom in cases where, as often happened, the landowner's estate was sold at auction.

A few additional steps were undertaken to lighten the burdens of the peasants: their transfer to mines was forbidden; their being rented out to owners of land or factories who had no right to hold serfs of their own was stopped; and provisions were made for the care of the needy. In outlying parts of the empire, the serfs benefited by so-called "Inventory Regulations," which served as a census and stipulated the amount of land and dues for each peasant.

Economy. The delay in settling the problem of emancipation reacted adversely not only on the development of agriculture, but likewise on the growth of industries, on financial policies, and on the whole Russian social structure. Essential economic improvements were retarded; yet Nicholas' capable finance minister, Kankrin, through strict economy succeeded in re-establishing Russian credit after the Napoleonic Wars. A stable currency was introduced by withdrawing the devalued paper money issued during the emergency. Agricultural and building activities and, through protective tariffs, industrial output were stimulated; a technological and a mining institute were founded, and monopolies were subjected to revision. Textile home industries were aided through equipment with better types of spindles; and looms and mills, particularly in the Polish parts, gained international markets.

Political Unrest. Involuntary servitude combined with these socio-economic changes led (in Russia, more than elsewhere) to serious difficulties. Revolts in agricultural districts occurred in alarming numbers; scrupulous historians have counted as many as five hundred and fifty-six during Nicholas' reign of thirty years. Likewise, labor troubles, typical for industrialized countries, began to appear. The military colonies were reluctantly continued by Nicholas, and contributed their share to the spirit of rebellion. To deal with prevailing unrest, a new department was added to the imperial chancellery; this was the famed "Third Section," which assumed police functions and soon became a byword for autocratic oppression. Through it, revolutionary movements were brutally put down, religious sectarians were persecuted anew, censorship of books was enforced, liberal newspapers were suppressed, and universities were strictly supervised. The educational system was geared to making "good subjects" of the young; vocational training, useful for the state, was emphasized, and culture in its broader aspects was neglected.

1848. When the Revolution of 1848 broke out in Paris and swept over most of Europe, Nicholas sent troops abroad to quell the movement in Hungary before it could reach the Russian border, and at home all possible precautions were taken. The number of students in any university was limited to three hundred, and liberal groups were checked by police spies; the Petrashevtsy circle, a radical group to which members of the highest nobility belonged, was broken up and twenty-one were exiled to Siberia, the novelist Dostoyevsky among them. Through these measures Nicholas himself believed he was serving the true interests of the country, the care of whose spiritual and material well-being he considered his God-ordained duty.

PROBLEMS

1. State the social theories behind the Dekabrist rising.
2. Discuss the policy of "Autocracy, Orthodoxy, and Nationalism."

CHAPTER XXIII

SLAVOPHILS AND WESTERNIZERS

The progress of Russia's political and social conditions did not take place without sober questioning from the more thoughtful people in the country, who strove to sound the spiritual basis, the existing status, and the future direction of Russia's destiny. Two schools of thought, particularly, took part in the investigation: the Slavophils and the Westernizers. Both were separated by an unbridgeable gulf from the uninterested and inarticulate masses of the Russian people.

PHILOSOPHIES OF SLAVOPHILS AND WESTERNIZERS

Ideology. The two groups, as the names indicate, were opposed to each other because the one looked toward the "Slavic soul" for the salvation of Russia, the other toward Western methods. Despite such divergent attitudes the two groups had much in common. Adherents of one not infrequently changed over to the other or shared its views, and many held an intermediary position.

GROUNDS IN COMMON. What connected the Slavophil and the Westernizer was their mutual dependence upon Europe's great philosophers. Hume, Voltaire, Saint-Simon, and Proudhon exercised

135

wide influence, and the great German philosophers gave direction to their thoughts. The writings of Kant, Goethe, and Schiller and particularly those of Schelling, Hegel, Feuerbach, Stirner, and later of Karl Marx were scrupulously examined; and the demands of the Russian political schools were formulated either in conformity with the views of these men or in opposition to them.

Westernizers and Slavophils had in common also a love of Russia, around which all their work and efforts centered. Both feared the incompetence of the existing Russian government. Westernizers and Slavophils alike idealized the Russian peasant and defended the *mir* or village community, this peculiarly Russian institution in which all saw the sound foundation of the past and the basis for a desirable new Russian society. Both opposed a bourgeois society as it existed in Western republics—with "two classes, exploiters and exploited." Both hoped for a better balance between industry and agriculture, brought forth by Russian civilization. The work of both schools promoted new thoughts, led to a re-evaluation of the past, and resulted in valuable new historical and legal studies.

DIFFERENCES. They differed fundamentally, however, in their political aims. The Slavophils originally considered themselves nonpolitical, and many became conservatives later in life. The Westernizers were avowedly radical, some of them believing in the necessity of a class struggle, others envisaging progress within the capitalistic system. Influenced by the Christian romanticism of Chateaubriand, the Slavophils worked for a spiritual reform within the Russian people. The Westernizers, on the other hand, regarded the state not as a moral, but as a purely political institution properly functioning for the welfare of the individual. The Slavophils believed in Orthodoxy; religion was part of the very basis of their views and Orthodoxy expressed for them divine will and eternal truth. The Westernizers were often atheists; at least they saw no place in their system for a state religion. They believed in the rights of the individual, whereas the Slavophils opposed individualism because, in their view, it led from freedom of thought to license.

The evaluation of Peter the Great's achievements further separated the two groups. The Slavophils extolled the advantages of Russian ways before the reign of Peter. They thought that Peter's reforms had interrupted a healthy and natural development and that his work constituted a "negation of a sacred mission." They felt that it had created a barrier between classes by separating the educated from the folk. Conversely, Peter's work was held in high regard by the Westernizers, who saw Russia as but a part of Europe.

AIMS. If the Slavophils considered the West with its industrial development, bureaucracy, and urbanization to be bad and poisonous, the Westernizers exaggerated and idealized the virtues of the West. As the Slavophils pointed out, they overlooked a lack of spiritual depth. This lack was felt particularly in the Western law system, which the Slavophils regarded as the "law of the conqueror," including many meaningless formalities, whereas the Russian law system sprang deep from the roots of a "pacific people." The West, the Slavophils asserted, fostered ambition and looked for outward comfort and shallow luxury, whereas typical Russian traits were simplicity, humility, and patience—leading, they held, to true contentment.

Attitude of the Government. The Russian government looked with equal disfavor on both philosophies, and representatives of both suffered censorship and exile. The revolutionary tendencies of the Westernizers were naturally condemned, but the ideas of the Slavophils likewise were found objectionable. It was feared that the latter would interfere with the Russification policies in the non-Orthodox parts of the empire and lead to a breakup of the national entity.

LEADING THINKERS

The representatives of both groups were numerous:

Slavophils. The Slavophils represented no homogeneous group; as time went on, they showed consistent changes in their philosophy, their ideals, and in the character of their aims.

NICHOLAS KARAMZIN (1765–1826) is often regarded as a precursor of the Slavophils. He believed in autocracy, which he considered characteristic of and necessary for Russia. He opposed any constitutional system as developed by Western countries, and advocated the division of Russia into fifty provinces each of which was to be ruled over by a paternalistic, benevolent governor responsible to the autocrat and directed by his Christian conscience.

IVAN KIREVSKY (1806–56) was the first acknowledged leader of the Slavophils. From a study of the Greek church fathers he arrived at the conviction that Christianity was deeper, purer, and more closely interwoven with Russian life than with that of any other country. He hoped that through the Orthodox faith Russia would gain inspiration. He explained the growth of the Russian character on the basis of the historical evolution of the nation, which should not be interrupted by the influx of non-Russian ways. In the same spirit, he extolled communal ownership as exemplified by the *mir*. Although he acknowledged the possibilities of the United States (which, however, he considered handicapped by the one-sidedness of its English heritage), he believed that Russia would fall heir to the greatness of Italy, Germany, and France.

ALEXIS KHOMYAKOV (1804–60) extended the conclusions of other Slavophils to all Slavic people of Orthodox faith. He insisted that all Slavs were more or less similar in character, and that unlike the heritage of the conquest-minded Romans and Germans, theirs was a peaceable one. But his generalizations, unsupported by historical evidence, failed to convince the serious student.

KONSTANTIN AKSAKOV (1817–60) followed Kirevsky and Khomyakov in their explanations of Russian ways and in attesting to their peaceful character, for which he gave as example the deliberative assemblies of the past—the *vieche*. He affirmed that not majority but common consent represented the true will of a people and that it alone could establish acceptable law. European ways led for him to the destruction of liberty; for liberty "could never survive in countries where governments and peoples were separated by divergent interests." The formation of a Russian state along European lines seemed to him destructive and practically impossible.

IVAN AKSAKOV (1823–86) survived most of the other prominent Slavophils and demonstrated by his example the dead end to which their philosophy led. Convinced, as were the others, of the decadence of the West, he personified the transition from a philosophical and religious system, founded in the soul of the people, to a practical political nationalism (Pan-Slavism) and, ultimately, to reaction.

Westernizers. The Westernizers likewise underwent a change, beginning like the Slavophils in the field of philosophy but ending with socialism and anarchism when attempting practical application of their theories.

P. CHAADAYEV (1794–1856) may be considered as their precursor. His *Philosophical Letters,* published in 1836, exposed the cultural "isolation" of Russia, doubted the greatness of her past, and denounced Orthodoxy, which—unlike the Catholic church in Europe—had failed to provide a sound spiritual basis for the Russian mind.

VISSARION BELINSKY (1811–48) is considered the dominant figure among the Westernizers. He devoted his work to literary activities, and literary criticism offered him in censor-stricken Russia the best field for the promulgation of his political ideas. He joined the Slavophils in their contention that society had precedence over the individual, but he maintained that society had to reserve room for the expression of individual activities and rights. He vigorously denied to Orthodoxy the place in Russian life assigned it by the Slavophils, believing that reason was the tool of civilization and of true justice. Knowledge, not autocracy or theocracy, he considered the main cultural power. Belinsky's chief importance lay in the influence which, after his premature death from consumption, he exercised upon the younger generation, for which he opened the road to socialism.

ALEXANDER HERZEN (1812–70), the illegitimate child of a Russian nobleman and a German woman, continued and perfected Belinsky's work, though not always agreeing with him. Under the influence of the writings of Voltaire, Schiller, Saint-Simon, Proudhon, and especially Hegel and Feuerbach, he became a protagonist first for liberal and later for socialist ideas. In 1847 he left Russia never to return. His chief influence was exercised through a paper, *The Bell* (*Kolokol*), which he published in London from 1857 to 1867 and which, though forbidden, was widely read in Russia—even by the Tsar.

Herzen believed in a combination of the aims of the French Revolution and the concepts of German idealistic philosophy. He hoped for a new law, replacing the old Roman law, which was to lead to materialistic socialism and atheism. Inasmuch as he despised a bourgeois republic as thoroughly as a monarchy, he was looking for a true folk state with the hope that in evolving it Russia would be able to skip altogether the stage of the bourgeois state. Yet, he was ready to allow for the lethargy of the people and their persistence in old ways, until the practices of his new state could gradually replace them. From his exile he fought first of all for emancipation of the serfs, greeting with joy the steps taken towards such reform. After seeing emancipation come true in 1861, he increased his demands, asking for constitutional rights, common ownership of land, and self-government of the people.

Mikhail Bakunin (1814–76) went far beyond the aims of other Westernizers. Described as a "product and victim of Russian conditions under Nicholas I," he fought valiantly throughout his life in his struggle against all existing order. He was one of the great agitators of all times, a man who by extraordinary and persistent deeds tried to bring about his utopian form of society.

Born of a wealthy, cultured family, he studied in Berlin and Paris and in 1848 took an active part in the revolution in France. He never relented in his fight against organized authority. From Paris he rushed to Prague, then to Dresden, to participate in revolutions there. Twice imprisoned, twice sentenced to death and reprieved, he was finally extradited to Russia. There he spent the years 1851–54 in prison, and afterwards was exiled to Siberia until he escaped. Subsequently he participated in the Polish uprisings in 1863, worked with the revolutionaries of Italy until 1868, and became leader of the revolution in Lyons in 1871. Denounced by Karl Marx, he was excluded from the International Workingmen's Association; in 1874 he once more participated in uprisings (at Bologna), and finally he died in Switzerland.

Ardent for action, he denounced all compromise including that of democracy. Destruction came first with him; for the new world, he thought, had to be created from the start. Freedom was his religion; state and church were his two "black beasts." Although believing in immortality, he did not believe in God. According to him, a world without God and without law could alone be free. He recognized no moral responsibility of the individual, as long as no one could escape the political and economic inequality of society as it was. This society he wanted first replaced by voluntary contracts in the sense of Proudhon. Unlike Karl Marx, who relied on the city proletariat, he believed that Russia with its millions of suffering peasants could lead on the road to such a new world.

Proponents of Other Systems.　Bakunin and Ivan Aksakov represent the ultimate products of Westernism and Slavophilism, both going far beyond the original principles of either school. Between them, there were many men of lesser influence, representing all shades of opinion from the theocratic and apocalyptic dreams of a Vladimir Solovëv, from Juri Samarin's and Pisarev's and Chernyshevsky's systems, to the practical political programs of the materialists. It was in this climate of opinion that the great reforms of Russian society were undertaken.

PROBLEMS

1. Discuss the trend of political ideas in Russia in the middle of the nineteenth century.
2. Discuss the philosophical background of the Russian thinkers.
3. Trace the transition from thought to action in the second half of the nineteenth century.

CHAPTER XXIV

EMANCIPATION

ACCESSION OF ALEXANDER II

The first of the great reforms was the liberation of the serfs. The need for it had long been recognized, but emancipation was delayed less because of opposition to the measure itself than because of uncertainty and fears of its implications. With tens of millions of people involved, no one doubted that emancipation would necessitate a series of additional changes, and that these were bound to interfere with the maxim of "Autocracy, Orthodoxy, and Nationalism" which Nicholas had considered the basis of the Russian state. Yet, even he realized the inefficiency of the existing system when he saw his country defeated in the Crimean War by the far inferior forces of Western nations, and shortly before his death in 1855 he advocated emancipation. His son and successor, Alexander II (1855–81), elected to support the emancipation movement, not out of any liberal spirit but because he feared revolution unless the government remedied the evils "from above."

ACT OF EMANCIPATION

Preparations. The practical solution began with the working out of certain principles and the adoption of a procedure. Abolition

142

of serfdom was accepted in principle, and it was decided that personal liberty alone would not do; the peasants were to receive land as well as freedom. Likewise it was established that such land was not to be secured by confiscation, but that the landowners were to receive due compensation. The procedure was to be systematic, beginning with the gathering of all available material and the sifting and discussion of it, and ending with a finished and effective emancipation plan to be submitted to the Tsar. The co-operation of all was solicited: of the idealists who, whether as members of the intelligentsia or of the imperial household itself, advocated it for humane reasons; of the economists, who in view of population pressure and increasing scarcity of cultivable land feared the collapse of the financial structure of the empire; of the state functionaries, who found themselves unable to erect a stable, modern government upon the archaic institution of serfdom; and, most of all, of the landowners themselves.

Economic Problems of Emancipation. When work began, the problems appeared to be overwhelming. There were regions with a surplus of workers and others with too few; there were districts with rich "black" soil and others of very limited fertility; there were serfs paying *obrok* and earning part of their living through industrial activities and those altogether engaged in agriculture under the *barchina* system; there were household serfs and artisans and factory help completely separated from the soil. No uniform solution was possible; on the contrary, circumstances demanded a separate system of emancipation for each group and region. The size of future land allotments for freed peasants and the compensation to owners had to be worked out according to local conditions. The decision had to be made whether to include in the compensation a sum for the loss suffered by the owner upon being deprived of the labor of his former serf. If he was to be compensated for both land and labor, who was to pay—the state, its treasury sorely depleted after a lost war, or the peasant, who possessed nothing and could only rely on future earnings from the land to be apportioned to him? If the latter plan were accepted—and under the circumstances it appeared the only feasible one—provisions had to be made to guarantee his payments, necessarily spread over many years, by retaining some sort of control over him.

Social Problems of Emancipation. Similar unfathomable problems were raised by the social aspects of emancipation. What would be its reaction on the peasant and his productivity, which formed the backbone of the state economy? How would the shattered finances be affected? What would be the effect on the liberal bourgeoisie and on the industrialists? Certainly, the danger of revolutionary outbreaks could not be discounted if the peasants were led to expect too much; and the peasants could be prevented from too great expectations only by public instead of secret sessions of the committees charged with emancipation legislation—and this in itself constituted a danger. Furthermore, the possible effect of any measure upon the landowning nobility had to be considered, since it was this class whose services had chiefly sustained autocracy.

Method of Emancipation. In the face of these thorny problems, the task was resolutely undertaken in 1857 and was successfully carried through owing to the devoted work of the high functionaries. Committees of landowners were formed, and plans from their midst as well as from outside sources poured in. In February, 1859, an "Editing Commission" was established to sift the various programs. Under the broad-minded chairmanship of Count Rostovtsev, and later of dutiful Count Panin, and with the help of progressive statesmen such as Minister of the Interior Lanskoy and Under-Secretary N. A. Milyutin, the work was taken up by three subcommittees in its judicial, administrative, and economic aspects. It was agreed to free the serf, to grant him a land allotment, and to fix a transitory period during which he was to pay for the acquired land while still obligated to perform some of his former duties. The state was to guarantee or advance the payments to the landowner, while the peasants were to continue through village communities (*mir*) to repay the government for all sums advanced to him. For the fulfillment of the obligations of each peasant, the *mir* remained collectively responsible. Attempts by reactionary landowners to sidetrack the decisions by giving the peasants only temporary use of the land were thwarted; and heated discussions over the amount of compensation, the size of the allotments, and the judicial status of the freed peasant were brought to final conclusions. After a protracted session of more than a year and a half, the findings were submitted to a "Main Commission," which accepted the proposals of the Editing Commission with one special amendment. With joint consent of both landowner and serf, the allotment could be reduced to one-quarter of the legal size, and in that case the peasant was exempted from each and every redemption payment and service. Many were to avail themselves of the opportunity and accept a small but outright gift of land in preference to a larger piece burdened with dues.

Emancipation Proclamation. On February 19, 1861, the solemn emancipation manifesto was signed. Twenty-two and a half million peasants were thereby freed. This tremendous work, which anticipated by four years the Thirteenth Amendment abolishing slavery in the United States and which was carried out on an infinitely larger scale, was achieved without civil war and without devastation and armed coercion; and yet it provided not only for freedom but also for the economic future of the freed. The state and court peasants were also freed, this act being promulgated in 1863, and the provisions for them were still more liberal than those for the landowners' serfs.

AFTERMATH OF EMANCIPATION

Status of Freed Peasants. Enthusiasm in Russia as in all of Europe was enormous, though it was soon dimmed by a realization of the burdens still resting upon the peasants. Although an end had been put to the jurisdiction and arbitrariness of squires, full citizenship was not granted and the peasantry was to form but a "tributary order." For a transition period of nearly fifty years, the peasant was still tied to his *mir,* which distributed the allotments, regulated the dues of each, and was obliged to assume joint tax responsibility for all members. Private land property was not recognized for the individual peasant, but the allocations in each village were held in common property by the *mir.* Unless sufficient guarantees were given to meet future obligations, no one could move from his village without relinquishing his title to a share of the common land. The burden of taxes—now payable, in money or in work, to the state instead of the squire—was heavy because taxes included compensation for both land and lost bondage rights. The burden was distributed according to the number of "souls" or male workers and the amount of livestock of each peasant. The land allotments were often not sufficient, considering existing cultivation methods; from one-quarter to one-half of all former serfs had to lease additional land in order to make a living, and often had to lease it at extravagant rates. Misery was greatest in the fertile but densely populated black-soil areas. Laziness and drunkenness, compatible with the status of serfdom, were not miraculously abolished nor was a feeling of responsibility or a desire for initiative engendered.

Effect on Peasants. The peasants were bitterly disappointed. Since they had not followed the proceedings, despite all publicity, the mistaken feeling grew among them that they were being deceived by greedy landowners and that the true intentions of the government were being thwarted. They resented not receiving all the land formerly tilled by them, they objected to the burdens, and they felt encumbered by a *mir* which was often under the undue influence of a village priest or a rich peasant (*kulak*).

Effect on Landowners. The landowners were not less dissatisfied. Only the more progressive among them succeeded in adjusting themselves to the new conditions by reasonable arrangements with their former serfs. The majority found great difficulties and lived by selling instead of cultivating their estates. By 1905, out of the land left to them after the emancipation in 1861, approximately one-half had passed into the possession of peasants. The redemption payments from the state had been insufficient to provide the former owners with a new start, for a large part was simply used by the government to cancel existing debts and the remaining payments were made in bonds which shortly became salable only at a loss. Industries monopolized much needed help, particularly in sparsely populated northern districts, and fields remained uncultivated.

Peace Mediators. To deal with existing unrest and to quell riots, the government appointed peace mediators. Though many of them were corrupt or inefficient, their task as a whole was well performed. Many difficulties were eliminated; time helped to settle remaining problems, and despite shortcomings and dissatisfaction, the gigantic work of emancipation was carried out with an astonishing measure of quiet and success.

PROBLEMS

1. Discuss the problems of emancipation.
2. Discuss the effects of emancipation.
3. Compare the social conditions of the peasants before and after emancipation.

CHAPTER XXV

ERA OF REFORM

SIGNIFICANCE OF EMANCIPATION

Emancipation introduced a new stage in Russian history, the short transition period of the "Liberal Age," which saw bureaucracy triumphant over the country as well as over the autocrat himself. The long era from Ivan the Terrible to Nicholas I, in which the service-nobility and its ideology had dominated Russian development, had come to an end with the Crimean War. The new period was more in line with the spirit of Europe than any other in modern Russian history, and it was marked by a series of progressive steps, of which emancipation was but the first.

REFORM LEGISLATION

Financial Reform. In 1862, legislation embodying some of the proposals of Speransky was set in motion to co-ordinate the financial structure of the empire with the needs of a new era. A ministry of finance and a state bank were created; and a regular budget was introduced, to be supervised by the finance minister. Tax collection was removed from the hands of private financiers, and a large government staff was organized to deal with the taxpayers, whose ranks were swelled by the multitudes of emancipated serfs.

Educational Reform. In 1863 a second great reform, that of the educational system, was undertaken. Popular education was widely extended; secondary schools were opened to women, who were also permitted—though sometimes only as auditors—to enroll at the universities. Universities were granted greater autonomy, but after the revolutionary disturbances in the seventies this autonomy was again limited through state supervision.

Judicial Reform. A third step, in 1864, consisted in the reorganization of the judiciary. Since the squires' jurisdiction had been eliminated with the abolition of serfdom, the state was obliged to assume their functions. Secret interrogation was abolished, equality before the law was decreed, new courts with a jury system—though limited in scope—were introduced. Special *volost* (district) courts for peasants and justices of the peace dealing with minor offenses were set up. The judicial agencies were freed from bureaucratic interference, trials were speeded, and the existing tortuous process of judicial appeal was restricted.

Administrative Reform. Likewise in 1864, local self-government through a Zemstvo system was instituted and became a progressive factor of outstanding importance. In three separate *curiae* (estates)—the landowners, the village communities, and the townspeople—delegates were elected to district and provincial assemblies. These assemblies, called *Zemstvos,* were bodies attending to local administration. They dealt with education, welfare, health problems, the organization of communication systems, and industrial construction, and through them state and local taxes were levied. Unfortunately, the funds at the disposal of the Zemstvos were often insufficient; yet, the Zemstvos contributed much to the betterment of conditions and served as schools for future political leaders. In the revolutionary eighties their work, like that of the new courts, was interrupted; but later they gained increased prestige.

Revision of Censorship. In 1865, edicts were issued to reduce censorship.

Insufficiency of Reform Legislation. The great reform laws of 1861–65 altered the structure of the empire fundamentally, but years were to elapse before their practical effect was fully felt. Only gradually could sincere co-operation on the part of officials be secured and the state machinery as well as the minds of the masses be adjusted to the new situation. In the meantime the progressives, belonging to all classes of the population, became impatient. Socialist tendencies increased, and in 1863 a revolt occurred in Poland which was suppressed with unnecessary brutality. In 1866, in a growingly tense atmosphere, an attempt on the life of the "Tsar Liberator" was made.

Further Reforms. Most Russian historians take this event as a milestone marking the interruption of the reform work. Facts, however, indicate that with the accomplishment of the financial, judicial, educational, and administrative reorganization of 1861 to 1865, the legal changes necessitated by emancipation had been essentially effectuated before 1866; the execution of further adjustments in line with the trend of the times could be stopped as little by the displeasure of the Tsar at the ingratitude of the people as by the appointment of reactionaries to high positions. Thus in 1867 protective tariffs were revoked; in 1870 a reform of municipal administration along the same lines as the Zemstvo government was carried out; and four years later universal military service was introduced. The number of years of service was radically reduced, a system of exemptions for breadwinners and a system of education for all soldiers were instituted, and much of the inequality and abuse resulting from the existing military organization was banned.

Beginning in 1863 and extending for three decades, various acts were passed which regulated and lightened the financial burden of the peasants under the emancipation act.

SHORTCOMINGS OF REFORM WORK

How did it happen that this enormous reform work—perhaps occasionally retarded by so-called reactionary trends yet never seriously interrupted—failed to satisfy the needs of the country? The chief causes may be found in various factors: delays in carrying out the laws in the immense country with its often unreliable bureaucracy; antiquated agricultural methods still practiced by the peasants after their emancipation; rapid industrial development which ran parallel with and always outdistanced the administrative reform work; and dissatisfaction of the intelligentsia at the persistency of a paternalistic regime which showed no intention of giving way to constitutional or popular rule.

Agriculture. In agriculture, especially, the beneficial effect of the reform work was slow in coming. The land distribution caused widespread injustices. Many farms, owing to their small size, proved unworkable under existing cultivation methods; capital was lacking for modern improvements; and famines still occurred regularly. In the black-soil districts, the need for land to provide for a rapidly increasing population was keenly felt, but intensified cultivation profiting from mechanical inventions was neglected. Agricultural production between 1860 and 1900 was raised only slightly, and necessary government credits for extensive improvements were not available. An undue share of the crops was used for exports to secure gold needed for interest payments on foreign loans. The lazy peasant profited from the industry of his neighbors in the same *mir;* drunkenness and illiteracy led to low living standards. Thus, despite emancipation and judicial, financial, and administrative changes, the agricultural system of Russia was still far from up to date.

Industries. Conversely, industries developed far too rapidly in comparison with the over-all progress of the country; and industrial crises, in themselves a factor sufficient to cause grave difficulties and revolutionary activities, were added to the agricultural problem. To be sure, at first after the emancipation edict of 1861, production fell because many of the erstwhile forced laborers left their working places and because lack of capital slowed down important improvements. But gradually factories adjusted themselves to the new situation, joint-stock companies were founded, and better wages and living conditions were offered. The transportation system, which had been grievously neglected, was improved. After its slow, fitful growth, which had followed the construction of the first railroad in 1838 and of the main line connecting Moscow and St. Petersburg in 1851, large-scale railroad-building activities began in 1870 under D. A. Milyutin, capable war minister and brother of the advocate of emancipation. In 1877 an additional impetus to industrialization resulted from the reintroduction of protective tariffs, although they exercised adverse influence on the price level of industrial products, since even with low trade barriers Russian industries could have found sufficient markets for their limited production.

In 1881 one of the periodic world-wide depressions hit Russia, but from 1885 industrialization again took a strong upswing.

PROBLEMS

1. Discuss the need for further reform legislation after the emancipation of 1861.
2. Discuss the attitude of the tsarist government toward reform.
3. Discuss the influence of the reforms on industrial life in Russia.

CHAPTER XXVI

INTELLIGENTSIA AND PARTIES

SOCIAL CURRENTS

Intelligentsia. In an atmosphere replete with reforms that never kept pace with the needs, political agitation persisted under the direction of the so-called "intelligentsia." Unlike the agitators of Western Europe, these Russian intelligentsia were not essentially bourgeois, nor were they close to the soil and the people living on it. They were recruited largely from the professional classes and from the nobility; they were city- and university-bred men distinguished by a strong social consciousness. Like the eighteenth-century philosophers of the French Enlightenment, they little valued the religious spirit of man and its expression through the church; they were socialistically inclined and were preoccupied with the material needs, the individual well-being, and the security of man.

POPULISTS. The intelligentsia were divided into various groups and "circles." Some of the circles were not unlike the "salons" before the French Revolution, where revolutionary ideas were discussed theoretically. But many of the intelligentsia, fearing the sterility of their endeavors unless fructified by practical knowledge and experience and aware of their lack of understanding of the masses, tried to gain a better idea of existing needs by establishing artificial contact with the people and by sharing their life. Under the guidance of Bakunin and Lavrov, they combined this purpose with an endeavor to inspire the people with revolutionary ardor. This Populist movement became known as *V narod* ("To the people"), and secret societies such as the *Zemlya i Volya* (1878–79) and *Narodnaya Volya* (1879–84) tried, though without success, to co-ordinate idealistic reasoning with practical demands of the day.

NIHILISTS. Others, lacking such practical experience and driven by theoretical materialism and scepticism, formed a special political school which became known as "Nihilist" after a term used by the novelist Turgenev. It aimed to free the individual altogether from the duties imposed upon him by family, state, and church, and to destroy the foundations of existing society through acts of terror. Whereas the *V narod* program asked for theoretical preparation, for practical experience, and for scientific investigation of social and economic conditions, the Nihilists called for action, subordinating social to political aims. Believing in the urgency of directing general attention to the dire need of constitutional reform as an essential condition for improving the status of the masses, they proceeded to do so by means of all kinds of propaganda, using terror as their chief weapon.

Terror. Under the aegis of the Nihilists, a number of outrages were committed without regard for the lives of guilty or innocent. In 1878, when general dissatisfaction with the government prevailed because of the lack of results from the Turkish war, the first great terrorist act was committed and the chief of the secret police was killed; in 1879, the governor-general of Kharkov was murdered, as was the new chief of police; in the same year, two attempts were made on the life of the Tsar, both miscarrying but exacting the lives of innocent victims. In the following year, another attempt was made by undermining the imperial palace. In 1881, the Tsar's "dictator," Loris-Melikov—an able, progressive statesman—was the object of a plot. Co-operating with the only elected popular representation, the Zemstvos, he had envisaged liberal reforms whereby the influence of the radical groups was to be reduced and a constitutional system gradually created. Finally, in March, 1881, Alexander II, while engaged in putting into practice the constitutional plans of Loris-Melikov, was assassinated by a bomb.

REACTION AND PROGRESS

Alexander III. The murder of Alexander II interrupted the progress of political reform, but did not stop the process of industrialization and social change. Under his son, Alexander III (1881–94), work on the constitution was halted, autocracy revived, and censorship restituted in an intransigent form. Loris-Melikov and the Slavophil friend of the people, the imperialist N. P. Ignatiev, were dismissed. Konstantin Pobedonostzev, tutor of Alexander III and superprocurator of the Holy Synod, a narrow and selfish reactionary, gained dominant influence; his assistants were Aksakov and Katkov, two former liberal Slavophils, but by now old and likewise reactionary. N. K. Bunge, finance minister until 1887, was the only prominent liberal among Alexander III's advisers.

Revival of Paternalism. The Zemstvos, which had grown in importance and which had laid a basis for a certain amount of self-government, were deprived of their representative character and became a part of the civil service. The so-called Zemstvo-Liberals were persecuted when they tried to organize co-operation among the various Zemstvos all over the empire and to develop the institution into a large-scale political factor, and their state-wide planning was discouraged. Through the church special influence was exercised on the curricula of the schools, and the police supervised most intellectual activities in the country. In line with Pan-Slavist programs, Russification was sponsored in the border regions, in Poland, Finland, and the Baltic countries. Under Alexander III, furthermore, persecution of Jews was intensified; they were allowed to settle in restricted areas only; certain professions were barred to them; purchase of real estate was prohibited; and schools were ordered to accept only a low percentage of Jews.

Gains of Peasantry. This return to the principle of "Autocracy, Orthodoxy, and Nationalism" of Nicholas I was not paralleled by a reactionary tendency in economic and social conditions. On the contrary, the reign of Alexander III showed the continuance of the progressive trends noticeable since emancipation. The peasantry gained considerable advantages: in 1882 the redemption payments were reduced, and in the same year an inheritance tax was introduced by the able finance minister Bunge, who thus for the first time laid the larger share of the financial burden on the shoulders of the wealthy and privileged classes. From 1883 to 1886 the poll tax was abolished, and following this the village authority over the peasant was eased by opening the way for appeals to higher courts.

Industrial Working Conditions. Likewise, the needs of the working class caused by the rapid industrialization of the country were realized, and legislation in its favor was drafted. Emancipation had little improved the laborer's low standards of living, as the country with its economy based on agriculture was not ripe for industrialization. Only 8 per cent of the population lived in cities, from which new industries springing up all over the country could draw their labor supply. Living quarters, hastily and penuriously constructed, were often of a most disgraceful type. Sometimes numerous families dwelt together in large sleeping halls, and immorality, drunkenness, and filth prevailed. The health of young and old was undermined by the vices of the towns and was no longer even partly balanced by strength-giving rural activities which in earlier days had formed a vital part of the industrial serf's life. Working hours were long; whole families were occupied in plants, and the care and education of children were sorely neglected.

Social Legislation. But plans to ameliorate conditions were put into practice under Alexander III. In 1882 child labor was regulated and working hours were reduced, and during the following eight years laws were promulgated regarding compulsory education for minors working in factories and curtailing nightwork of women, unjust fines, and payment of wages in kind instead of money. Factory inspectors were named to enforce this legislation and to supervise the laborer's living and working conditions. Gradually Russia, "backward, but not stagnant," caught up with social measures in Western countries, although, largely because of corruption, the application of the law often lagged behind the spirit.

FORMATION OF PARTIES

Liberal Parties. Alexander's vigorous rule of political conservatism and economic advance necessitated a change in the position of the various groups among the intelligentsia. The incoherent, utopian movements had to make room for more practical political parties. Populists, Nihilists, and Anarchists disappeared; capable organizers, both liberal and Marxist, emerged and with their help the *V narod* movement developed into what was later called the "Social Revolutionary party," and the Zemstvo-Liberals gave rise to the "*K*onstitutional *D*emocrats" (Kadets). In contrast to former radical groups, both these parties were progressive and fought determinedly with the use of peaceful propaganda and legal means for abolition of class differences, freedom of speech and press, equality before the law, a constitution, and betterment of social conditions.

Revolutionary Parties.

SOCIAL DEMOCRATS. Yet parties of a more revolutionary character were also created—parties ready to use Marxist tactics. The Social Democratic party as such was organized abroad by G. V. Plekhanov in 1883. The Social Democrats shared the desires of the Zemstvo and popular groups with regard to equality before the law, freedom of the press, and civil liberties; but they concentrated on practical economic aims—the gaining of higher wages, better working conditions, and shorter working hours. They organized strikes and unionized workers. Though active underground, they found themselves, paradoxically enough, not infrequently encouraged by secret government agents and spies who wanted to divert attention from political goals. The police, who succeeded in placing agents in key posts right within socialist ranks, actually co-operated with labor unions in the economic struggle when to do so served the political intentions of the government.

MENSHEVISTS AND BOLSHEVISTS. The growth of the Socialist party suffered at first from the smallness of the industrial proletariat and from the peasant's aversion to innovations. Violent strikes, which were organized in 1896 and in 1897 after Alexander III's death, proved a failure; and eventually, because of lack of success, the over-cautiousness and opportunistic policies directed by Plekhanov led to a schism in the socialist movement. In 1903, the "majority party," the Bolshevists under Vladimir Ulyanov (later known under his pseudonym "Lenin") seceded, while the "minority," the Menshevists, continued to follow Plekhanov. By working together with other liberal parties, as in other countries, and by participating in popular agencies and representations, this more moderate wing of the Socialists sought the realization of socialist objectives not through violent and revolutionary, but through evolutionary and parliamentary, means.

PROBLEMS

1. Discuss the position of the intelligentsia toward the social system of Russia.
2. Discuss the economic policies of the government under Alexander III.
3. Trace the emergence of political parties in Russia.

CHAPTER XXVII

REVOLUTION OF 1905

NICHOLAS II

Social legislation and political growth were constantly endangered because of the government's failure to adjust itself sufficiently to the changing conditions produced by rapid industrial progress. In 1894 Alexander III's son, Nicholas II (1894–1917), last of the Romanov rulers, had come to the throne. He may have been personally engaging, well-intentioned, and devoted to his duty, but he was also narrow-minded, autocratic, and politically weak and inconsistent.

INDUSTRIALIZATION

Introduction of Modern Economy. During the first decade of Nicholas' reign, an attempt was made to continue the paternalistic course set by Alexander III. The dominant figure in this period was Sergius Witte, appointed in 1892 by Nicholas' father to the post of minister of finance. Witte was ruthlessly efficient, a Westernized statesman of considerable ability, politically a conservative but economically a progressive; he never found himself in the good graces of the Tsar or in the favor of the people. Nevertheless, his contributions were outstanding; he concluded trade treaties, granted subsidies for industries, and introduced protective tariffs; he built railroads, secured loans from abroad, introduced the gold standard, and developed new industrial centers, such as the rich Donets basin. In the thirty years before World War I, although per capita production lagged considerably behind Western European countries, Russian coal output climbed more than tenfold and iron production was twice tripled, so that Russia came to hold third place in the world as a producer of these. The number of spindles in the textile mills was increased to nine million; some of the largest plants of Europe were found near Moscow and Narva, and Russia rapidly climbed to fourth place among the world's textile producers. Through cotton grown in newly acquired regions in central Asia, she freed herself by more than 50 per cent from her dependence on foreign—mainly American—imports. Oil production in the Baku region was doubled, platinum production provided nine-tenths of world supply; the paper industry was extended, and copper, silver, gold, zinc, and manganese were mined in increasing quantities.

FOREIGN LOANS.   But this enormous progress was bought at considerable sacrifice. Loans, needed from abroad and proffered chiefly by France, could be secured only at the expense of political concessions which later were to contribute to Russia's involvement in the First World War. Outside influence increased; commercial activities were channeled in an unfavorable direction, and the fruitful supplementation of mutual needs of Russia and Germany suffered. Forced and unprofitable exports became necessary to establish further credit and guarantee punctual interest payments. The cycles of prosperity and depression haunting the industrialized nations struck Russia also; and the country, already confronted by its many political and social problems, was exposed to all the consequences which the full impact of industrialization and radical economic shifts had brought about.

Political Oppression.   As Alexander III's progressive course was followed, though at a considerable price, in promoting industrial expansion, so were his conservative policies continued in the political field. No more was done to introduce a modern political order than had been done during his reign. The liberal policies of the Zemstvos were consistently opposed, Jews were persecuted more ruthlessly than ever, Orthodox sectarians were subjected to similar sufferings, and an intransigent policy of Russification of border lands was carried out. What had remained of autonomy in Poland, in the Baltic states, in the Ukraine, and in Armenia was destroyed. Finland suffered most: the guarantees given her under previous reigns were disregarded; and in 1899, under the pretext of unconstitutional demands by the Finns, the autonomy of the country and its legislature were abolished.

REVIVAL OF TERRORISTIC ACTS. As a result, popular discontent and tension increased, and shortly after 1900 new terroristic outbreaks occurred. In 1902 the minister of the interior was assassinated; in 1904 the hated reactionary finance minister Plehwe, who the year before had replaced the able Witte, was murdered; in the same year the governor-general of Finland was killed.

REVOLUTION

Road to Revolution. Within ten years of incongruous administration, the country thus headed toward radical change, and the struggle prepared by the liberal and Marxist intelligentsia came to pass. A second stage of Nicholas' rule began in 1904 and lasted until 1907. However, only Western, and mainly Anglo-Saxon, thinkers considered as a true accomplishment the progress made during these years in the direction of Western democratic concepts. In Russia, except for a small group, the trend toward democratic liberalism was regarded as being of not more than temporary use; if it were to serve Russian good, it would have to lead promptly to the next stage. For, in the minds of the Slavophils and Westernizers, of adherents of autocracy and of socialization, liberal bourgeois ways were typical for Western countries; in Russia, they were to make room quickly for a society based less on individualism than upon a communal spirit, and Russia's future was to be anchored in Russian and not in Western ideas.

BLOODY SUNDAY. The forces for reform found an opportunity for pressing their demands when, in 1904, the government engaged in war against Japan and needed their support. In November, representatives of the Zemstvos met in St. Petersburg and asked for popular representation and civil liberties. As their demands were not heeded, notwithstanding the fact that defeats in the war revealed the weakness of autocracy, more radical groups took over and began to organize strikes and foster disorders. These culminated on a January Sunday in a great procession of workers—men and women who, under the leadership of a priest, Father Gapon, marched to the Tsar's palace to present a petition asking for political freedom, equality before the law, lower taxes, and better working conditions. In the absence of Nicholas II, the marchers were received with rifle fire, and "Bloody Sunday" ended with the murder of hundreds of the defenseless, singing petitioners.

October Revolution. Agitation for violence was thereupon renewed. In February the ruthless Grand Duke Sergius was assassinated, and late in February the Tsar found himself compelled to make a first concession by promising the convocation of a consultative representative assembly, a *Duma*. Such representation—to be elected by three separate *curiae,* the landowners, townsmen, and peasants— failed, however, to satisfy the demands; and agitation was renewed. The Zemstvos organized new nationwide congresses of their various delegates, the intelligentsia increased their propaganda, the factory workers formed revolutionary unions, and even the peasants, who had so far remained inactive, began to stir. In line with the progressive economic program inherited from Alexander III, joint tax responsibility through the *mir* had been ended in 1903, and flogging was abolished in 1904; but now the peasants joined with their co-operative associations in political demands for more land and full civil rights. In August the Tsar found himself compelled to make a second promise— the granting of popular representation with wider consultative tasks and the right to propose drafts of laws. But this concession failed to stem the tide. The Socialists steadily gained in strength; and in October a general strike was staged by quickly formed revolutionary *soviets* (councils), paralyzing all activities. Revolution was now in full swing. Leadership was assumed by the Socialists under Khrustalev and Trotsky and by the Kadets under Milyukov; and many members of the various professions hastily formed unions of their own and joined in the movement.

COMPROMISE. Fearful disorders followed, which the government found impossible to curb even with the most ruthless measures. Mutinies flared up in the navy and, with somewhat less vigor, in the army. The nationalists rose in Finland, the Baltic states, Poland, and the Ukraine; the Jews vigorously supported the revolt against their oppressors; the peasants attacked landlords and pillaged estates; and strikes spread throughout the country affecting the whole economy of the nation. In the midst of the turmoil, Count Witte was reappointed by a frightened Tsar and given special powers. He determined upon a decisive concession promising fundamental civil liberties and regular popular representation with a certain amount of legislative power. This, in connection with extensive promises given several weeks later regarding franchise, appeased the liberals and, combined with energetic support to all conservative groups, isolated the Bolshevist-dominated soviets. Pobedonostzev, for three decades evil genius of the Tsars, resigned and with his elimination the issue became clearly a struggle for power between government and soviets. The former received support from France as well as Germany and succeeded toward the end of the year in arresting the revolution. When in December the soviets called for renewal of the general strike and for further violence, the government acted energetically. With the help of the army, risings were suppressed, the members of the soviets were arrested, additional promises regarding the franchise were made, and then elections for the Duma were held.

CONSTITUTIONAL REGIME

First Duma. Although the revolution thus failed to bring true success, it did evoke political consciousness among all classes and augured disaster for the bureaucracy which had overshadowed autocracy and held the reins of government since the Crimean War. In May, 1906, the Duma convened. According to Witte's plan, it was elected by *curiae* of large and small landowners, the former enjoying plural vote, and of an urban population likewise divided according to property and profession. Suffrage was indirect and unequal; clergy, students, soldiers, and nomads possessed no vote at all. Nevertheless, the peasant representatives and the Kadets held the majority; and Count Witte, who had assured the Tsar of a "pliant Duma," was dismissed.

DISSOLUTION OF DUMA. The life of the first Duma was short. Through so-called "fundamental laws," control of the finances and of the military forces as well as special legislative powers, and thus supreme authority, still remained reserved for the Tsar, and the government was responsible to him personally. The representatives tried to do away with such prerogatives and to push through a truly liberal program. Demanding a general amnesty, control of the budget, expropriation of landowners, factory reforms, and parliamentary ministerial responsibility, they still found their aims irreconcilable with those of the government, which after a short time summarily dissolved the assembly.

Agrarian Reform. Revolutionary activity was promptly renewed. The ex-representatives convened at Viborg, Finland, to protest and to continue their work until the convening of a new popular representation. The government—now under P. Stolypin, a man of energy and progressive leanings, yet a political conservative and supporter of Tsarism—countered with efficient and strong measures. On the one hand, it resumed repressive steps, and on the other, many social and peasant reforms were decreed "from above." The peasant, whose balances on the redemption tax dating back to emancipation had been cancelled in the previous year, received his land as inviolate private property and was allowed to leave his village community at will, yet retain his share of property. By this measure, Stolypin succeeded in avoiding the partitioning of the landowners' estates and in dividing the peasantry, the more wealthy members of which were satisfied and began to lend their support to the government.

Second Duma. Then elections for a second Duma were held. However, they turned out as unfavorable as those for the first Duma; for, although the Kadets lost rather heavily, the Socialists, who had not participated in the first Duma, won many seats. In a more radical assembly, inciting speeches were made and again demands for extensive changes were formulated. This led to the dissolution of the second Duma.

Third Duma. The Tsar now chose to alter arbitrarily the electoral law. Through a different curial system and redistribution of electoral districts, the peasants and workers were deprived of some part of their votes, and the representation of the always obstructive national minorities, foremost the Poles, was drastically cut, whereas the landowners and wealthy classes gained additional franchise. The third Duma, elected according to the new method and convened in November, 1907, was consequently chiefly composed of conservatives and moderates. Though not representative of the Russian people as a whole, it introduced for the first time some sort of representative government in Russia and, as it happened, exercised no inconsiderable influence on national and international relations. Although its legislative powers were small and censorship continued, a number of progressive measures were worked out, not the least among them being a plan for universal education to be completed in practice by 1922.

The third Duma served its full term from 1907 until 1912 and was then followed by the fourth Duma. It introduced the third stage in Nicholas' rule, which belongs to the history of the First World War.

PROBLEMS

1. Discuss the significance of the work of Witte for the economic growth of Russia.
2. Discuss the chief causes of the revolution of 1905.
3. Discuss the aims of the agrarian reform work under Stolypin.

CHAPTER XXVIII

THE ARTS IN RUSSIA

Life and conditions in every country find their expression through nonmaterial as well as material media—through the use made by people of their leisure; through the works of art produced within the atmosphere in which they live; through the thoughts expressed in their literature; through their costumes, dances, music, and play. No description of such activities can be satisfactory; for each has its own medium of expression and must be seen, heard, or felt rather than listed or described. But an indication of their scope, direction, and significance in the body politic has a place in the work of a historian.

ARCHITECTURE

Leadership of Kiev. The first concrete form of expression of artistic feeling with Russian as with many other cultures is found in architecture. As in the West, Christianity provided the moving impulse, and except for northern Russia, Byzantine influences were predominant. The early Christian churches were often shed-like buildings. The first wooden cathedral of more elaborate design was built in Novgorod in 989; it was much imitated all over the country, but wars, invasions, and fires have destroyed many of the best.

The first stone church was begun in Kiev in 991. In 1017, under the influence of Byzance and with the help of Greek artisans, the great Cathedral of St. Sophia in Kiev was begun; it was provided with many domes and beautified by mosaics and paintings. St. Sophia served as a model for future building, which combined "lusty northern strength, mystical Byzantine piety, and a haunting Orientalism." In the twelfth, thirteenth, and fourteenth centuries was developed the peculiar bulbous roof—born out of climatic considerations—combining cupola with pyramid. It survives to this day as a mark distinctive of Russian churches. However, nothing was brought forth during this time which, to the Western eye, would compare with the mighty perfection of German or French Gothic cathedrals, though the serenity and unique grace of the Russian churches, adapted to the Russian landscape and of special beauty in their natural setting, could not fail to inspire the people for whom they were created.

Predominance of Moscow. Attracted by possibilities offered in the growing country of the Moscow grand dukes, master architects from many parts of Europe arrived, some from the south, others from east and north. But they failed to develop further the Russian style, for they were bound by rules of the Orthodox authorities and had to conform to rigid traditions. Not even the mighty movement of the European Renaissance during the fifteenth and sixteenth centuries was powerful enough to change the trends in Russia and imbue the art of building with new vigor. Still under the influence of early wooden architecture, the two great Moscow cathedrals erected in the fifteenth century, the "Assumption" and the "Annunciation" —the former built by an Italian, the latter by a Russian—profited but little from European examples. St. Basil, created in the sixteenth century, alone represented a certain departure from earlier structures.

Among secular buildings, houses and fortifications of more elaborate construction emerged in the thirteenth century which began to show an unmistakable influence of Tartar traditions spread by the conquerors. The subservience of the Muscovite grand dukes increased these influences, which found their reflection in the palaces the grand dukes constructed for their own glorification.

Hegemony of St. Petersburg. It was in the seventeenth and eighteenth centuries, after baroque and rococo architects had replaced the great artists of the Renaissance, that contact with the West, established by Peter the Great, allowed the infiltration of new ideas.

Italian, German, and French style, entering through Poland and the Ukraine, began to influence and later to dominate Russian architecture. Palaces, bridges, portals, and streets, if not churches, took on the stamp of a different spirit. In 1757, the Academy of Fine Arts was founded in St. Petersburg; from it were graduated native artists, many of them serfs, who at the request of their Westernized patrons and masters imitated chiefly the French and Italian schools. In the nineteenth century, the German classicist style dominated. But in Russia, as in other countries, nothing original of durable value was born; and the former spiritual creative impulse was supplanted by an inspiration which came chiefly from commercial, military, and self-glorifying projects.

PAINTING, MUSIC, BALLET

Painting.

ICONS. The history of painting follows a different pattern. Introduced through frescoes of Greek artists during the eleventh century, the art was soon adopted by Russians, whose *icons,* with their pure colors, their gold and blue, showed unusual beauty, depth, simplicity, and grace. Later, the art of painting icons flourished particularly in Suzdal and Novgorod, where far from Byzance it was enriched by national elements and where red, yellow, and green coloring came to supplement blue and gold. It reached its peak around 1400 with Andrew Rublev, whose tender, timeless work is well comparable to that of Giotto and other inspired masters of the early Renaissance. Rublev was not a solitary figure. Several artists shared with him the beautiful achievements of Russian icon painting, and the art flourished despite Tartar occupation and Western influence. It failed, however, to progress; its course was arrested rather; and, in the fifteenth and sixteenth centuries, it was cheapened and finally degraded by conventionality and a mercenary spirit. Unlike the situation in the West, the church succeeded in stifling the further evolution of painters through its opposition to pictures of secular topics; and despite the examples of the great Dutch, German, and Italian artists, Russian painting became untrue to the spirit of its time. It was only late in the seventeenth century that successful opposition arose to old traditions and that the technique was improved by perspective and attention to background. Yet, it was not before the eighteenth century, after the foundation of the Academy of Fine Arts, that painters of eminence appeared. Then, although old church art persisted, the interest of the painters was directed to and began to include secular themes and their horizon was widened through travel and studies abroad. But even so, lack of originality and imitation of the French and Italian prevailed.

MODERN PAINTING. The first masters of independent merit came after 1800, in the Romantic period, with Levitsky, Bryulov, and Ivanov; and it was the genre picture (Venetsianov) which in the nineteenth century began to pay special attention to the Russian national scene. By then the Academy, whose influence on the development of arts had been beneficially felt during the earlier period, had assumed a dogmatic character, and in 1863 a number of members revolted against it. A patron of art, Paul Tretyakov, supported their ideas and a new school arose which, instead of imitating foreign tastes, took its inspiration from Russian history and daily life and marked the rising spirit of "social consciousness." Its followers in the second half of the nineteenth century, N. Gay ("Crucifixion"), I. Repin ("Barge Haulers on the Volga," "Ivan the Terrible and His Son"), V. Surikov ("Execution of the Streltsi"), and others often not known by name in the Western world, belong to the best masters of their times. They introduced a period when Russia, accepting and influenced by the impressionists and expressionists, shared in the international development of painting. The constant social preaching of the artists, however, was eventually resented, and the period before the First World War witnessed a return to earlier purely aesthetic concepts.

Music. In music, Russia produced little of outstanding merit until the nineteenth century. Russian folk songs, with their "elemental power" and expression of tenderness and melancholy, were deep and inspiring like the musical treasures of other peoples. Collections of these folk songs exist, and many of their themes and rhythms have found a reflection in the masterpieces of later periods. But the sacred music possessed little of the general and timeless appeal of that of the Western world, and there is nothing preserved that compares with the majestic medieval Latin hymns or with the fundamental works of Renaissance and Reformation. In the eighteenth century, opera was introduced from Italy. The first Philharmonic Society was founded as late as 1802, when the works of the Germans—Bach, Haydn, Mozart, and Beethoven—inspired the Russian world. But in this field more speedily and effectively than in others, the Russians emancipated themselves from foreign influence and, deep from the springs of their soul, began to create their own music, imbuing it with such spirit as to give it significance beyond the national borders. Glinka (d. 1857) with his *Life for The Tsar* introduced the great period of Russian music. In the agitated times of emancipation and reform when national aspirations and social questions involved every feeling artist, Tchaikovsky (d. 1893; symphonies, *1812 Overture*) Musorgsky (d. 1881; *Boris Godunov*), and Rimsky-Korsakov (d. 1908; symphonies, *Scheherazade,* collection of folk songs) created their immortal works. In the twentieth century, Rachmaninoff and the "modernists" Scriabin, Stravinsky, and Prokofiev maintained the tradition of Russian accomplishment, versatility, and social consciousness.

Ballet.

BEGINNINGS OF BALLET. Of special interest is the development of a Russian specialty—the ballet. The first performance of a play took place in 1672 before Tsar Alexis. It dealt with a biblical topic, *Esther,* and it was succeeded by a dance performance, *Orpheus and Eurydice,* and by another biblical play, *Holofernes and Judith.* But after Alexis' death, reactionary tendencies prevailed, and the stage was closed except for private performances. The theater was revived by Peter; and in 1735, before his niece, Tsarina Anna, the first regular ballet was staged by Landé, dancing master of the Military Academy. He founded in 1738 "Her Majesty's Dancing School," accepting pupils from the age of seven on, many of them children of serfs; and ballet presentations soon became fashionable. The topics were mainly of foreign and mythological origin, but gradually folk dances and Russian themes gained in importance. By the beginning of the nineteenth century the ballet was well established: the government supervised and paid for the school; children of serfs were "ascribed" to it; no one could leave before the lapse of ten years; the star, rather than the ensemble, was emphasized; and musical composition, mimicry, and pantomime were greatly improved. The Mazurka from Glinka's *Life for The Tsar* was staged and a great director, Didelot, and excellent performers increased the reputation of the Russian ballet.

ZENITH OF BALLET. After Didelot—through bad administration and conventionality, poor education, and low moral standards—the work of the school was menaced until, in the fifties, reforms were introduced. Under the direction of two Frenchmen and with the help of fine dancers, the ballet re-established its reputation and led in creative and inspiring methods. Through grace, as opposed to "acrobatics," the St. Petersburg ballet gained fame and world-wide appreciation. It maintained this reputation because of its faculty for consistent evolution, reform, and resistance to outmoded traditions. In the 1890's it witnessed a great revival; and men like Sergius Diaghilev and Michel Fokine, supported by musicians and painters of merit and training in ballet composition and by the great dancers Anna Pavlova, Adolph Bolm, and Waslaw Nijinsky, led the art of Russian ballet to new heights.

LITERATURE

Early Literature. In literature—of which, as in other arts, no understanding can be gained except by direct contact—Russia had likewise little to offer before the nineteenth century, if we are to judge from what has been preserved. The most prominent work was the twelfth-century epic, *The Lay of Prince Igor*. Church literature flourished in the Kiev region in the eleventh century, and around Suzdal and Moscow in the twelfth. It included contemporary chronicles and stories—foremost the *Chronicle of Nestor;* but though it may be dear to the historian and Slavophil, it failed to lay a basis for the development of a Russian national literature. Fables, folk songs, and epic songs, the *byliny,* constituted a more important part of the Russian art of expression. The printing press was not introduced until the middle of the sixteenth century, and even then played but a small role for another two hundred years.

Linguistic Reforms. Under Peter, interest was taken in foreign works and many imitations and translations were published; but not even under Elizabeth, vaunted for her Russian leanings, was native literature fostered. Likewise the three outstanding writers of the time of Catherine the Great—Novikov and Radishchev (both pamphleteers as well as literary men) and G. Derzhavin—failed to reach the level of contemporary European poets. Some of the difficulties for Russian authors consisted in the tradition of the church, in the differences between the written and the spoken word, and in the complexities of alphabet and grammar. Linguistic studies therefore had to precede other accomplishments and pave the way for poetic literary expression. Three names were chiefly connected with this task: Lomonosov (1711–65), professor at the Academy of Sciences, a polyhistor, philosopher, poet, historian, physicist, and chemist; Karamzin (1766–1826), historian and poet, whose romantic novel, *Poor Lisa,* was a milestone in the field of the Russian art of writing; and Zhukovsky (1783–1852), famous for his grammar and translations.

Nineteenth Century.   Once the basis for literary expression was laid, writers of ability and profundity were not lacking. In line with the spirit of the nineteenth century, interest in religious, philosophical, psychological, and social aspects rather than in literary problems and fantasy dominated. Although Russian writers greatly admired and were influenced by German idealism, by Schiller and Goethe, as well as by the romantics Schlegel and Fichte, art for art's sake and classical serenity and detachment never gained widespread favor in Russia. "Art [is] an expression of the spirit and tendency of society in a given epoch," said the great literary critic Belinsky, and, added Herzen, "Man is not born for logic alone,— but also for the social-historical world of moral freedom and positive action." It is in this spirit and in a definitely national yet "all human" atmosphere that the greatest works in Russian literature and their creators must be viewed: Pushkin (1799–1837), famed for his poetry, for *Boris Godunov,* and for *Eugene Onegin;* Lermontov (1814–41), known for *A Hero of Our Times;* Gogol (1809–52), who wrote *Dead Souls* and *The Revizor;* Turgenev (1818–83), author of *Fathers and Sons;* Dostoyevsky (1821–81), writer of *Crime and Punishment, The Idiot, The Brothers Karamazov;* and Tolstoy (1828–1910), who wrote *Anna Karenina, War and Peace,* and *The Death of Ivan Ilyich.* In an interplay of nationalism and practical religiosity, the prominent Russian poets demonstrated their deep trust in the Russian people and in Russia's destiny.

The literary tradition of the great Russian authors and their many distinguished contemporaries was continued in the following generation by Anton Chekov (1860–1904), D. Merezhkovsky (1865–1941), V. L. Andreyev (1871–1919), and the fighter for the new revolutionary world to come, Maxim Gorky (1868–1936).

PROBLEMS

1. Discuss the foreign influences on Russian art.
2. Discuss the importance of "social consciousness" among Russian artists.
3. Discuss the scope of artistic achievement in nineteenth-century Russia.

CHAPTER XXIX

RUSSIA AND EUROPE

The rhythm of domestic change in Russia is traceable also in external affairs. A distinct connection between international and internal policies can be observed, for instance, in the defeat in the Crimean War and its reaction upon the emancipation of serfs, in the Congress of Berlin and nihilistic activities, in Far Eastern involvements and the Revolution of 1905.

NEAR EASTERN PROBLEM

The Near East. During the eighteenth century and Napoleonic times, Russia's chief preoccupation in external affairs had been with her northern and western neighbors, Sweden and Poland. During the nineteenth century, Russia centered her attention upon the south, upon Turkey and the Straits of Constantinople. Down to 1914, the strategic Near Eastern problem runs like a red thread through the history of Russian international activity in Europe, giving direction to her plans and her wars and alliances. Yet, despite many a victorious enterprise against Turkey and notwithstanding the dissolution of the Ottoman empire, the gains were insignificant; the aim, Constantinople, was not reached, and by 1914 Russia had hardly improved her position over 1815. In all her enterprises she found England to be her chief obstacle, and it is her dealings with Great Britain which offer a key to an understanding of Russian diplomacy in the nineteenth century.

Principle of Legitimacy. The Napoleonic Wars saw Russian troops victoriously marching into Paris, but Constantinople was still out of reach. At Tilsit and Erfurt, Napoleon had refused any concessions with regard to Constantinople, which he called the "capital of the world." After his abdication, the Congress of Vienna established—in contrast to the liberty and equality of the French Revolution—the principle of legitimacy, which guaranteed the "legitimate" rulers their pre-Revolutionary territories. Russian aspirations in the Near East were thereby stalled, for the legitimacy of the Sultan's rule could not be disputed; and Alexander, founder of the Holy Alliance, concentrated his attention upon remoter problems. He participated in the Congresses of Aachen (1818), Carlsbad (1819), Laibach-Troppau (1820–21), and Verona (1822), which after the Napoleonic catastrophe and in line with the principles of the Holy Alliance were held to deal with threats to peace. He occupied himself with questions of French occupation and reparations, with revolutionary movements in Germany, Italy, and Spain, with American slave trade, and with the struggle for independence in South America.

Greek War of Independence. But in the meantime, the Eastern problem emerged with redoubled force. In 1821, the Christian Greeks began a war of independence against the Turks. Since traditional Russian policy favored any action which served to undermine Turkish power, whereas the principles of the Congress of Vienna prescribed the subduing of all revolutionary activities against legitimate rulers, Alexander found himself in a dilemma. Under the influence of Austria's minister Metternich, he decided to observe the principle of legitimacy; but after his death this policy was reversed. By the Treaty of Akkerman (1826) the Turks were forced to respect previously undertaken obligations regarding Christian minorities in the Balkans; and when they again procrastinated, intervention in favor of Greece was decided upon. In conjunction with France and England, Russia dispatched a fleet to force the Sultan to accept Allied mediation between him and the insurgents. Against the original intentions, this Allied armada struck a decisive military blow at Turkey and destroyed, at Navarino, the fleet which had come from Egypt to support the Sultan.

Turkish War. The attack was represented in the English Parliament as an "untoward" accident, and was certainly unwelcome to the British to the extent that it increased Russian influence in the Mediterranean. They therefore withdrew from further action, with the French following in their wake. But the dismayed Turks declared a holy war, and Russia decided to profit by this opportunity and continued her campaign. While General Paskevich seized the fortress of Kars in the Caucasus sector, the main body of the Tsar's troops, led by General Diebitsch, crossed the Balkan mountains under great difficulties and took Adrianople, key to the road to the Straits.

Adrianople. Defeated Turkey was obliged to sue for peace in 1829 (Adrianople). She ceded all her territories in the Caucasus and accorded Russia a protectorate over the Danubian provinces of Moldavia and Walachia. The treaty marked an important moment in history, for Russia established herself thereby as protagonist of the Christian states in the Balkans in their struggle for independence from Turkey and as a power on the Balkan peninsula. With her sponsorship, Greek independence was declared and guaranteed by the European powers, and Serbia as well as the Danubian principalities gained autonomy.

Unkiar Skelessi. A new success was scored in 1833, when a rising of the Egyptians forced Turkey to appeal for help to the European powers. In exchange for assistance, the Sultan concluded the Agreement of Unkiar Skelessi with Russia. This treaty accorded the Tsar the right to use the Bosporus and the Dardanelles for his warships and closed them to other nations, thus establishing a virtual Russian protectorate over Constantinople. The treaty was supplemented in the same year by an arrangement with Austria which provided for co-ordinated policies of the Tsars and the Hapsburgs toward Turkey.

Straits Convention. The position thus gained, however, could not be maintained against the misgivings of England and France, which in 1838 seized upon the opportunity afforded by new troubles between Turkey and Egypt to weaken Russia's protectorate. This time, in alliance with Austria and Prussia, they did not allow Russia to act independently, but insisted upon their right to have a voice in affairs pertaining to Turkey and the Near Eastern problem. After long negotiations, which were complicated by France's desire for prestige and her alignment with Egypt, a new convention was concluded in 1841. It replaced the Russian protectorate over the Straits by an international guarantee which deprived Russia of the military use of the Bosporus and the Dardanelles.

CRIMEAN WAR

Outbreak. The Straits Convention did not settle the Near Eastern problem, nor did it satisfy Russian ambitions or compose Anglo-Russian rivalry. It also failed to arrange the question of protection for Christians in the Balkans, among whom the Catholic minority looked for French, and the Orthodox majority for Russian, support; neither did it protect the vast French economic interests in the Near East. In 1850 the struggle was resumed when Louis Napoleon, then President of France and thirsting for recognition and glory, demanded from Turkey the right of French control over holy places in Palestine for the protection of Catholic monks. This reopening of the Eastern question induced Tsar Nicholas not only to demand like privileges for the Orthodox clergy and a protectorate over all Orthodox Christians, but also to suggest to England a final settlement of the whole Near Eastern problem: he proposed in 1853 the outright partitioning of Turkey. The offer, which ran counter to the British policy of keeping "life lines" through the Mediterranean intact and unimperiled, was categorically declined. Suspicions and fears in London rose to a high pitch, and the Turks were incited by England to reject a simultaneous Russian ultimatum demanding a protectorate over their country. Tsarist troops thereupon invaded the Danubian provinces, and the Sultan, relying on British backing, declared war. Prussia took no part in the hostilities, and Austria confined herself to keeping a menacing but noncombatant attitude so long as Russia did not transgress on the Danubian region. But Britain, France, and later Piedmont actively intervened in favor of the Turks; their fleets sailed through the Straits into the Black Sea and the Crimean peninsula was invaded.

Defeat. The Allied forces reaped little glory. Poor leadership and bad organization led to unnecessary loss of human life and waste of material, and ultimate success was due only to the technical inferiority and still greater incompetence of the Russians. Corruption of the bureaucracy, failure of the supply system, and lack of equipment and particularly of medical help rendered useless the bravery of the Russian soldiers and the valiant efforts of such capable leaders as General Totleben, defender of the key fortress of Sevastopol. In

view of their losses and the exhaustion of their finances, after Tsar
Nicholas I's death in 1855 the Russians were obliged to put an end
to the struggle, which seemed to prove the superiority—at least militarily—of a "degenerate" yet industrially developed Western world.

Peace of Paris.   Peace was concluded at Paris in 1856. In pushing Russia's frontiers back and stripping her of naval power, it served
mainly English interests. The mouth of the Danube and Bessarabia
and parts of earlier conquests in the Caucasus region, including the
fortress of Kars, were forfeited by Russia; she had to renounce any
existing or future unilateral protectorate in Turkey, to remove her
warships from the Black Sea, and to scrap her shore fortifications.

Political Reorientation.   The stipulation dealt a severe blow
to Russia and led to a reversal of her policies. The old foreign
minister Nesselrode was replaced by A. M. Gorchakov; a rapprochement with France was promoted and the alliance with Austria, which
had proved so unsatisfactory, was discontinued. A firmer alliance was
sought with Prussia, where Gorchakov's friend and "pupil" Bismarck
came to power in 1861; and steps were taken to recover lost prestige through enterprises in the Far East.

POLAND

The realignment in foreign affairs, combined with the internal
reforms of 1861, made it possible for Russia to meet a crisis which
arose in 1863. This time not Turkey but Poland was involved.

Revolution of 1830.   The Poles had been granted autonomy
within the Russian empire by the Congress of Vienna: their country,
"Congress Poland," which corresponded approximately to existing
ethnographic facts, had been made a kingdom with Russia's Tsar as
king of Poland, and they had been accorded a separate administration and constitutional rights. But this arrangement had deprived
them of coveted eastern territory and had failed to satisfy their
national ambitions. The resultant unrest led to infringements on
Russian suzerainty, and in 1830, following uprisings in Paris, a
revolution broke out. Faced by the brutal might of the Russian army
under Diebitsch and Paskevich, and hindered by their own disunity
and the greed and reactionary spirit of their leaders, the Poles
emerged defeated and deprived of many of their previous rights.

Revolution of 1863.   When the Revolution of 1848 swept Europe, Poland dared not join in the movement; but in the following

decade, after the Crimean War and during the early reign of
Alexander II, Tsar-Liberator, hopes in Poland were reawakened.
Alexander's conciliatory attitude encouraged the Poles to demand
concessions and territorial aggrandizement. Unrest grew and culminated in 1863, after the introduction of a revised conscription law,
in a new revolt. With the assistance of Bismarck and because of
continued disunity among the Poles, this revolt also was suppressed,
and it led to the abolition of Polish autonomy. Emancipation of the
serfs was decreed; and in order to break the hold of the Polish
nobility and gain the sympathies of the people, it was carried out
under particularly generous conditions for the peasants. Measures
for the Russification of the country were proclaimed and harshly,
though unsuccessfully, applied.

Internal consolidation and recovered prestige opened the way
for Russia to concentrate again on her most important foreign
problem and to resume her Balkan policies.

PROBLEMS

1. Discuss Russia's drive to gain domination of the Straits.
2. Discuss the influence of Russo-Turkish relations on Anglo-Russian
   relations.
3. Describe the status of Poland under Russian rule.

CHAPTER XXX

INTERNATIONAL REORIEN- TATION

WAR WITH TURKEY

Background and Events Leading to War.

ABROGATION OF BLACK SEA CLAUSE. The first move in Russia's renewed drive for the penetration of the Balkans consisted in the abrogation of the most burdensome stipulation of the Peace of Paris. In 1870, while the attention of the world was focused on the Franco-German War and the collapse of Napoleon III's empire and while England and Austria were preoccupied with the issues arising from these, Russia swiftly repudiated the clause which banned the maintenance of warships on the Black Sea.

EXPANSIONIST PAN-SLAVISM. Emboldened by the inability of their treaty partners to challenge the act, the Russians undertook the next step and began to reclaim from the Turks the parts of Bessarabia ceded at the Peace of Paris. Their drive gathered momentum under the leadership of the Pan-Slavs, who—as political heirs of the Slavophils—preached the collaboration of all Slavic nations, the common interests of all Orthodox peoples, and the "great civilizatory mission" of the tsarist empire. Anti-Western, and particularly anti-British, propaganda was promulgated; the competitive and oppressive system of the West was denounced; and the salvation of all Slavic brethren from oppression was fiercely advocated.

RUSSIA AND CENTRAL EUROPE. Behind the profession of lofty Pan-Slav aims stood the practical desire for the possession of Constantinople. The Russians realized, however, that no possibility existed for taking the city against the concerted opposition of the European powers. They therefore made a number of compromises, the most important of which consisted in the renewal of good relations with the Austrian empire. So long as Russia and Austria were confronted by a strong Turkish power threatening the existence of both, they found collaboration expedient; but when the Turkish danger subsided and Austrian and Russian spheres in the Balkans moved close together, tension arose, increasing in proportion to the growing ethnic and religious aspirations of Slavophilism. These aspirations ran counter to Austria's plans for aggrandizement and her resolve not to permit the emergence of a strong Slavic power which, like the old Ottoman empire, could threaten her from the rear. Now, however, a reconciliation of Russian and Austrian aims was sought; and a willing hand was lent by Bismarck, chancellor of Germany, who was anxious to strengthen his newly created empire through friendship with his eastern neighbor. Under his auspices, a "Three Emperors' League" was formed in 1872, based on the analogous monarchical structure of Russia, Austria, and Germany.

RESURGENCE OF THE BALKAN PROBLEM. The alliance was never wholehearted: Austrian and Russian policies in the Balkans remained opposed despite formal co-ordination, and Germany's feelings were alienated when in 1875 Gorchakov, fancying himself in the role of a European arbiter, interfered in Franco-German relations. Nevertheless, the alliance survived and enabled Russia to further pursue her Balkan plans. She had not long to wait for a propitious moment. In 1875 and 1876 continued Turkish oppression led to revolts in Bosnia, Herzegovina, and Bulgaria. Promptly Russia and Austria dispatched an ultimatum to the Sultan, known as the "Andrassy Note," and—Germany, France, and England concurring —demanded from him long overdue reforms in favor of the Christian states in the Balkans. The Turks made promises but took no action, and the revolts spread. In 1876 Serbia and Montenegro declared war against Turkey.

The Turkish War. This situation gave Russia the sought-for opportunity to resume her Near Eastern drive. After assuring herself of Austria's acquiescence by a convention (at Reichstadt) which set aside Bosnia as Austria's and Bessarabia as Russia's sphere of influence, she actively intervened with the Sultan on behalf of the revolting Balkan nations. The Pan-Slav Ignatiev was sent to Constantinople and took up the cause of Serbia and Montenegro, demanded the cessation of Turkish oppression, insisted on the introduction of reforms which tended to break up the Turkish empire, and thus tried to re-establish Russian hegemony in the Balkans. In vain did England sponsor an international conference in order to prevent the Russians from solving the Near Eastern problem in their own way. The negotiations brought no result, and with Turkey still obstructive, Russia declared war in April, 1877. Despite valiant defense of the fortress of Plevna by the Turks and the persistent incompetence of Russia's military and administrative leaders, the tsarist army, greatly outnumbering the enemy, eventually reached the gates of Constantinople.

PEACE OF SAN STEPHANO. At this point the advance was halted by the decision of the Russian general staff not to risk a long, costly, and possibly unsuccessful assault on the Turkish capital and by the action of the British, whose fleet entered the Marmara Sea and threatened to fulfill Turkish hopes for intervention. The Russians decided to conclude peace (San Stephano, 1878). They forced Turkey to recognize the independence of the Slavic nations in the Balkans, created—under their own protectorate—a large autonomous state of Bulgaria with a port on the Aegean Sea, and recovered Batum and Kars. By also demanding recognition of additional rights for Christians within the Turkish empire, they secured permanent domination of Turkish affairs.

CONGRESS OF BERLIN. This Russian solution of the Balkan problem might have brought a beneficial and durable settlement; but in going beyond the Reichstadt Agreement it antagonized the Austrians, who found their own Balkan plans menaced; and, more important, it revived the familiar fears in London. Disregarding the inefficiency and barbarity of Turkish rule, England demanded, under threat of war, a revision of the Treaty of San Stephano; and the Russians found themselves in no position to oppose her. After separate negotiations in Vienna and London, an international congress for the settlement of the Eastern problem was convened in 1878 in Berlin. Bismarck presided as mediator and "honest broker"; Disraeli represented England and Gorchakov, Russia—the latter being a rather unfortunate choice, for he was old, deaf, and vain, and his claim of "having saved European peace" in 1875 had cost him the friendship of the Iron Chancellor. At the Congress, the British did not yield; determined to make war rather than allow the execution of the Peace of San Stephano, they found support from Bismarck, who was resolved to avoid war at any price and therefore supported their demands. The Russians were forced to rescind the Treaty of San Stephano, to consent to a radical reduction of the territory assigned by them to Bulgaria, and to forego access to the Aegean Sea via a Bulgarian port. The border lines of the Christian states, whose independence was recognized, were redrawn—unsatisfactorily for them and for Russia; the Straits were once more closed to all non-Turkish warships; and the cession of the port of Batum to Russia was made dependent upon its complete demilitarization.

RAPPROCHEMENT WITH FRANCE

Three Emperors' League and Reinsurance Treaty. The Congress of Berlin marked a turning point in Russian external relations. It exposed the unreliability of any power combination in which the Russian and the Austrian empires were partners; it proved England's resolve to impede Russian access to the Mediterranean even at the cost of war; it divulged Germany's primary concern with friendly relations with Austria and England; and it demonstrated France's inability to help Russia within the existing system. The subsequent forty years Russia therefore devoted to attempts to build up a different, more reliable alliance system and to temporize in questions referring to Turkey and the Straits.

For the time being, and only through Bismarck's exertions, the Three Emperors' League was renewed in 1881. Bismarck considered friendship with the Slavic neighbor "the pivot" of German security, and in order to avoid new friction he endeavored to direct Russian attention to tasks and opportunities in Asia. But the Balkan problem could not be subdued. In 1885 troubles flared up in Bulgaria and again proved the incompatibility of Russian and Austrian plans with regard to the Balkans. Not even Bismarck's skill, prestige, and acknowledged peaceableness could restore harmony among the three empires. The League expired, and in 1887 Bismarck found himself forced to renounce the idea of renewing it. He had to confine himself to preserving friendship with Russia through a separate secret alliance. This so-called "Reinsurance Treaty," defensive in intent, served the cause of understanding only briefly; for in 1890 Bismarck was forced to resign, and without his support the Reinsurance Treaty was allowed to lapse. Once more isolated, Russia this time turned to France.

Entente with France. Friendly relations between Russia and France had existed for some time, and immediately upon the nonrenewal of the Reinsurance Treaty in August, 1890, an official political agreement was made. An exchange of diplomatic and military courtesies followed; and in August, 1891, despite the Tsar's reluctance and against the protests of liberal and socialistic-minded quarters in France which recognized the threat to peace, an *entente* was established. It provided for consultation in international questions and mutual support in case of war. In the following year it was supplemented by a military convention of aggressive character, and in 1895 and 1896 the treaties were disclosed to the world. Russia gained economically, for she received loans of almost one billion dollars which were fundamental to her progress on the road to Westernization and industrialization. Politically, the balance was less favorable. On the one hand, Russia could use France as a counterweight and emancipate herself from dependence upon the central powers. On the other, she became subservient to chauvinistic French interests, found herself launched on an anti-German policy contrary to her growing trade interests and leading to a long-drawn-out tariff war with Germany, saw the security of her western border imperiled, and continued to be thwarted in her Near Eastern plans.

Relations with Other Powers. Several vain attempts were made to escape this political bondage without losing access to the French money market. In 1899 a conference was held at The Hague at Tsar Nicholas' suggestion in an endeavor to halt the armament race and ease the financial burden on Russia. In 1905 an agreement was signed at Björkö by which the Tsar and Emperor Wilhelm II tried to revive the former friendship between their two countries; in 1907 a second peace conference was held at The Hague; and in 1908 a new convention was entered into with Austria at Buchlau, dividing the spheres of interest in the Balkans and laying a basis for a new advance on Constantinople. But the Hague peace conferences failed to promote the cause of disarmament and understanding; the Björkö negotiations were disavowed and blocked by both Russia's and Germany's foreign ministers—the one out of consideration for France, the other for Austria—and the Buchlau bargain turned out to the unilateral advantage of the Austrian empire. Whereas Russia encountered an insurmountable obstacle in England when trying to secure her share of the deal, the Austrians, to the utmost indignation of Russia, quickly grabbed the parts allotted them.

Thus, after one hundred years of diplomacy, the Russians found themselves still hopelessly stalled in the pursuance of their primary aim, the seizure of Constantinople. England still blocked the free exit from the Black Sea; Austria frustrated Russian Balkan schemes; Germany, whose friendship had been forsaken and who consistently supported Austria, threatened the western border; and France dragged Russia into Western European problems alien to the needs of the tsarist empire. Combined with internal difficulties, the whole situation boded ill for Russia.

PROBLEMS

1. Discuss the relations of Germany and Russia, 1870–1905.
2. Trace the causes for the Franco-Russian alliance of the 1890's.
3. Discuss the antagonism of Russia and Austria, 1870–1905.

CHAPTER XXXI

EXPANSION IN ASIA

THE "FRONTIER"

Like the westward movement in America, the eastward expansion of Russia bears witness to the historical hunger of all agricultural peoples for more land. There, as in the United States, the movement was spasmodic. All fields of human endeavor were touched, so that several separate "frontiers"—political, agricultural, economic, and cultural—can be discerned, each progressing eastward and southward, one following the other.

Advance of Frontier. The changes of the political frontier may be surveyed in four stages: (1) from 1580 to 1650, expansion from the Urals to the Pacific, in a general northeastwardly direction, followed by a hundred years of intensive exploration; (2) from 1785 to 1830, conquest of the lands between the Black and Caspian Seas; (3) from 1850 to 1860, annexation of the Amur River region and penetration through Manchuria, followed by economic exploitation; (4) from 1865 to 1885, incorporation of Transcaspia and Turkestan, and penetration of central Asia.

CAUCASUS

Annexation. The first stage ended with the mapping of the confines of Siberia in the middle of the eighteenth century. The second

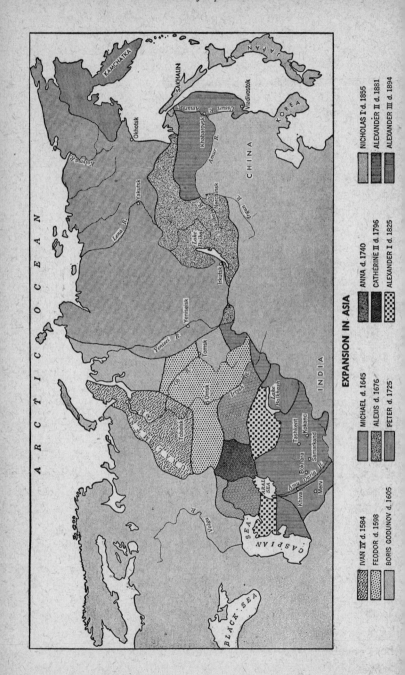

EXPANSION IN ASIA

IVAN IV d. 1584
FEODOR d. 1598
BORIS GODUNOV d. 1605

MICHAEL d. 1645
ALEXIS d. 1676
PETER d. 1725

ANNA d. 1740
CATHÉRINE II d. 1796
ALEXANDER I d. 1825

NICHOLAS I d. 1855
ALEXANDER II d. 1881
ALEXANDER III d. 1894

consisted of an unrelenting struggle for possession of the area between the Black and Caspian Seas. This region was of high value
because it included the strategic passes and roads through and
around the Caucasus range and possessed the economic advantage of
considerable mineral wealth, particularly oil. Although inhabited by
different nationalities—Armenians and Georgians—the territory belonged geographically and politically to Persia and Turkey. Peter
the Great in his time secured some of the Persian sectors in the
eastern Caucasus region, but under his successors these had to be
relinquished. During the reign of Catherine II, encroachments were
made on the Turkish parts and culminated in the submission of local
princes in Georgia; but no definite Russian suzerainty was established. Under Paul I, further expeditions and negotiations were undertaken; yet only during Alexander I's rule, in 1813, was the full
incorporation of Georgia, including Baku, accomplished. The struggle
for the surrounding land went on for another decade or more. It
was not until the Peace of Adrianople (1829) that Russia could
consider all of the Caucasus as hers, together with the lands extending south to the strategic town of Erivan.

FAR EAST

Period of Neglect. The third stage of Russian eastward movement comprised expansion beyond Siberia. Until the nineteenth century, Russian progress there had been slow. After the exploration
of the country, attention had been centered less on its exploitation and
expansion than on discoveries in other regions. A number of expeditions were undertaken such as that around the world in 1803,
another to explore the coast of America in 1815, and an Antarctic
expedition in 1819 to 1821, while in Siberia proper the government
confined itself to administrative reforms. According to plans drawn
by Speransky the region was divided into two governor-generalships,
and some attention was paid to the settling of the land.

Revived Interest. It was only after England's Opium War
against China had divulged the weakness of the Chinese empire and
the possibility of European political and economic infiltration that a
commission was set up to investigate economic opportunities in the
regions bordering on China. In 1847, N. Muraviëv was appointed
governor-general of eastern Siberia. His initiative and energy, supported by a more determined government at St. Petersburg, changed
the existing policy of passivity. Muraviëv turned his attention to

the Amur region, which since the Treaty of Nerchinsk had been reserved for China. In line with the imperialistic urge of the age and contrary to the stipulations of Nerchinsk, he founded a city, Nikolaevsk, on the Amur estuary. Soon thereafter the island of Sakhalin and territory in Korea were occupied, and in 1853 Alexandrovsk was built on the De Castries bay. Peasants were settled in the Amur region and, for the sake of defense, organized as Cossacks; and an "Amur Company" for promotion of Russian interests was founded.

Annexation of Amur Region. The Crimean War, which broke out in 1854, further stimulated these activities; for in view of the imminence of a Franco-English attack in the Far East, Muraviëv was forced to strengthen and expand Russia's hold. Chinese protests notwithstanding, he took possession of the whole course of the Amur. Specially built steamships were sent down the river to its mouth to protect and provision the new settlements and, despite the unhealthy climate, thousands of colonists were assigned to the region of the Amur's estuary. Chinese immigrants were attracted, and solid fortifications to protect against possible landings of the enemy were erected.

Crimean War. In the same year, 1854, a combined Franco-English fleet opened hostilities by attacking the fortress of Petropavlovsk in Kamchatka. Despite the seizure no advantage was gained, and in 1855 the British and French shifted the scene of action southward in an attempt to destroy Russia's Far Eastern fleet. They succeeded in blockading the Russians in what they took for a bay west of Sakhalin; but in reality, this bay was an open waterway through which the Russian fleet sailed unharmed while its enemies lay in wait at the southern entrance. In the following year, the Peace of Paris put an end to the futile campaign.

Treaty of Peking. After the Crimean War, in 1858, the annexation of the Amur region was legalized by a treaty with China. Pressed by British infringements in the south and threatened by Russia in the north, the Chinese agreed, through the Convention of Aigun, to the cession of the left bank of the Amur and to commercial privileges for Russia not unlike those granted earlier to England. Two years later when the British and French occupied Peking in order to put down a Chinese independence movement, the Russians extended their hold and founded Vladivostok on Chinese territory.

In 1860 they also made a new treaty at Peking whereby both sides of the Amur estuary were acquired in addition to all the country south to Vladivostok. A new border along the Ussuri River was established, and economic concessions were made by China. In addition, the Russo-Chinese border in central Asia, in Turkestan, was subjected to a revision; and it was to this latter region that Russia, from 1860 on, began to shift her attention.

CENTRAL ASIA

Early Failures. Ever since the early eighteenth century, the country lying east of the Caspian Sea had attracted Russian interest. During the rule of Peter's niece Anna, local princes in the regions of the storied cities of Khiva and Bokhara had pledged their submission to the great neighbor. But not until the following century did political and economic reasons call for steps beyond formal submission. Only then did industrialization and the attendant race for raw materials and markets, imperialism, and the missionary spirit renew the desire for the neglected region. For despite its deserts and mountains Turkestan was rich in hemp, tobacco, silkworms, and cattle, and it possessed unexploited subsoil wealth. Moreover, Khiva was famed for its gold mines, its horticultural opportunities, and its horse-breeding areas. In 1834 Russian domination was therefore extended east of the Caspian Sea, and five years later an expedition against Khiva was undertaken. Unprepared for the extremely rigorous climate, it came to a disastrous end, but not without alarming the English, who saw an additional sphere of conflict added to the many already existent in areas situated between their possessions and life lines and those of Russia.

Conquests. For two decades after the failure of the Khiva expedition, no further attempts were made by Russia; the humiliation of the Crimean War, however, released a new urge to resume activities in central Asia. This prestige motive was coupled with a realization of the strategic need for securing the southern borders of Siberia against possible British inroads and for eliminating the pillaging attacks of roving tribes. Furthermore, the demand for cotton by the textile mills of Moscow and Narva grew steadily, and it seemed possible to partially satisfy it with the products of central Asia. A few enterprising and energetic governors, such as General Kaufmann, were aware of these trends, and a period of rapid and highly successful expansionist activity was initiated by them. In 1865 Tashkent was seized; in 1866 Bokhara was invaded and in 1868 ancient imperial Samarkand fell; in 1873, after great losses, Khiva was taken; and in 1876 Kokand was occupied. The inhabitants, many of them Mohammedans, were brutally subjected, and thousands fled across the Chinese border. Turkestan itself was constituted a governor-generalship. In 1881 Geok-Tepe was stormed, and under the leadership of the harsh governor-general of Transcaspia, General Skobelev, Turkomania was added to previous conquests.

Conflict with England.　Imperialism triumphed. With increased misgivings the English watched the steady approach of Russia toward India. Determined not to yield, they emphasized their own aspirations and determination; they had their queen crowned "Empress of India"; they occupied Baluchistan; and they made wars and treaties with Afghanistan. Yet, the Russian drive advanced inexorably: in 1884 Merv submitted to Russia, opening the road to Herat, gateway to India. Remembering the days when Persia, acting for Russia, had taken possession of Herat in 1856, the British now decided to put a definite stop to the Russian advance; they negotiated a treaty delineating the northern frontier of Afghanistan, beyond which the Russians were not to go.

Economic Penetration.　This enforced pause in the advance of the Russians turned out to their own advantage, for instead of wasting their strength by further expansion which would have served none but some private banking and trading interests, they began to consolidate their rule in the conquered areas. They strengthened military installations, promoted cultural interests, and opened the country by constructing railways. The economy of the occupied territory was remodeled, new markets were created, and new products won. Despite great difficulties, the Transcaspian railway line in 1888 was continued to Samarkand and later to Orenburg and Tashkent; and strategic stations and ports were built at the crossroads of the tradeways. The whole area was made part of the economic, political, and strategic structure of the empire. Ultimately—though only in postrevolutionary times—the civilization of the West and of European Russia reached the native populations of central Asia.

Persia.　After Russia's position had been consolidated in Turkestan, her influence was spread further. Particular attention was paid to Persia. The Transcaspian and Transcaucasian lines were extended to the borders of that country and a number of concessions were gained. Russia was granted the right to install telegraph service in Persia, to organize steamship companies, to veto foreign railroad construction, to build up fisheries, and to found a bank for financing imports from Russia. A special hold over Persia's internal affairs was gained by receiving, as a guarantee for Russian loans, the privilege of supervising the country's income from customs duties. Economic relations became very lively: Russia exported sugar, oil, and textile goods, and imported cotton, fruits, opium, rice, and fish, so that by 1914 the total value of trade exceeded sixty million dollars.

PROBLEMS

1. Trace the regions of chief expansionist interest of Russia in Asia.
2. Discuss the political and strategic significance of Russian expansion in Asia.
3. Discuss the economic advantages derived for Russia from Asiatic expansion.

CHAPTER XXXII

RUSSO-JAPANESE RIVALRY

TRANS–SIBERIAN RAILROAD

Railroad Planning. Important though the results of railroad building and economic penetration of central Asia turned out to be, the most ambitious commercial scheme of Russia in the second half of the nineteenth century concerned Siberia and the Far East. From approximately 1850, plans for railroad connections there had been proposed for strategic, economic, and cultural reasons. Regardless of its original efficiency, the existing mail and river transport system, which extended over thousands of miles, was no longer adequate; not even the steamship lines, operating since about 1840, sufficed to provide for the growing population and the demands of the Far Eastern military forces. It was therefore first proposed to supplement the steamboat service by railroads which were to connect the main river network; and later, a through line extending from the Urals to the Pacific was suggested. As in the United States, the advantages of a northern, a central, or a southern route were for a long time vainly debated, while an attempt was made to gauge also the implications of the construction as such. Some feared undesirable economic, social, and international repercussions; conversely, others considered

188

these unimportant in comparison with the railroad's strategic and commercial value.

Construction of Trans-Siberian Railroad. No practical step was undertaken until 1884, when a line was constructed across the Ural range connecting the Volga and the Ob basin and servicing the mining districts in between. Although this railroad eventually formed no part of the Trans-Siberian system, which was to run to Irkutsk between 53° and 55° latitude, it served to stimulate final planning. In 1891 actual work on the main line was begun and simultaneously carried on in different sections, reaching Irkutsk in 1898. Because of climate and expense, the last sector—from Irkutsk to Vladivostok— presented the greatest difficulties. Eventually, Chinese permission was given to lay track through Manchuria; and in 1903 the Trans-Siberian railroad, extending five and a half thousand miles to the shores of the Pacific Ocean, was completed. Constituting at first a drain on the resources of the government, it began to show profits from the year 1913 on; and only the First World War interrupted further progress.

Demographic Consequences. As in the United States, the railroad thoroughly transformed the country. Economic growth was stimulated, and a vast influx of settlers began. In 1861, after almost three hundred years of occupation, Siberia had contained no more than five million inhabitants; and during the thirty-year period following emancipation of the serfs, despite offers of free land and exemption from military service, immigration had accounted for little more than half a million colonists. In contrast to this record, the twenty years following the start of the railway project saw an influx of approximately four million additional settlers. Before the outbreak of World War I, more than eleven million people inhabited the country and great opportunities existed for many millions more.

Political Consequences. Politically, the railroad changed the picture by upsetting the balance of power in the Far East, affecting English as well as United States interests, Japanese aspirations, and Chinese conditions. In view of China's impotence and America's continentalism, counteraction was left to the initiative of the British and the Japanese. Both were determined to halt Russia's further advance and to prevent any scheme for establishing a hegemony on the Pacific coast. England had witnessed Russia's approach in the Near East to the Straits of Constantinople, in the Caucasus region to Persia, in central Asia to Afghanistan; she had seen the tsarist empire extend its feelers into Tibet and towards distant colonial prizes: Siam and Abyssinia. She now feared the emergence of additional spheres of conflict and so seized the opportunity to check Russia through collaboration with Japan.

RUSSO–JAPANESE WAR

Russo-Japanese Relations before 1900. Japan had entered into relations with Russia in 1855, but Muraviëv's occupation of Sakhalin had quickly brought dissensions. Sakhalin had been reached by Europeans in 1649, but since it held little attraction for them, it had formed an unchallenged field of activity for the Chinese and also, from about 1785, for the Japanese. Russia did not put forward claims until 1807, and Muraviëv's occupation of the island was the first practical evidence of her interest. The resulting conflict with Japan was not settled until 1867, when a convention stipulated common rights for Russia and Japan. This agreement, naturally of no permanence, was terminated in 1875, when Russia ceded southern Sakhalin to the Japanese in exchange for the Kuril Islands. After another score of years difficulties again arose when Japan, jealous of Russian railroad construction and penetration into Chinese territory, attacked China, defeated her, and wrested from her vast territorial and commercial concessions. Russia, in conjunction with other European powers which were interested in the independence of a weak and exploitable China, forced Japan to relinquish a part of her spoils. Following the example of various Western powers which had imposed trade concessions and annexed harbors from impotent China, Russia secured in 1898—to the great dismay of Japan—a twenty-five-year lease of the very harbor, strategic Port Arthur, which Japan had just been forced to withdraw from. The Russo-Japanese tension came to a climax during the Boxer Rebellion in 1900, when Russia extended her sphere by occupying Mukden and, instead of evacuating it after the suppression of the Boxers, made it an important railroad center and a flourishing commercial town.

Outbreak of War. Japan saw herself thus deprived of access to a region she considered important for her strategic security, vital for her surplus population, and necessary as a market for her coal and cotton exports and as a source for needed wheat, rice, and beans. In order to retrieve the lost ground, Japan therefore looked for allies and found unexpected support in England. In 1902, the two nations entered into a formal alliance. Thus backed, Japan started negotiations for Russian withdrawal from Manchuria; and as these did not bring results, she swiftly struck at Russia in 1904. The attack not only served Japanese interests, but put Japan in the role of an agent for various European powers: for France, which desired to see Russia more dependent upon her alliance; for Austria, which wanted the Tsar's attention diverted from the Balkans; and for England, which was determined to halt Russian progress in the Far East.

Peace of Portsmouth. The war itself turned out disastrously for the Russians. Although they won many an important battle and although within a year the Japanese were in serious financial straits, the victory was Japan's. Port Arthur was lost; and in the great naval battle of Tsushima the Russian Baltic fleet, after a long cruise around Africa, was virtually annihilated. Having underestimated Japanese strength, possessing weak communication lines, conducting a war from a distance of thousands of miles, and hindered by hostile public opinion at home and abroad, the Russian government found itself forced in mid-1905 to accept the mediation of Theodore Roosevelt and to enter into peace negotiations. Owing to the ability of Russia's plenipotentiary, Count Witte, and his shrewd estimate of Japan's financial weakness and material exhaustion, and as a result of American and English fears lest Japan emerge a more potent power on the Pacific than they desired her to be, the peace turned out to be less harsh for Russia than anticipated. It was concluded at Portsmouth, New Hampshire. It stipulated that the long-promised military evacuation of Manchuria was to be carried out forthright; that Port Arthur and half of Sakhalin were to be surrendered; that fishing rights in Russian waters were to be granted to the Japanese and their special interests in Korea recognized. But no indemnity was exacted from Russia, nor was she compelled to relinquish her railway line through Manchuria.

Thus ended, for the time being, Russian advance in the Far East.

PROBLEMS

1. Discuss the political significance of the Trans-Siberian railroad.
2. Trace the relationship of Russia and Japan until 1904.
3. Discuss the interests of the great powers in the outcome of the Russo-Japanese War.

CHAPTER XXXIII

RUSSIA AND THE UNITED STATES

RELATIONS UP TO THE AMERICAN CIVIL WAR

Russia and the Birth of the United States. It is of special interest to survey separately the relations of the United States and Russia. That the revolutionary foundation of a new commonwealth in opposition to its legitimate suzerain would find the approval of autocratic Tsarina Catherine, who ruled Russia during the American War of Independence, could hardly be expected. Yet, disagreements with England over the question of neutral rights on the seas forced Catherine to assume a friendly attitude towards the United States; and, peculiarly enough, the paradoxical situation of ideological opposition and political co-operation has remained until our own times.

Opening of Official Relations. The first hopes of the new United States concerned recognition of American independence, initiation of official relations, and regulation of commercial intercourse. As early as 1780 Francis Dana was sent by the Continental Congress on a mission to Russia, and in the last few years of the eighteenth century, Rufus King was commissioned to carry on negotiations. But in neither case, despite the unremitting efforts of the

192

United States, was recognition extended by Russia. More than a quarter of a century elapsed before official relations were opened in 1809, in the midst of the Napoleonic era. Then a minister to St. Petersburg was appointed in the person of John Quincy Adams, and Russia named Count Pahlen for the post in Washington; A. Dashkov was made chargé d'affaires; and consulates were established in both countries.

Napoleonic Period. The results of Adams' mission were disappointing; a commercial treaty could not be concluded, for Russia insisted on political concessions as well as economic arrangements. Anxious though she was, because of Napoleon's Continental system, to replace the English with American carrying trade, she insisted on a formal acknowledgment of her claims in North America (which extended, territorially, from Alaska to the Columbia River and to trading posts even farther south). Economically, recognition of Russian trade monopolies there was demanded. The prolonged negotiations were broken off in 1812 when Napoleon attacked Russia and forced the Tsar into an alliance with England, against whom the United States in that very year went to war. To bring the contradictory situation to an end, Russia offered her mediation between the United States and England. This proposal was anxiously accepted by the Americans; envoys were immediately dispatched, but the British refused to negotiate and the Americans were obliged to return empty-handed. Nevertheless, friendly contact was maintained with Russia, who in 1814 again was asked to sponsor peace with England. Yet, even after the signing of the Treaty of Ghent, the urgently desired commercial treaty with Russia was not concluded because political demands still stood in the way. Claims were brought forward by Russia not only on territory in America south to 51° latitude, but also on the entire northern Pacific Ocean, which Russia wished to declare a *mare clausum;* and these claims were emphasized by the renewal of the Russian-American Company, which had been founded by Paul I with the Tsar himself as a stockholder. Furthermore, no recognition was to be extended by the United States to the revolting Spanish colonies in South America.

Political Accord. The South American issue was eventually eliminated, first by United States recognition of Colombia in 1822 and then definitely by President Monroe's message to Congress on December 2, 1823. But Russian demands on the northwest coast remained, and not until the next year was a political settlement reached. Since the returns from the commercial investments in their American colonies were small and did not warrant a great military outlay for protection, the Russians finally declared themselves ready to conclude a treaty. Latitude 54°40′ was recognized as the southern border of Russian America, and the United States undertook to refrain from trade with Russian settlements there.

Commercial Treaty. Once political accord was reached, efforts for a trade agreement were resumed. After several attempts, yet not before the abrogation of the "Tariff of Abominations" in 1832, the long-delayed commercial treaty was concluded. Its immediate importance was small, for at the time Russo-American trade did not exceed one million dollars, of which Russian exports, mainly in hemp and iron, comprised about three-quarters; but the expectations of southern planters for increased cotton exports to Russia warranted the effort.

Dissatisfaction with Political Accord. Soon the commercial treaty began to overshadow the political agreement of 1824, and when in 1834 the ten-year period stipulated for the latter had passed, it was not renewed. During its course, Americans had continued to smuggle goods into Russian settlements on the West Coast; they had violated the stipulation banning shipments of munitions, arms, and liquor to the Indians; they had insisted on a different interpretation of Russian rights in the zone down to latitude 54°40′, Russia maintaining her right of jurisdiction, the United States allowing only that of settlement. Little chance for improvement existed; and, dissatisfied, Russia gradually lost interest in her American possessions. Some of these were eventually leased to the British Hudson's Bay Company, others were sold, and after the gold rush of 1848 had thoroughly altered the balance of power on the Pacific coast, Russia's colonial activities were increasingly directed to the vast spaces in Siberia.

Russian Weakness in America. The advent of the Crimean War further modified Russia's attitude. Alaska, lying open to seizure by England, would certainly have fallen to the enemy had the British not preferred an agreement with Russia to refrain from extending the theater of war to North America. For they realized that public opinion in the United States favored Russia and would never permit expansion of British rule contrary to the Monroe Doctrine. But Russia could not indefinitely rely on such a favorable constellation; indeed, hardly was the Crimean War over when new threats to Alaska arose. In 1863 a Polish uprising occurred, and the Tsar feared that it would be used as a pretext for a new attack by England and France. This time, the Russian-American possessions would be unprotected, for the United States was engaged in a civil war and the Russian fleet lacked appropriate support, coaling stations, and harbor facilities in the Pacific. Considerations of this kind led to the dispatch of the Russian Pacific fleet to the United States, a measure popularly interpreted as an act of good will towards the abolitionist North (Russia had abolished serfdom two years earlier), but simultaneously serving the cause of protection for Russian ships in neutral ports.

RELATIONS SINCE THE AMERICAN CIVIL WAR

Sale of Alaska. The recurring threats to Alaska caused the Russian government to seriously consider liquidation of Russian-American ventures and the sale of all possessions there. But serious objections to such a program were raised. Some feared a disturbance of the balance of power in the Pacific area and the possible emergence of the United States as a strong rival; others anticipated an imperialistic policy in the United States, which, once in possession of Alaska, might be desirous of extending its influence to the Asiatic continent. Again others considered the commercial disadvantages of selling Alaska, realizing its potential wealth, its use within the world-communication system, and its importance for shipping and telegraph lines. However, advocates pointed out that the sale of the colony would bring a substantial profit and that Russia should secure this rather than incur new expenses for defense which might yet prove inadequate. They felt that in view of vast migration of Americans to their West Coast and the resulting pressure, the continued possession of Alaska would disturb relations with the United States, as it had before; and they demonstrated that in the past the economic benefits had been disappointing. Furs were exhausted; little gold had been discovered; and, because profits could not be realized, the Russian-American Company itself had allowed its charter to expire in 1861. It was also feared that money invested in Alaska would divert attention from more profitable schemes nearer home. After full consideration, the government decided in 1867 to sell Alaska for $7,200,000—a small sum as measured by present standards, but at that time considered adequate by Russians and exorbitant by Americans.

Conflict of Interests. After the sale, friendly relations prevailed until the death of Alexander II. But with the accession of Alexander III, and more so when Nicholas II came to the throne, public opinion in America altered. Persecution of Jews and failure to introduce a constitutional system in Russia formed the ideological background for growing tension, and by 1903 ideas of official protests were entertained by the United States. Practical differences, however, played an equal, though never avowed, role. Imperialism on both sides of the ocean had brought American and Russian spheres close together in the Pacific area. Russia had established herself in Vladivostok, Manchuria, Sakhalin, and the Kurils, and the United States had penetrated beyond Alaska to Hawaii and the Philippines. Disturbances in China had opened the way for American commercial expansion, and an "open-door policy" was proclaimed which conflicted with monopolistic Russian penetration of the Chinese empire. The Boxer Rebellion and American insistence on the maintenance of China's *status quo* increased the tension. When the Russo-Japanese War broke out, the sympathies of the United States as well as her financial support went to the Japanese; and this aroused the bitter resentment of Russia. But fears of Japanese hegemony—after Japan's surprising victories—put an end to anti-Russian agitation and prompted Theodore Roosevelt to offer his mediation to the belligerents. The Peace of Portsmouth and subsequent steps towards constitutional government in Russia did much to bring about a gradual reversal of popular feelings. Russia's delegate, Count Witte, helped to spread a favorable opinion, convincing American press representatives as well as influential American Jews of future improvements within the tsarist empire.

Thus, revived hopes for improved domestic conditions in Russia coupled with comparative unconcern regarding her external policies prevailed in America until the outbreak of World War I; yet, even then, America's entrance into the war did not occur until after the overthrow of the tsarist regime.

PROBLEMS

1. Discuss the difficulties experienced by the United States with Russia during the first fifty years after gaining independence.
2. Discuss the factors prompting Russia to sell Alaska.
3. Describe the causes of discord between the two countries at the turn of the century.

CHAPTER XXXIV

ROAD TO WORLD WAR I

The Revolution of 1905 and the Japanese War ended an era of autocracy and imperialism without introducing a period of healthy national growth. The short "liberal era" which followed from 1907 to 1917 was one of reluctant and essentially fruitless governmental compromise with enemies at home and abroad. In domestic affairs these compromises, stimulated by the rapid economic expansion of the country, tended in the natural direction of greater freedom and social improvement, but failed to satisfy the progressives, whether liberal or Marxist. The gulf between government and populace remained unbridged.

INTERNAL CONDITIONS

The Court. At the head of the government was Nicholas II, inspired by his concept of duty yet unaware of the trends and needs of the time. His strong-willed wife, Alexandra—a German princess brought up at the court of Queen Victoria, where she had gained an ill-balanced notion of her position—more and more dominated the political scene, and insisted in a semireligious way upon an autocratic form of rule which her weaker husband was scarcely able to maintain. Behind her stood a number of strange religious and medical figures (the famed Rasputin prominent among them) who, though not always wrong or evil-intentioned, often used their influence for personal gain. A large and despised police force was necessary to support the tsarist system.

The Government. The chief ministers of the period were conservatives and bureaucrats. Many of them possessed considerable ability and were earnestly devoted to their tasks. With the aid of a class of educated and privileged officers, landowners, and administrators, and under the supreme authority of an absolute Tsar, they endeavored to guide the country along careful, beneficial, and paternalistic lines. The most important among them was P. Stolypin, a controversial figure who in 1906 introduced the peasant reform and who was assassinated in 1911.

The People. On the other side stood the intelligentsia and the masses, including the various national groups which formed part of the empire. All of these opposed the government, but for varied reasons and with different objectives in view. The intelligentsia demanded representative government patterned after the Western bourgeois states; they hoped to secure thereby greater freedom, extensive civil rights, and better social conditions. The proletariat envisaged a classless society, either of an anarchical character or under proletarian dictatorship; they were imbued with Marxist principles by radical organizers, and although as yet weak were most ably led. The peasants, faced with land shortage, desired the abolition of the large estates and additional land allotments for themselves. The Jews demanded equality and quite naturally joined the ranks of the dissatisfied, for they were still persecuted despite the warnings of far-sighted ministers such as Witte and Stolypin. The Finns, Poles, Armenians, and the growingly nationality-conscious Ukrainians sought independence or autonomy.

Economy.

INDUSTRIES. Despite the political rift between government and governed, considerable economic progress was made; favorable economic legislation was passed by the third and, from 1912 on, the fourth imperial Duma. Industries advanced at a rapid pace and economic expansion took place in various directions. Internal and external trade increased and foreign money markets became readily accessible to Russian enterprises. Living standards for the towns and for the industrial population as a whole were bettered, and educational facilities were spread by the Zemstvos.

AGRICULTURE. In the villages, various forms of co-operatives contributed to the advancement of peasant interests. Stolypin's peasant reform of 1906, which had broken the *mir* and communal ownership, had not succeeded in improving the lot of all peasants. Many who lived in the overcrowded black-soil districts or who possessed neither the industry nor the knowledge to improve their lands found themselves in as wretched circumstances as before and were forced to sell out and join the ranks of the landless proletariat; but there were other millions who benefited from the change. Certainly, the rise of a large class of small independent peasant proprietors was stimulated. The productivity of the land was increased; and, through reclamation projects in the old parts of Russia as well as in Siberia, the area under cultivation was considerably extended.

EXTERNAL CONDITIONS

Foreign Entanglements. But as in the times of the Crimean War or of the Russo-Japanese War, economic progress could not outweigh political dissatisfaction; and if there were external complications, lack of success was likely to topple the precarious balance. It was therefore of grave consequence when the government found itself inextricably involved in the complicated and war-breeding system of alliances which marked the late nineteenth and the early twentieth centuries. Indeed, the lost war against Japan entangled Russia still further in this system, for now she was compelled to seek a *modus vivendi* with her two most persistent antagonists, England and Japan.

Treaty with Japan. Treaties with both were concluded in 1907. Through a convention with Japan it was arranged that South Manchuria be reserved as a sphere of Japanese interest, and Korea was completely renounced by the Tsar and annexed by Japan in 1910. In exchange, Russia secured northern Manchuria, where the town of Harbin became a center of Russian activities and a railroad terminal. Settlers were attracted and a flourishing trade was built up, the mineral wealth of the country was exploited, and industries of large scope were founded. Russia also received a free hand in Outer Mongolia, although nominal Chinese suzerainty was retained there. Although the hold of the rich Chinese merchants persisted and counteracted Russian efforts to foster a separatist movement, new treaties made in 1912 and 1913 with Japan as well as China guaranteed the Tsar additional rights and extended them even to Inner Mongolia.

Treaty with England. The treaty with Japan found its counterpart in that with England; while the one drew a limit to Russian advance in the Far East, the other stopped Russia in central Asia and on the approaches to India. The agreement reached between the respective foreign ministers, Grey and Iswolsky, was to a certain extent the result not only of the lost Japanese war but also of friendlier public opinion in England which followed the introduction of a parliamentary regime in Russia. It also sprang from jealousy of the German advance in the Near East, where a railroad line was planned to connect Berlin and Bagdad via the Balkans and the Turkish empire, thus cutting through the hypothetical communication lines of both Russia and England. The Anglo-Russian treaty was intended to consign to the past all differences between the two nations. It dealt particularly with the rivalry of the two countries in Persia and stipulated that England should keep out of northern Persia while Russia should recognize southern Persia as a British sphere of influence. Subsequently, Russia promised also to refrain from penetration into Tibet and Afghanistan. In exchange, England extended loans to the tsarist government.

Triple Entente. Though the treaties served to eliminate causes of discord, they unfortunately did not further the cause of peace; rather, they form chapters in the melancholy story of how the nations "backed into" World War I. For while differences between Russian and British imperialism were composed, a general system of alliances was furthered which in itself bore the seeds of war. The rearrangements increasingly tied Russia financially to France and England, who shortly owned three quarters of all foreign investments in Russia, and made possible the finishing touches to the Anglo-Franco-Russian "Triple Entente," which implied grave political obligations for Russia.

Relations with Germany. From that time on, every European incident assumed proportions far beyond its inherent importance and led to tests of strength between the "Triple Entente" and the "Triple Alliance," the latter consisting of Germany, Austria-Hungary, and vacillating Italy. In many instances, Russia was but a pawn of the Western powers and found herself on the side opposing Germany when her own interests would have dictated a sympathetic attitude towards that country. For the political preponderance which Germany had possessed in Bismarck's time no longer existed; the customs wars of earlier periods were composed and almost one-third of all Russian foreign trade was carried on with Germany. The fears regarding the construction of the Bagdad railway were overcome in 1910 by an agreement at Potsdam, and the line itself was extended to provide for Russian needs. In the winter of 1913 to 1914, another source of friction was eliminated when the German General Liman von Sanders, who had been sent to reorganize the Turkish army, was appointed to another post at Constantinople.

Relations with Austria. Yet there remained the alignment of Germany and Austria, and Austrian interests continued to be incompatible with those of Russia in the Balkans. The two countries Russia and Austria watched each other jealously, in some cases preventing by mutual arrangements the progress of one at the expense of the other—as during the Turko-Greek War in 1898 or the Macedonian revolt of 1901—and in other cases taking advantage of a momentary opportunity. In 1908, common fears of a resurgence of Turkish power drove them once more to concerted action, when the so-called "Young Turk" revolt threatened to rejuvenate and reform the decaying Ottoman empire. At Buchlau they concluded an agreement which permitted Austrian annexation of Bosnia and Herzegovina and gave Russia free passage through the Straits. But in actuality this agreement brought new hostility: for Austria, acting quickly, annexed the region set aside for her, whereas Russia, facing the opposition of the Western European powers, found herself unable to take her share. In the resulting bitter diplomatic struggle Germany supported Austria's questionable action.

Relations with Turkey. The Buchlau bargain and its failure demonstrated the impossibility for Russia to come to a permanent good understanding with Germany as long as the latter country insisted on backing Austrian expansion southeastward. It also strengthened Russian determination to gain domination over the Straits, as previously arranged. Every opportunity was taken to achieve this aim by weakening Turkey, forestalling Austria, and gaining the consent of other powers. On this basis, Italy was allowed in 1911 to wrest Tripoli from the Turks, and in 1912 a war which Serbia, Bulgaria, Greece, and Montenegro declared on Turkey was greeted as a step towards the desired goal.

Sarajevo. The results of the Balkan War of 1912, which could not be checked by the halfhearted intervention of the great powers and which was followed in 1913 by a second war among the victors, were in line with Russian hopes. Except for the territory contiguous

RUSSIA IN 1914

to Constantinople and the Straits, Turkey was expelled from Europe; Austria's neighbor, Serbia, was enlarged and strengthened; and the whole situation remained sufficiently unsettled to foreshadow further favorable changes. Indeed, less than one year later an incident occurred which led to the next—and this time general—struggle. For on June 28, 1914, the Austrian Archduke Francis Ferdinand was murdered by a Serb national in the Bosnian town of Sarajevo. The outrage led to an Austrian ultimatum to Serbia with demands beyond those warranted by the murder; and, despite the guilt of some Serbian government agencies, Russia decided to take up the cause of her Slavic sister nation. In an atmosphere of chauvinism and imperialism, Russia's allies of the Triple Entente and Austria's partners in the Triple Alliance failed to counsel moderation. Hostilities began, and though wise statesmanship might have localized actual warfare, they were allowed to spread to Germany, France, and England. Thus began the First World War.

INVOLVEMENT IN WORLD WAR I

For the Russian government, the war was certain to turn out disastrously. The weakness of the existing social system, the pressure of new ideas, and the lack of progressiveness, combined with dependence upon uncongenial allies, portended defeat no matter what the military results. Nevertheless, Russia entered the war. Aside from the spirit of the time, the immediate practical political causes why she did so on the side of England and France may be approximated as follows:

1. *The existing system of alliances,* the Triple Entente and the Triple Alliance, which bound the countries to military support of their allied partners even when their interests were not directly involved. Thus, French thirst for revenge and Anglo-German naval and trade rivalry pushed Russia into action.

2. *Russian resentment against Germany,* surviving from the defeat at the Congress of Berlin, 1878, and the fear that Germany herself was to assume the leading role in the Near East. This resentment was increased by rumors that Germany had pushed Russia along the road to war with Japan and toward defeat and that, notwithstanding Germany's conciliatory attitude in the question of the Bagdad railway and the Liman von Sanders mission, she was endeavoring to draw Turkey into her own sphere.

3. *The leanings of some Russian circles,* particularly of the intelligentsia, towards a parliamentary system and civil liberties as found

in France or England, which seemed to them preferable to the parliamentary but paternalistic and ostentatious part played by the German imperial government.

4. *Irreconcilability of Russian and Austrian intentions* in the Balkans; fear of loss of prestige there if support were not given to Slavic Serbia, and hope that war would bring an opportunity for realizing domination over the Straits.

5. *The annexation of Bosnia* and the attitude of Vienna towards the Slavic nations in the Balkans and even towards those within the Austrian-Hungarian monarchy, which the revived Pan-Slavist movement regarded as the greatest threat to the fulfillment of its own mission.

6. *Personal intrigues* of diplomats, which were fostered by selfish, vainglorious men such as the Austrians Aehrenthal and Berchtold, the Russian Iswolsky, and many others in all countries. The position of the "autocrat" Nicholas and of the German emperor formed no political reality, despite all claims to divine rights, family ties, and personal friendship; the rulers' influence was in effect subordinated to the independent play of diplomatic forces and popular trends.

On August 1, 1914, war broke out between Russia, Austria, and Germany; France joined Russia according to treaty obligations, and England entered the struggle three days later. It came at a moment when, despite the great advance of the previous fifty years, the urgent problems besieging Russia—those of landownership, of industrialization, of democracy and class society, of education, and of strategic security—still remained unsolved.

PROBLEMS

1. Discuss the internal conditions foreboding ill for autocracy in the event of war.
2. Trace the steps towards the opposing political alignments of the Triple Entente and the Triple Alliance.
3. Discuss the factors dragging Russia into war.

CHAPTER XXXV

WORLD WAR I

WAR

The Early Campaigns, 1914–15. The Russian plan for the conduct of the war collapsed during its initial stages. While the Central Powers had calculated on a quick northward push from Austria into Russia, the Russians had intended to throw their forces southward, to invade Austria in Galicia and gain the support of the Slavs living in the region. But owing to the weakness of the French, the occupation of Galicia had to be interrupted; and instead, in order to divert German pressure from France, an attack on East Prussia was made. This saved France, by forcing the Central Powers to shift troops from their western to their eastern front, and thus perhaps constituted a decisive factor in preventing German victory in the First World War; yet it did not benefit Russia, for it resulted in terrible defeats in Prussia at Tannenberg and the Masurian Lakes. By the end of 1914 German armies under Hindenburg stood deep in Polish Russia, and the city of Lódź was lost. A Russian winter offensive failed to fully dislodge them, and only in Galicia were advances made; but lack of supplies endangered the newly won positions there. In the summer of 1915 a German-Austrian counteroffensive occurred which forced Russia to give up her conquests, and at the end of 1915 the Russians had evacuated all occupied foreign territory, while the enemy pushed beyond Kaunas, Warsaw, and Brest Litovsk. Likewise, Russia's allies in the Balkans were beaten, and Bulgaria joined the Central Powers.

The Brusilov Offensive, 1916. Despite these reverses, the Russians were called upon by their Western allies in 1916 to again relieve the critical situation in France. A new attack was therefore launched, called after the commanding general the "Brusilov offensive." The Russians succeeded in re-entering Galicia and won over many Slavs fighting in the Austrian army. But the advance constituted a Pyrrhic victory; for the terrific cost in men and matériel undermined the physical strength as well as the morale of the army, and more was lost than gained. Furthermore, Rumania, whose entry into the war was hailed as a welcome aid, proved a drain on Russia. Unprepared, she was soon defeated by the Central Powers; the country was occupied, and the Russian lines were exposed at their southeastern flank.

Rasputin. By the end of 1916, the Russian position had become precarious. Fifteen million men had been mobilized, the economy of the country was disrupted, yet success in the field was lacking. The original patriotic wave roused by the "great venture of war" had subsided; people and soldiers understood neither the causes nor the objectives of the war, nor did they cherish the immediate prospects. The number of prisoners and deserters multiplied, the enormous losses influenced the temper at home, and the whole country became weary of war. Moreover, confidence in the military and political leadership was fast waning. Prompted by his concept of duty, the Tsar, despite all warnings, had assumed personal command of the armies in the fall of 1915 after the great military disasters of that year. But owing to his military inexperience and his essential ignorance of the status of Russia—resulting from his autocratic seclusion—he proved unequal to the task. Increasingly he came under the influence of his wife, who through foreign education, autocratic pretensions, and mysticism was far removed from an understanding of popular trends and who followed blindly the advice of her friend G. Rasputin. This man had gained complete ascendancy over her when, apparently miraculously, he had saved the life of her son, a hemophiliac. She believed implicitly in his prophecies, some of which, perhaps because of his common sense, had come to pass. Because of his outward humility, mystic religiosity, and brusque manners—his coarseness, corruption, and debauchery notwithstanding—she regarded him as the incarnation of the spirit of the Russian peasant masses. Soon Rasputin dominated court intrigues, interfered (not always incapably) in state business, gave directions even to military authorities, chose and dismissed ministers, and directed the decisions of the Tsar. His financial malpractices, shameful private life, and evil ways did not come to an end until December, 1916, when members of the nobility and of the court, who feared for the survival of Tsardom, decided to do away with him. He was invited by them to a banquet and murdered.

Domestic Difficulties. The action came too late. As in the times of the Crimean and the Japanese wars, dissatisfaction was rife among the people. The inefficiency and waste of the bureaucracy were overwhelming; the military forces were left short of ammunition, and intended army reforms were not carried out. Heavy industries lacked the materials which they could no longer get from Germany, their former chief supplier; and skilled labor was unavailable in many fields. Despite improvements during the course of 1915 when the first military reverses demonstrated the critical situation, co-operation between government and people was wanting, and in view of prevailing low educational standards a realization of the issues at stake could not be evoked among the masses. Revenues dropped not only because of Russian isolation from abroad, but also because of prohibition of alcoholic beverages, which had provided a large share of excise taxes.

Growth of Opposition. Politically, the war accentuated the existing internal tension. Under the influence of the Tsarina and Rasputin, appointments to high offices were often injudicious; the war prime ministers, Goremykin, Stürmer, and Trepov, and most of their colleagues were essentially chosen from the conservatives and showed little ability and often still less uprightness. Their weakness strengthened those forces which the government had always tried to suppress; profiting from the wartime boom, the laboring class and the peasants increased their power. The intelligentsia, partly represented in a "Progressive Bloc" of the Duma, profited no less from war conditions and pressed for a parliamentary system embodying rights similar to those of the peoples in Western Europe.

REVOLUTION

February Revolution. In November, 1916, the final attack on the government was opened with a speech by Milyukov, leader of the Kadets in the Duma, who denounced the inefficiency or traitorous intent of the existing tsarist regime. The murder of Rasputin in the following month increased the tension, and in February, 1917, bread riots broke out in Petrograd (St. Petersburg). Strikes increased day by day. In vain did the president of the Duma, M. Rodzianko, beseech the Tsar to appoint a government which possessed the confidence of the people. Further disorders occurred, accompanied by clashes with the police and culminating in a mutiny of the Guards, who when ordered to fire upon strikers and bread rioters turned upon their own officers and sided with the masses. On the same day, the Duma was dissolved; thereupon the government resigned. To the cries for bread were now added demands for sweeping political changes. The Tsar tried to hurry back to Petrograd, but was stopped on the way and persuaded to abdicate. Subsequently he and his family were arrested. His brother, who was named successor instead of the sickly son, refused to reign without popular consent; and a provisional government, representing the "Progressive Bloc," was formed by a committee of the Duma. Prince Lvov, liberal head of the Zemstvos' Union, became prime minister; Milyukov, foreign minister, and A. Kerensky, leader of the Social Revolutionary party, minister of justice.

The Provisional Government.

BASIS OF NEW GOVERNMENT. The new regime was rooted in the middle class, which comprised but a small fragment of the Russian masses; as Leon Trotsky later pointed out, it was not truly revolutionary, since the change meant essentially that those who through economic position and education had, *de facto,* influenced affairs before, now officially assumed power. Being unprepared, they depended largely upon spontaneously formed councils (soviets) of soldiers and workmen. Thus, the new government was forced on a middle road and, lacking a broad basis, into a dead end. Its desire not to disorganize the country in the midst of war was greater than that for immediate execution of social and political reforms.

THE SOVIETS. From the beginning the radical forces, though inferior in numbers, proved exceedingly powerful and determined, and they were in close contact with the smoldering trends set in motion by the Russian masses. For the time being, however, the soviets, which represented these radical forces, were quite willing to allow the provisional government to bear both the official burden and the responsibility. They confined themselves to the organization of their own agencies, they instituted an "Executive Committee" of their own, and they took precautions against the return of autocracy. They undermined discipline among their opponents, abolished officers' ranks, and demanded peace. They also disseminated antibourgeois propaganda. Realizing the hesitancy of the government, they incited the peasants to seize the long-coveted land and aroused the workers to take possession of their factories. When Nikolai Lenin (speeded from Switzerland through Germany with the consent of the German High Command) arrived in Petrograd in April and Leon Trotsky arrived from America in May, the real struggle began; for Lenin, denouncing the provisional government as subservient to bourgeois England and France, demanded immediate concentration of all forces upon truly revolutionary tasks.

INCREASE OF RADICALISM. The first swing to the left—typical of all revolutions—soon came with the question of ending the war "without annexations and without indemnities," as demanded by the soviets. In May the moderates, including Milyukov, resigned. But the soviet representatives who replaced the outgoing ministers belonged essentially to the moderate Menshevist wing and failed to sufficiently strengthen the government. Reforms were postponed, in particular that concerning distribution of land, and the general desire for peace remained unfulfilled. Instead, a new and mighty offensive was undertaken in July, intended to serve as much the strengthening of the government at home as the cause of the Allies abroad. This "second Brusilov"—or "Kerensky"—offensive achieved surprising success in its initial stages, but it could not be sustained. Its failure coincided with growing difficulties at home; economic deterioration, rising inflation, and struggle over the nationality rights of Poles, Finns, and Ukrainians brought a severe crisis and led to the withdrawal of all Kadet ministers from the government.

RESIGNATION OF GOVERNMENT. This moment seemed opportune to the Bolshevists, who within the radical soviets made up but a small left wing, to launch a bid for power, or at least an attempt to increase radical influences and to push the country farther along the road to revolution. Relying on the revolutionary mood of the masses which had been evidenced in June in a convention of delegates from the soviets all over the country (First All-Russian Congress of Soviets), they organized riots and sponsored strikes, and finally incited uprisings. These, however, were quickly checked by government forces. Lenin had to go into hiding and Trotsky was arrested. Nevertheless, Prince Lvov, following the example of the

Kadet ministers, now resigned and Kerensky became prime minister; General Brusilov was replaced by General Kornilov.

Kerensky. Kerensky, though vain and ambitious, was patriotic and possessed of ability; but his ideas did not reflect Russian trends and he proved unequal to the task of guiding the imperiled nation and of directing the course of the Revolution. He lacked the support of the army, which felt that resistance to Germany was useless though preparations for peace were not made. He could not rely on the garrison of Petrograd, which was important because of the continued German advance on the capital. Likewise, he found himself unable to establish a working coalition with the soviets, to gather all military resources of the country, and to reorganize resistance. In September his authority and good faith were further shaken by a *coup* which General Kornilov undertook in order to seize power. Kornilov marched on Petrograd, but his troops deserted his cause and the scheme collapsed, thus adding to the revolutionary agitation of the day.

Achievements of the Provisional Government. Under such conditions, constructive work, which normally the provisional government might have achieved with considerable benefit to the Russian people; became impossible. Even so, what was done was by no means negligible. An end was put to autocracy and the entire tsarist system and, in September, Russia was declared a republic; the nationality problem was courageously, though not always judiciously, attacked; the Poles and Finns were started on the road to independence; cooperatives were supported instead of private enterprise; legislation was enacted concerning civil rights, prison reform, equal rights of women, universal suffrage, and religious freedom. Yet, the most pressing problems—the question of further prosecution of the war, the scope of internal reforms, and the partition of land—were postponed by the Kerensky government. The military position of the country deteriorated rapidly and the whole empire, disorganized and irretrievably split, was faced with dissolution. It was in this situation that the chance for gaining control presented itself to the Bolshevists.

PROBLEMS

1. Discuss the domestic influences checking the successful progress of the war.
2. Describe the February Revolution and its relationship to the soviets.
3. Discuss the significance of the Kerensky government.

CHAPTER XXXVI

INTRODUCTION OF BOLSHEVISM

OCTOBER REVOLUTION

Bolshevist Realism. Neither determination, nor political organization, nor the use of physical force suffices to explain the rise of the Bolshevists to power in 1917. The essential causes for their success must be sought in their realization of the ultimate trends of the Revolution and in their readiness to face and satisfy the two chief demands of the Russian masses—peace and land. In order to gain these objectives, they undermined the authority of the Kerensky government not only with the industrial proletariat, but also with soldiers and peasantry—those segments of the population which theoretically did not constitute potential Marxist recruits. Kerensky was unable to offer more attractive aims, and his assumption of dictatorial powers lacked a sound basis and remained without political reality.

Bolshevists in Majority. Late in September, shortly before elections for important town and provincial soviets were held, new strikes and food riots occurred. The Bolshevists profited from these anarchical conditions; promising nationalization of land as well as of banks and industries, elimination of the bourgeoisie, election of a constituent assembly, and—most of all—peace, they secured for the first

211

time a majority in the soviets. Trotsky was elected president of the Petrograd Soviet. The government—which could rely on the Social Revolutionary and the Menshevist parties only, neither one of which was ready to identify itself with the masses and fulfill their wishes —was thus forced into trying to gain Bolshevist support. The Bolshevist leaders increased their propaganda for "direct action," formed their own "Red Guards," and furthered the disorganization of the regular armed forces. As a result, soldiers quit the ranks in steadily increasing numbers, while peasants continued to seize lands of proprietors and began to plunder and murder.

"Victory of Socialism."   In October, Lenin returned to Petrograd where, ostensibly for the defense of the capital, he organized a "Military Revolutionary Committee" which assumed the right to countersign orders issued by the regular general staff. Lenin also secured control of the Petrograd garrison, of the Peter and Paul fortress, and, indirectly, even of the army in the field. Relying upon such formidable backing, he proceeded to prepare an armed uprising. Too late did Kerensky order countermeasures. The authority of his government was insufficient, and a "Pre-Parliament," convoked early in October, 1917, to bridge the time until the convening of a constituent assembly, failed to support his measures. The Bolshevists grew stronger daily; and on the day set for the convening of an "All-Russian Congress of Soviets," October 25 (November 7), they executed a long-planned *coup* and overthrew the Kerensky government. They seized railways, bridges, telephones, and banks of the capital; and when Kerensky left to secure help from the army, the members of his government, who had sought refuge in the old imperial Winter Palace, were captured after some resistance. The Pre-Parliament was abolished. Lenin proclaimed the "victory of socialism"; and without much difficulty Bolshevist rule was extended to Moscow, where the Kremlin was taken.

Bolshevist Legislation.   Once in power, the Bolshevists, in contrast to the hesitant provisional government, acted with speed and energy. They disregarded personal and political consequences and concentrated on the two fundamental points—nationalization and peace. Executive power was assumed by a "Soviet of the People's Commissars" with Lenin as chairman, Rykov for the Interior, Trotsky for foreign affairs, and twelve other members—Stalin becoming commissar of affairs of the nationalities. Within less than three months, from October, 1917, to January, 1918, the most radical changes were enacted. All large estates of state, church, and private owners were confiscated and turned over to *volost* land committees. Workers' control over the means of production and over the sales and finances of industrial and commercial enterprise was established. Eight-hour work laws and legislation for the protection of women, minors, and mine workers were passed. Civil ranks and classes were abolished and social insurance and price regulations were introduced. Banks were nationalized and banking was declared a state monopoly. All tsarist prewar loans were declared null and void. By decree, none but civil marriages were legally recognized; registry of all births was required and equality was decreed for legitimate and illegitimate children. Divorce by petition of one or both parties was made possible. Measures for expansion of educational and library facilities were adopted, and separation of church and state was instituted.

Bolshevist Administration. In December a "Supreme Council of National Economy" was created and the food supply for the capital, although remaining insufficient, was augmented. The foundations for a special "Red Army" were laid and the country was reorganized on a federal basis. Provincial soviets were charged with regional administration, and a People's Court with elected members was instituted. Revolutionary tribunals were authorized to deal with cases of sabotage, treason, or even opposition; special agencies were formed to supervise the press, and a new police force (Extraordinary Commission—"Cheka") was formed. The nationality problem was solved on the promised basis of the rights of the people to self-determination, and the various national groups of the empire were authorized to constitute themselves as independent states. Following the Finnish and Polish example, the Ukraine, Bessarabia, and the Caucasus regions availed themselves of this right.

Dissolution of Constituent Assembly. A last blow was dealt the dying system when in January, 1918, the recently convened Constituent Assembly was summarily dissolved. Elected in November, it was chiefly composed of Kerensky's Social Revolutionaries and of Menshevists. The Bolshevists were determined to make impossible its interference with their program; and upon losing their fight for the presidency and the first test vote, they immediately withdrew. Within twenty-four hours, supported by the galleries and the Petrograd garrison, they dispersed the convention.

PEACE

Armistice. With equal assurance, speed, and radicalism, the Bolshevist government turned to external affairs. Immediately announcing their intention to conclude an armistice, they confronted the world with a demand for peace on a nonimperialistic basis, without annexations or indemnities, and with self-determination for all peoples. Since England and France (and later the United States) refused to negotiate on such a basis whereas the Central Powers declared themselves willing to accept the terms, separate peace was decided upon and armistice negotiations commenced in November.

Soviet Dynamics. Despite their military and domestic predicaments, the Russians were in no wise in a weak position. Taking up the cause of workingmen the world over, they had reason to hope that by using propagandist speechmaking and by prolonging the negotiations, they would be able to rouse the working masses in Germany and, perhaps, in the Western countries. They knew the strength of their appeal to self-determination of the people, which threatened to sway the minorities in the Austrian-Hungarian empire; and they were also aware of the military difficulties besetting the Central Powers, who were anxious to shift troops from the east to an endangered front in the west.

Peace. The Russian delegation handled the situation astutely, but was unable to come to an agreement because Germany, after seeing the Russian border states released from Russian suzerainty, wished to control them. Furthermore, the Central Powers were resolved not to permit self-determination or political dissolution in their own realms and were as intent upon averting revolution in their own countries as the Russians were anxious to promote it. As no progress was made and as the Germans were threatening resumption of hostilities, the leader of the Russian delegation, Leon Trotsky, finally declared that he would sign no formal peace, but that his country would withdraw from war and forthwith cease combat. Such action, however, was unacceptable to the Central Powers, who countered by first concluding a separate peace with the Ukraine and then, in February, 1918, reopening the campaign against Russia. By a vigorous push deep into the country they forced the resumption of negotiations and now, under stricter conditions, secured the conclusion of a formal peace (March, 1918, Brest Litovsk). The Russians bitterly denounced the dictate as imperialistic and as a blow to the working class; but in order to fulfill the domestic promise for peace and to maintain Bolshevist rule, they nevertheless signed it.

CONSTRUCTION OF SOCIALIST STATE

Nationalization.

AGRICULTURE. The cessation of hostilities was utilized by the soviets to concentrate on the work of building a socialist society in Russia and spreading the Marxist doctrine from this center to the other countries of the world. With this in mind, the Bolshevist government concentrated its attention, notwithstanding increasing internal disorders and foreign intervention, on the task of reshaping the entire national system. Between February and December, 1918, many new laws were promulgated. Private ownership of all land, including that of the peasants themselves, was abolished. Anyone who wanted land to cultivate without hired labor could get it from the state. A central food control was introduced, prices were fixed, a corn monopoly was established, and, with the help of the armed forces, grain control was taken over by the state and a share of the harvest was collected from farms. Special "Committees of Poor Peasants" were set up to prevent the clandestine resurgence of wealthy landowners. In February, 1919, the first state (Soviet) farms were created; collective farming was sponsored with the aid of state loans; and the establishment of farm associations (*artels*) was furthered.

INDUSTRIES. In industries, whole branches, rather than individual plants, were nationalized; and the coal mines, oil fields, and railway works were declared public property. In May, 1918, the first "All-Russian Congress of the Soviets of People's Economy" met and set in motion the process of planning typical of later Soviet policy. Projects were devised for the financing of state industries and trade establishments. Co-operatives were incorporated into state institutions; a "People's Commissariat for Food Supply" took over sugar, meat, textile, and other retail establishments; the tobacco, oil, and sugar trades became state monopolies. All foreign trade was nationalized and likewise turned into a state monopoly. The right of inheritance was abolished. A new "Labor School Statute" with emphasis on manual training was promulgated.

Soviet Constitution.
These changes were embodied in a fundamental law or constitution covering at first only a part of the former empire, Russia proper. Under the dictatorship of the proletariat, it

provided for a "Federation of Soviet National Republics" in which all class divisions were abolished. All peoples of the Federation were declared equal and sovereign by a decree issued in October, 1918, and their right to self-determination and secession from the Federation was reasserted. The abolition of private ownership of land, banks, and all means of production and transportation was confirmed. War, imperialism, and colonization were denounced. Anyone could profess any or no religion. The church was no longer recognized as a juridical person; it could own no property and was fully separated from the state. Education was made free. Universal military training was ordered and the duty to work established. Supreme authority was vested in the "All-Russian Congress of Soviets," which was to elect an "Executive Committee," which in turn chose the highest state functionaries in the "Council of People's Commissars." Local and district soviets were created and their jurisdiction circumscribed. Suffrage was confined to soldiers, laborers, and peasants; merchants, *rentiers,* and former members of the police, of the ruling house, and of the clergy were disfranchised.

Results of Bolshevist Revolution. In less than twelve months, the Bolshevists thus not only extirpated the roots of autocracy as they had existed in Russia for hundreds of years, but they also abolished by law those fundaments on which a "liberal democracy" could be built. As envisaged by nineteenth-century radicals, the stage of the bourgeois state was skipped. Instead, true to Marxist concepts, the legal foundations for a new type of society were erected in which classes were leveled and equality was to reign; in which the church as a political factor was eliminated, and private property, ownership in land, and wealth of every kind were abolished; in which the means of production and most of those of distribution passed into the hands of the state, which was ruled by soviets of formerly "exploited" classes. But it remained to be seen to what extent, if at all, this transformation could in practice be accomplished; and urgent appeals were made by Lenin to strain all resources and work toward the goal.

PROBLEMS

1. Describe the methods applied by the Bolshevists in gaining power.
2. Discuss the immediate measures carried out upon assumption of power by the Bolshevists.
3. Discuss the importance of external peace for the survival of Bolshevist rule.

CHAPTER XXXVII

CIVIL WAR

PARTIES IN THE WAR

While the work of socialization was in progress, Russia found herself exposed to internal disorders and external dangers which had been unequaled except during the Time of Troubles. As then, national unity was broken and a triangular or multilateral struggle raged in which external and domestic, political and social issues were hopelessly confounded. There were the Bolshevists or "Reds," rulers of Russia and fully on the defensive, and the counterrevolutionaries or "Whites," divided into many incoherent groups of former officials, nobles, military men, Westernized liberals, and moderate socialists. There were external enemies. On the one hand stood the Germans, favoring the Reds in Russia proper because they were responsible for the withdrawal from the war, but attacking them in the newly created border states of the Baltic region and in Poland and the Ukraine—all of which the Central Powers wished to dominate and use as buffers against the rising social danger. On the other hand stood the Allies—France and England, joined by the United States— equally apprehensive of the "Red peril," but at first particularly anxious to reopen an eastern front against Germany. They continued their interference on the side of the counterrevolutionary

Whites long after the war with Germany was terminated. There were also the Japanese, interested in the more practical aim of wresting Far Eastern territory from an apparently disintegrating Russian empire.

REDS AND WHITES

Foreign Intervention. Civil war began immediately upon assumption of power by the Soviets; Allied intervention followed five months later. The first efforts of the Whites, commanded by two former chiefs of staff, General Alekseyev and General Kornilov, came to naught in the spring of 1918; and new operations under a more efficient leader, General Denikin, were begun from the Ukraine and the Caucasus. Simultaneously with Denikin's campaign, Allied intervention was undertaken. In April, 1918, the British and Japanese landed in Vladivostok, and they were followed in August by contingents from the United States, which was interested as much in checking Bolshevism as in keeping an eye on its allies, the Japanese. In the summer British troops descended on Murmansk; they were followed by French and, in September, by American detachments. English forces landed also in Estonia, Russia's western gate, and at Baku in the south, while French help, military and financial, was extended to Denikin's army. Thus Soviet Russia found herself menaced from north, south, east, and west, cut off from the seas, and isolated from contact with other nations.

Comparison of Reds and Whites. Against the overwhelming forces of its enemies, the Bolshevist government had to struggle until October, 1920, when French, English, and American troops were finally all withdrawn and civil war was ended. The Bolshevist government managed to survive only because of the lack of co-ordination of its enemies—the natural consequence of their utterly divergent aims. On the side of the Soviets were patriotism, enthusiasm, and fear—patriotism to defend the country against foreign invaders, enthusiasm to promote a "classless society," fear (on the part of the masses, and particularly of the peasants) of losing the economic advantages gained through the Revolution. On the side of the Whites were expert military men, zeal for constitutional freedom, and the vast resources of the foreign interventionists. But the Whites lacked a common objective. Some were desirous of the return of monarchy, others of some kind of democratic republic; yet all were in the unhappy position of fighting their own country and were unwilling to make the necessary social concessions. They fought in separate groups over interrupted lines of communication, and there were many unreliable subordinates lacking in discipline. The Bolshevists, on the other hand, had the strategic advantage of easily defensible interior lines, unified command, and a devoted Red Army, capably organized and led by men like Trotsky. The Whites were also dependent upon help from foreign powers which, like the Poles in the Time of Troubles and Napoleon in 1812, did not understand the social aspects of the struggle.

Civil War Fronts. The only objective common to all Whites was the overthrowal of the Bolshevists; up to November, 1918, the chief aim of the foreign powers consisted in the reopening of a second front against Germany. After the end of World War I in November, 1918, the Allied aim became identified with that of the Whites. But very little was effectively done to make their cause triumphant, and at no time was concerted action carried on. When Denikin launched his main offensive in the south, the other fronts wavered; nearing Moscow, he had to give up his drive for want of support. In 1920 he was replaced by a leader with more statesmanlike abilities, General Wrangel, who operated until November, 1920, in the Crimea but achieved no better results. When at another time, in the fall of 1919, the western group under General Yudenich pushed from Estonia eastward on Petrograd, neither Denikin nor the Allied forces co-ordinated their actions with his. Indeed, the Allies were forced just at that time to quit the northern sector and to flee from Archangel; thus, Yudenich's attempt also miscarried. When the White forces in Siberia under General Khorvat, Admiral Kolchak, and Captain Seménov started their operations, they met with the same fate. Favored not only by their remoteness from Soviet strongholds and easier access to foreign supplies, but also by the social and economic structure of Siberia, they actually came closest to success. They sponsored an autonomy movement which resulted in a provisional Siberian government with headquarters at Omsk, and in November, 1918, Admiral Kolchak was proclaimed "supreme ruler" of all of Russia. But the Bolshevist power of resistance combined with dissensions in Kolchak's own camp overwhelmed him. After holding out until February, 1920, he was betrayed, captured, and executed. Seménov, who continued his anti-Soviet activities through two decades and supported the Japanese in World War II, was seized, tried, and executed in 1946. The Siberian autonomy movement, sponsored and artificially upheld by the Japanese, collapsed.

EFFECTS OF CIVIL WAR

Death of Tsar. In addition to the organized resistance groups, there were also roaming bands of all kinds which contributed to the agony of the country in the post-Revolutionary era: war veterans who could not reach their homes; young people who were orphaned or who had left their homes because of the general disintegration; German war prisoners, released but unable to gain their homeland; and others. Among these different groups was also a large band of Czechs, at one time numbering several hundred thousand, who had deserted the Austrians and had joined the Russian armies. After the Peace of Brest Litovsk, they were to have been shipped to the western front in Flanders. They reached Vladivostok, their port of embarkation, but at the instigation of the Allies they were turned back into Siberia to fight the Bolshevists. Joined by Kadets, Social Revolutionaries, and Cossacks, they seized large sections of the Siberian railroad and marched upon Moscow. Only after entering European Russia were they repelled. They returned to Siberia, where they terrorized the population, sometimes fighting against the Soviets, sometimes joining the Red forces. An indirect result of their actions was the death of Nicholas II, the last Romanov ruler. When a Czech detachment reached the region of Ekaterinburg (Sverdlovsk) where the monarch had been brought, he and his family were executed by their guards, lest they be liberated by the Czechs.

Polish War. Following the Civil War, although in many respects a part of it, there occurred an external war against the Poles which resulted from Poland's support of the counterrevolutionaries in the Ukraine. The Poles seized the occasion offered by Russia's civil strife to take Lithuanian and White Russian regions which had once belonged to their medieval empire. The war, beginning in May, 1920, with their occupation of Kiev, might have been disastrous for them—the Reds ousted them in June and actually reached the suburbs of Warsaw—had they not rallied on their own territory and received the help of the French, who were particularly insistent in their opposition to Bolshevist rule. Thus, the tide turned in August, 1920; the Reds were forced to retreat from Warsaw and give up their conquests. In May, 1921, Russia was obliged to consent to the Peace of Riga, which deprived her of all territory coveted by the

Poles, notwithstanding the decision of a commission under Lord Curzon, which, in accordance with ethnographic realities, had fixed a different, more equitable, eastern border for Poland.

Famine. While the Poles were penetrating into Russia, at the end of 1920, a new disaster befell the country and added to the horrors of civil and external war and the accompanying Red and White terror which had cost hundreds of thousands of lives. A terrible famine occurred—the result of war and revolution as much as of the experimenting with new social systems and methods. But military intervention being over, the outside world was now willing to intervene with helping hands. Foreign churches, nations, and humanitarian groups such as the Quakers and the Red Cross took part in relief, and the efforts of men like Fridtjof Nansen and Herbert Hoover served to ameliorate the worst suffering.

Survival. Despite famine, despite economic collapse, despite internal and foreign wars, despite physical demolition and the destruction of existing law, despite the disintegration of society, the Bolshevist government succeeded in surviving. But only a gigantic effort and a large-scale reversal of the accepted program saved the communist system.

PROBLEMS

1. Compare the respective aims of the Reds and the Whites during the Civil War.
2. Discuss the causes for the success of the Bolshevists.
3. Discuss the implications of the Polish-Russian war of 1920 and its effects.

CHAPTER XXXVIII

RECONSTRUCTION

LENIN

The year 1921 brought the adaptation of communist Russia to demands and needs within a noncommunist world. The dominant figure in achieving this adjustment was Nikolai Lenin. Born in 1870 Vladimir Ilich Ulyanov, the son of a teacher belonging to the lower nobility, he became involved in the revolutionary struggle at an early age. The execution of his elder brother, who had participated in an assassination attempt on Alexander III, left a deep impression upon him. Much of Lenin's life was spent abroad, gathering and guiding the forces for the overthrowal of the tsarist government. Lenin consistently advocated the extreme revolutionary course and was the chief agent in splitting the Socialist party in 1903, when as leader of the Bolshevists he rejected the parliamentarian tactics of Plekhanov.

Like many of the great figures in Russian history, Lenin possessed a dual personality. Utterly ruthless in his methods, sacrificing without compunction the lives of hundreds of thousands, both guilty and innocent, he yet had a feeling heart and his actions were dictated by humanitarian considerations. He was a practical follower of a materialistic school, but simultaneously a fervent adherent of a faith which included many idealistic elements. In the sense of Bismarck, he considered politics as "the art of the possible," and was ready to compromise without losing sight of his ultimate aims. He assumed dictatorial powers in a society intended to be the most democratic; and although he misjudged the chances for the Russian experiment in other countries, he proved a farsighted, soberly evaluating statesman for his own country. His ability as an orator was not outstanding, yet he knew how to inspire people and to command their loyalty.

CONDITIONS AT END OF CIVIL WAR

International Position. It was under Lenin's guidance that— up to the time when he suffered a stroke in 1922 and then, diminishingly, until his death in January, 1924—the transformation of Russia into a working "Soviet Union" took place and that her international position was re-established. By the end of 1920, the Soviets had succeeded in gaining official recognition from their four Baltic neighbors, Estonia being the first of these nations to sign a treaty with them; commercial intercourse was secured with Germany and Sweden. In 1921 Poland, Turkey, and Afghanistan extended their recognition; and in 1922 the first great power, Germany, followed. Russia's former allies, however, who enjoyed greater freedom of action than Russia's neighbors, still held aloof. Since the Soviets had withdrawn from the war in 1917, they were refused a voice in the peace conferences and in planning a future which they had not helped to prepare. A meeting to ascertain their wishes, held on the Turkish island of Prinkipo, came to naught, since the Allies insisted on consulting also the counterrevolutionaries (who, however, refused to appear). As a consequence, the new Europe was drafted by the Western powers not only without the co-operation of defeated Germany, but likewise without that of Russia; and it showed all the shortcomings of a one-sided arrangement. The Soviet Union bitterly denounced the Versailles Treaty (although it rescinded the stipulations of its own peace treaty of Brest Litovsk) as a continuation of the old imperialistic policies of Western powers, and predicted the collapse of the Versailles system before the proletarian advance.

Comintern. In opposition to the traditional "war-breeding" policies of the Western powers, a new "international ideal" was set up in Russia by the institution of the Third International (Comintern). Under Lenin's leadership the first Congress of the Comintern was held in 1919, and a second followed in 1920. These Congresses were directed "against chauvinism as well as pacifist hypocrisy" and aimed at world peace through world revolution, at abolition of capitalism in all countries, and at federation of communist parties everywhere. Nationalization of the press and confiscation of factories, lands, buildings, and banks in all countries were demanded. In advanced countries, the aim was to be achieved by revolts of the proletariat, in colonial areas by risings of the oppressed.

Economic Weakness.

INDUSTRIES. The real test of the Soviets' strength and future position, however, depended less upon their relations with other European powers than upon their ability to consolidate their rule and to build a society at home which could secure for the Russian people benefits unparalleled in tsarist times. A proof of their strength was obviously given by the success of the new government in surviving the Civil War; but the growth of their system depended upon the success or failure of economic reconstruction. Foreign intervention and civil war, which had been fought with unspeakable brutality, had ravaged the country; and the speed and radicalism of governmental policies had intensified the state of disruption in which the Russian empire found itself at the end of 1920. Food and fuel were lacking, money was worthless, and black markets and speculation flourished. Nationalization of industries, extended to embrace all enterprises employing more than ten workers, had been carried out in a haphazard way by inexperienced officials sometimes for purely ideological reasons, sometimes for economic reasons, and in other instances for the sake of revenge. Managerial experience was lacking; productivity fell by one-half and more and in some oil, coal, and metal industries amounted to no more than 10 per cent of the prewar level. Labor had to be conscripted; workers were sent against their will wherever needed; and the advantages of nationalization which should have resulted from correlation of industries, standardization, and planning were more than outweighed by discontent and disillusionment. Contrary to their hopes at the beginning of the Revolution, the workers had not become employers: government agencies and officials now controlled their labor, using former owners and foremen as industrial managers and mercilessly punishing slackness or non-co-operation.

AGRICULTURE. In the field of agriculture, conditions by the end of 1920 were equally desperate. Productivity had sunk to a new low; no peasant was interested in producing more than his own needs demanded, and anticommunist feeling ran high among the peasantry. The state, and not they, had—at least legally—taken over all the land and had partitioned and redistributed it. Farms, no matter how unlucrative, were overcrowded; for bad conditions in the cities forced millions to migrate to the land. Moscow had declined to one million inhabitants. Compulsory grain deliveries, brutally enforced, lessened interest in tilling the soil and this caused widespread famine.

TRADE. Trade had necessarily followed the trends in industry and agriculture; most of it, with the exception of black markets, had come to a standstill for lack of production. In 1920, all private trading had been prohibited; small factories, shops, and stores were closed, the owners arrested, their goods confiscated. House owners were dispossessed, the homeless being quartered in available rooms. Gold, silver, and jewelry above a small amount were confiscated, and all cash had to be deposited with the state bank. Consumers' co-operatives were brought under state control and food was rationed, the rationing system itself serving as a political tool and lever.

NEW ECONOMIC POLICY

N.E.P. In the face of these conditions and the discontent of the masses, the Soviets in 1921 relinquished, at least for a transitory period, the original program and accepted a compromise with Marxist ideology. This compromise covered all phases of public life and became known as the N.E.P. (New Economic Policy). In order to revive production, to increase the output of the individual working-man, to re-establish the transportation system, to revive a feeling of responsibility among all citizens, and to check spreading discontent—which in March, 1921, had found expression in a mutiny of sailors at Kronstadt—a series of fundamental changes was undertaken. After three years of experimenting with communistic organization, a department for economic planning was now created (*Gosplan*) which began the task of scientifically outlining measures for Russia's political, economic, and social development. A considerable amount of private trade was reintroduced and, to stimulate it, the hoarding of cash and the functioning of private mutual banks were no longer prohibited. Not only was the individual's right to property partly recognized, but permission was given to leave to heirs sums up to five thousand dollars—for existing conditions, a considerable amount. Large factories were removed from the control of the workers and brought directly under that of the state; considerable differentiation was now made in the remuneration of the worker on the basis of the quality and quantity of his work. Money recovered its value and stability, co-operative societies gained new concessions, and many of the smaller industries were denationalized, although at times, for lack of capital, they remained dependent upon the state. Treaties with capitalistic countries were concluded and concessions were granted to foreign private entrepreneurs.

In agricultural districts, where discontent with the political structure was greatest, requisitions of grain according to fixed quotas were stopped. Instead, the peasant was allowed to sell on the free market that part of his crops which exceeded a fixed food tax. A program of rural electrification was worked out to increase agricultural production and to raise the tiller's living standard.

EVALUATION OF N.E.P. The N.E.P. marked a retreat from the uncompromising theoretical position of communism by allowing capitalistic activity and by promoting individualistic business endeavors. It has therefore been bitterly denounced by some groups within the Communist party who insist that it prevented the progress and success of the cause of the proletariat. But it does not seem to have constituted a permanent renunciation of the communistic goal, nor did it sacrifice more ground than special conditions temporarily demanded. Its results justified the expectations. Although communistic principles and the classless society were endangered, and although poverty, low wages, and lack of such essentials as fuel persisted, the Soviet regime was saved. The first winter following the inception of the plan was hard. Famine and epidemics ravaged the country, all food rations for workers had to be reduced, and church goods were confiscated to help purchase food for the starving. But under the new policy, and with the help of relief organizations, many Russian peasants resumed work on the land, and agricultural production increased rapidly. Trade and industrial production followed, and illegitimate trade could be curbed. Technical experts were secured, railroads regained their pre-Revolutionary standards, and attention could again be devoted to education and recreation. A normal, though very low, state budget was drafted and further planning was put on a sound basis.

Labor and Land Codes. The plan was supplemented in 1922 by a Labor Code and a Land Code. The Labor Code provided for collective agreements through trade-unions of the workingmen. The regulations regarding working hours and labor of women and children were revised, and new laws were passed for health and accident insurance. Old-age insurance, however, was postponed until 1928. The Land Code abolished "once for all" private property in land, forests, and rivers, and forbade purchasing, selling, and mortgaging, while providing for gratuitous leasing if the land were kept under cultivation.

Revision of Constitution. Many of the changes were embodied in the fundamental law (constitution) which was re-edited in 1923 on the basis of the political events that had taken place simultaneously with the economic recovery under the N.E.P. In December, 1922, the first Congress of the United Soviet Socialist Republics had been held and Joseph Stalin had delivered the main report. A Union of Soviet Socialist Republics was declared, comprising the Russian, Ukrainian, White Russian, and Transcaucasian republics, the last consisting of Georgia, Azerbaijan, and Armenia. This union ended all separatist tendencies, which had been particularly strong in the Ukraine and had led there in 1918 to a chauvinistic, anti-Semitic, and anti-Soviet regime under Petlyura. Foreign policies, foreign trade, over-all economic planning, the army, civil and criminal legislation, and education and health services were unified for the whole country. Supreme authority was vested in a central executive committee, which in turn elected a presidium of nineteen members. A Council of People's Commissars retained executive powers.

PROBLEMS

1. Discuss conditions in Russia at the end of the Civil War.
2. Discuss the advantages and dangers of the New Economic Policy.
3. Describe the organization of the U.S.S.R. under the constitution of 1923.

CHAPTER XXXIX

THE STRUGGLE FOR POWER

THEORY AND REALITY

Party Friction. The N.E.P. solved, but also created, economic problems. At the same time, through departure from original social-istic theory, it exercised far-reaching influence on the ideological de-velopment of Soviet Russia as a communist state, and harmony within the ranks of the revolutionaries was endangered. In May, 1921, before Lenin had even formulated the new policy, dissatisfac-tion came to the fore, evidenced by the resignation of G. Zinoviev, one of the prominent Bolshevist leaders. In the following year, the government found it necessary to reinstate the Cheka (secret police), known since as the Ogpu, and to outlaw tendencies conflicting with the official Party program. As the years went on, disunity and difficulties increased, revealing a tripartite rift between government forces, antirevolutionaries, and ultrarevolutionaries. Failing health prevented Lenin from settling the struggle which soon engulfed two of his most influential collaborators, Trotsky and Stalin. Shortly before his death in January, 1924, a clash occurred openly at the Congress of the Communist Party. Called to discuss problems of economic reorganization, social insurance, and international rela-tions with Western capitalistic powers, it brought forth sharp controversies among the contending factions. In an atmosphere of distrust and acrimony, demands were promptly voiced for the forceful suppression of all dissenters and of all factions within the Party.

Break in the Party. After Lenin's death the need for demonstrating unity and determination, lest the Western world seize a chance for overthrowing the Bolshevist regime, held the Party together. A. I. Rykov was chosen chairman of a new government, S. S. Kamenev became vice-chairman, G. V. Chicherin took the commissariat of foreign affairs, and Trotsky the commissariat of war. The Party was likewise reorganized; but despite their disagreements Zinoviev, Trotsky, and Stalin remained members of the Central Committee and of its executive committee, the Politburo. Stalin was also renamed Secretary General, an office which he had held since 1922. N.E.P. policies were reaffirmed and plans were drawn for balancing the budget, increasing exports, and further reducing "profit-seeking private capital." But peace within the Party did not last. The existing breach was widened by acrimonious denunciations among the various factions, and before the year was over, Trotsky was stripped of his powers.

Stalin and Trotsky. The struggle, which thereafter increased in violence, was, as always, evidenced by ambitious personalities: the one, Stalin, then forty-six years old, a practical politician, born in Georgia, child of an Orthodox family, trained in the revolutionary movement, essentially an accomplisher and executor of ideas; the other, Trotsky, a professional revolutionary, offspring of a well-to-do Jewish family, intellectual, a founder rather than an accomplisher, an originator of ideas and not an executor. But behind the two men stood, as in every important struggle, issues which overshadowed the human beings who represented the two sides. These issues concerned essentially the relationship of the individual to society and his right to self-assertion and initiative within the communistic world. This basic problem led to clashes on questions of Party discipline, Party policies, planned economy, and the immediate practical issues of tactics regarding the furthering of world revolution, the training of the young generation, the relationship of town and country, the communization of the peasantry, and the right to independent trade-unions and other agencies outside the Party. Trotsky, who was essentially a theoretician and who never held a position of final responsibility, generally advocated the liberal and anarchical side of the program and a materialistic, classless, and communistic world; Stalin,

Sherrill,

a practical statesman, emphasized the need for adjustment to existing conditions and for discipline, which he considered necessary to guarantee the success of the revolution in Russia and the preservation of a proletarian dictatorship. Both insisted upon their exclusive understanding of true materialistic socialism and upon their adherence to and furtherance of it, and each accused the other of betraying the work of Karl Marx and Lenin.

Stalin's Triumph. After a bitter struggle, success came ultimately to the party of Stalin, not only because he controlled the better organization, the Communist party itself, but also because of the realism of his policies and the inherent disruptive tendencies among his opponents. Trotsky, who several times recovered his position in Party and government, was unable to hold the opposition together. Ideological issues divided it into so-called "right" and "left" oppositions. Prominent members among the rightists were Rykov, Bukharin, and the trade-union leader Tomsky; the dominant figures among the leftists, aside from Trotsky, were Kamenev and Zinoviev. In 1926 the latter three were successively deprived of their positions. In 1927 Trotsky was expelled from the Politburo, and in the following year he was banished to Siberia, while Kamenev and Zinoviev, who recanted, escaped with a light sentence of exile to European Russia. Even in Siberia, Trotsky continued his opposition and intrigues, and in 1929 he was expelled from the Soviet Union for organizing secret antigovernment societies. He went first to Constantinople and then to Mexico, from where he hurled his denunciations and accusations against the Stalin regime. He was murdered in 1940. His followers, the so-called Trotskyites, were persecuted with unrelenting bitterness and many were banished to remote regions or they fled or perished.

Rightist Opposition. No sooner was Trotsky expelled than the fight was extended to the "right opposition." The right's insistence before the Party congress of 1927 that everyone should enjoy the privilege of criticism, although he might be compelled to obey the final Party decisions, was rejected. In May, 1929, Rykov was removed as chairman of the Council of the People's Commissars—an office taken in 1930 by V. Molotov; in June, Tomsky lost his position as head of the trade-unions; and in July, Bukharin was deposed as head of the Comintern. In the following year, a great trial was started against another rightist group, the "Industrial party," which was accused of Menshevist heresy. Denounced for conspiring with foreign enemies, principally England and France, and for sabotaging the industrial program by false propaganda and incorrect planning, all participants were condemned.

Purges. The emergence of Hitler as Germany's chancellor and the resulting external threat to the Bolshevist government increased the necessity and accelerated the process of disposing of all disuniting forces. From the year 1934 (when the murder of one of Stalin's friends, Sergius Kirov, in Leningrad was interpreted as an attack on Bolshevist rule) each year witnessed trials, courts-martial, purges, and executions. Rightists and leftists alike found themselves accused and repeatedly tried, and ultimately all lost their positions and many their lives. Tomsky committed suicide. Zinoviev and Kamenev were executed in 1936, Bukharin and Rykov in 1938, and each time many followers died with them, while less conspicuous figures were imprisoned or exiled. In 1937 the purges were extended to the Red Army, and Marshal Tukhachevsky and seven other generals were executed after a secret court-martial. Those who escaped trial but who were not considered fully reliable were removed from their offices, so that in 1939, when the Second World War began, few of the prominent leaders of the Bolshevist Revolution held leading positions in Russia.

PARTY POLICIES

Party Congresses. The fight of the Party under Stalin against the Trotskyites and the rightist opposition could never have been won had it not been supplemented by constructive political and economic programs worked out by the Party. Party congresses were regularly held and, in the early years of the Revolution, were of great significance because they acted as a barometer of popular trends and frequently challenged the policies of the leaders. Later they lost some of their democratic importance and served to ratify and propagate the programs of the leaders. Of special importance was the fourteenth congress, held in December, 1925, during the course of which a vast industrialization plan was announced; all forces of the Soviet Union were called upon to co-operate lest the capitalistic West, recently strengthened by the Locarno Pact with Germany, put an end to the communist experiment. Also, a change in the policies regarding the peasantry was proposed. One year later, at the fifteenth congress of the Party, which was remarkable for its intransigent attitude towards the opposition, the reshaping of Soviet agriculture was again emphasized. But a change was noticeable in international policy, inasmuch as the drive for world revolution was slowed down. Stabilization in Germany and most other countries rendered the outbreak of world revolution problematic, and only England, hit by a crippling strike of the miners, and China, disturbed by civil warfare, seemed to offer any prospects. Hence, co-operation with capitalist countries to secure credits for industrialization was envisaged.

Tenth Anniversary of Revolution. The following year, 1927, brought the tenth jubilee of the Red Revolution. At the celebration in November, Stalin reviewed the achievements of the past, and far-reaching plans for the future were laid. Chief points of the program were the creation of a mighty industry, the radical abolition of private property among peasants and the collectivization of villages, the spread of education to eliminate illiteracy and drunkenness, and the extension of diversified cultural activities. Provisions were made to reduce or cancel the debts of all poor peasants, to decrease taxes, and to raise old-age and veterans' pensions. The death penalty was to be abolished, except for treason, desertion, and corruption; equality for women, wherever still lacking, was to be provided for; and a general amnesty for former political opponents was granted. In foreign affairs, peace, self-determination of the peoples, and intercourse with all nations replaced earlier formulas.

Twentieth Anniversary. The program of the Jubilee year was followed and reaffirmed by every new Party congress. It became the chief weapon against the opposition and its consistent execution the keystone for the success of the Communist party. In 1937, when the twentieth anniversary of the Revolution was celebrated, Soviet power rested more than ever on the Communist party, centralized under its leaders and determined to follow a practical course consistent with external realities and internal contingencies.

PROBLEMS

1. Discuss the issues involved in the struggle between Trotsky and Stalin.
2. Discuss the role of the Party in the building of Soviet Russia.

CHAPTER XL

CONSTITUTION AND GOVERN-MENT

STALIN CONSTITUTION

Socialist Basis. The consolidation and centralization of the Soviet government found its reflection in a new fundamental law which was promulgated in 1936 (Stalin Constitution). Like the pre-existing law, it provided for a Union of Soviet Socialist Republics based on socialist ownership of the means and instruments of production. Socialist ownership would consist (1) in the form of state property (land, subsoil wealth, banks, factories, the bulk of the dwelling houses, state farms, and transportation already belonged to the state), and (2) in the form of co-operative enterprises (including collective farms, *kolkhoz* markets, and farm machinery). But in addition, the law would now allow for a small private economy as long as this was based on the personal labor of peasants and artisans and excluded the use of the labor of others. Personal property within defined limits would be permitted; and savings, houses, and furniture could be inherited. The guiding principle was not the slogan "To each according to his needs," but "From each according to his ability; to each according to his work."

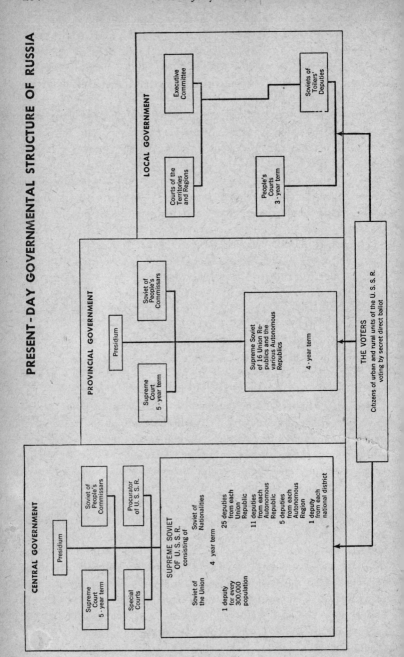

PRESENT-DAY GOVERNMENTAL STRUCTURE OF RUSSIA

CENTRAL GOVERNMENT

Presidium

Supreme Court
5 - year term

Special Courts

Soviet of People's Commissars

Procurator of U.S.S.R.

SUPREME SOVIET OF U.S.S.R.
consisting of

Soviet of the Union

1 deputy for every 300,000 population

Soviet of Nationalities
4 - year term

25 deputies from each Union Republic

11 deputies from each Autonomous Republic

5 deputies from each Autonomous Region

1 deputy from each national district

PROVINCIAL GOVERNMENT

Presidium

Supreme Court
5 - year term

Soviet of People's Commissars

Supreme Soviet of 16 Union Republics and the various Autonomous Republics
4 - year term

LOCAL GOVERNMENT

Executive Committee

Courts of the Territories and Regions

Soviets of Toilers' Deputies

People's Courts
3 - year term

THE VOTERS

Citizens of urban and rural units of the U.S.S.R. voting by secret direct ballot

Political Structure. The Union was now composed of eleven republics: the Russian, Ukrainian, White Russian, Azerbaijan, Georgian, Armenian, Turkmen, Uzbek, Tajik, Kazak, and Kirghiz; to these, during and after the Second World War, were added the Karelo-Finnish, Moldavian, Lithuanian, Latvian, and Estonian republics. Each republic possessed sovereignty except for the powers exercised by the Union, which included questions of war and peace, defense, foreign trade, economic planning, banking, transport, and communications. Each retained the right to secede. International relations formed part of the tasks of the Union until an amendment of 1944 allowed Union republics to enter into direct relations with foreign states. In addition to the Union republics, there existed Autonomous republics and Autonomous regions and National districts which were organized along parallel lines but which enjoyed a lesser degree of independence. Special guarantees were given the numerous ethnic minorities in the Union; they were allowed to develop their cultural heritage and to retain their own languages and their customs and individual institutions as long as these remained "socialist in content."

Executive, Legislative, and Judicial Structure. The highest authority of the Union was vested in the Supreme Soviet, which consisted of a Soviet of the Union and a Soviet of Nationalities, both elected by the people for a term of four years. The Soviet of the Union was composed of one delegate for each 300,000 of the population; that of the Nationalities, of a fixed number of delegates representing each Union republic, each Autonomous republic, and each Autonomous region. The Supreme Soviet possessed exclusive legislative powers and was charged to elect the presidium of the Supreme Soviet and to appoint the government (the Council of People's Commissars), which exercised the highest executive and administrative functions. It likewise chose, for a five-year term, the highest judicial organ, the Supreme Court of the Union. People's courts were to be elected for each district by its citizens for a three-year term; area, regional, and territorial courts by corresponding soviets for five years; and supreme courts of Autonomous and Union republics for a similar term. Unlike the practice in the United States, no separation of powers was introduced; the final authority was vested in the legislature, which, after fully debating issues, generally took decisions unanimously.

Rights of Citizens. Full equality was guaranteed all individual citizens, regardless of race and nationality; punishment was provided for those who preached race prejudice or inequality. Each citizen received the right to employment and to payment for his work—a right ensured by the "elimination of the possibility of economic crises and the abolition of unemployment" because of the "socialist organization of the national economy." He had the right to rest, to leisure, to maintenance in old age, sickness, and disability, and to education. Women were assured of equal rights with men in all fields. Freedom of conscience—i.e., of religious worship as well as of disseminating antireligious propaganda—was likewise ensured to all. Freedom of speech, press, assembly, and demonstrations was proclaimed, as was inviolability "of the person" and "of the home of the citizen," including privacy of correspondence. Universal military service was made compulsory, and offenses against public property were punishable.

Franchise. The most important change, compared with previous constitutions, consisted in the elimination of the disabilities formerly imposed on priests, merchants, and ex-members of tsarist authorities. Now that the bourgeoisie was virtually eliminated, all citizens were to be equal, with equal ballot rights. Candidates for office were to be nominated by public organizations, such as the Communist party, trade-unions, co-operatives, youth organizations, and cultural societies. The election of deputies was secret, and deputies were subject to recall at any time by a majority of the electors.

Amendments. The constitution itself could be amended by a two-thirds majority in the Supreme Soviet of the Union.

COMMUNIST PARTY

Membership. The Communist party was mentioned only twice in the constitution and was defined as the "vanguard of the working people in their struggle to strengthen and develop the socialist system," and as the society of the "most active and politically most conscious citizens in the ranks of the working class." It was the only party in the Union, and admission was difficult. In 1918 it numbered no more than 115,000 members; in 1923, 75,000; by 1928, it had increased to about one million out of a population of one hundred sixty million, but repeated purges had kept it down to a nucleus of devoted adherents. New members were often recruited from suborganizations such as the Communist youth group, the *Comsomol*.

After 1928 the membership continued to fluctuate; yet by 1941 the Party counted two and one-half millions. The decision to end the system of periodical purges and to admit millions of soldiers to the privileges of membership brought a large influx of new members during the Second World War.

Position of Party. The Party was given no official status as a government agency, but it held vast powers. Through its members, its youth organization, and its right to nominate candidates for offices, it secured a dominant position in internal affairs; and through its connection with the Third International it exercised extensive influence in foreign policies. The decisions of its executive committee, the Politburo, were of no less importance than those of the Soviet government, whose directing members generally held positions in both. The Party exercised influence on law courts, whose task it was to further the interests of the proletariat.

Trade-Unions. Unlike the Party, factory soviets and trade-unions, which at the beginning of the Revolution assumed great responsibilities, soon lost their importance. The nationalization of industrial plants made their control by the workers illusory, and in line with this development trade-unions began to function as government agencies. Although trade-unions strove to protect the interest of the workers, the nature of the Soviet state, which accorded many privileges to the manual worker, turned the trade-unions into executors of the government's over-all policies; and these were not necessarily in line with the specific interests of each individual group of workers. M. Tomsky, head of trade-unions, fell out with the Party leadership over just this question, and his resignation and later suicide were the result of his disagreements over the position of trade-unions as instruments of the state. However, Stalin ordered a change in 1935, and "democratization" of trade-unions was provided in order to enable them to represent the workers' cause to the government rather than vice versa.

FINANCES

State Control of Finances. Unchecked by trade-unions and controlled by a party which did not allow for deviations, the government as conceived in the Soviet constitution found itself in a unique position. In contrast with capitalistic countries, where the authorities find checks on their power through the strength of private capital, the Russian government enlarged its constitutional supremacy by securing direct control over practically all the financial resources of the country. During the first few years after the Revolution these were necessarily small, and most of the state's income was derived from confiscation and disposal of the wealth accumulated in tsarist times. Printing of paper money likewise served to bridge the initial need. But, in line with the New Economic Policy, a state bank was founded in 1921 and the entire banking system was changed. Whereas during the time of civil war the existing private banking facilities had simply been taken over by the state, an intricate branch system of the central bank was now introduced; special credit institutions for the various branches of trade and industry were created, and in 1923 Soviet Savings Banks were founded. All financial operations were made dependent upon the state and its planning commissions, which issued loans to buyers who in turn used these to advance payments to their suppliers. Money markets, in the sense in which they existed in capitalistic countries, ceased to function in Soviet Russia.

Currency. The year 1922 brought also a currency reform and a stable money unit, the chervonets, guaranteed by a 25 per cent bullion reserve. Two years later, the chervonets was replaced by the ruble which was fixed at one-tenth of a chervonets. Lacking intrinsic value and serving only as a means of facilitating the exchange of goods and services within the country, the ruble was artificially kept stable and since 1936 has been pegged at 19 American cents. The commodities produced in Russia and at the direct disposal of the government served to guarantee its value. Foreign debts contracted by the Soviet state were conscientiously honored, and many internal loans for financing industrialization were successfully floated. The interest rate of 8 to 9 per cent in 1929 sank by 1940 to 3 to 5 per cent, but many issues carried no interest at all and instead were raised as lottery loans.

Budget.

REVENUES. The budget increased enormously. In 1922, when stabilization began, it amounted to one and a half billion rubles; by 1929, it was eight times as high; and during the following twelve years it increased again eightfold. The 1946–47 budget anticipated a total of not less than 300 billion rubles. The main income was derived from the surplus ("gains") of state-owned industries and from the sales tax of the co-operatives. These surpluses corresponded to the profits of industries in capitalistic countries, which in the true sense of the word did not exist in Russia; for within a socialist society, not supply and demand but the needs of the state governed the profit or surplus; and prices were fixed sometimes below cost, sometimes far above, but in all cases according to over-all plans and general political considerations. The rest of the state income was made up chiefly by income and inheritance taxes and customs revenues. For the major part of the Soviet Union's existence, the income taxes were based on class principles, private traders paying up to 55 per cent of their often small earnings, while journalists and actors paid from 18 to 30 per cent, workmen and employees still less, and peasants from 3 to 30 per cent. The inheritance tax was graduated, reaching a maximum of 90 per cent.

EXPENDITURES. On the passive side of the budget, the main expense factors were those for defense and for industrialization, the latter actually constituting less an outlay than a capital investment. Smaller amounts were disbursed as health and educational obligations and as interest on government loans.

PROBLEMS

1. Compare the centralization of power in the U.S.S.R. and in the United States.
2. Discuss the relationship of Soviet government and Communist party.
3. Describe the financial basis of the Soviet government.

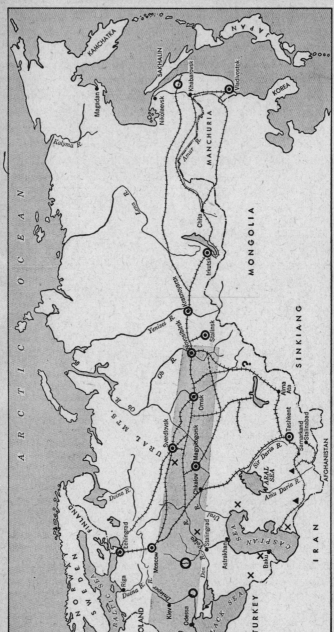

ECONOMIC MAP OF U.S.S.R.

○ INDUSTRIAL CENTERS (Iron and Coal)   ✕ OIL   ▲ COTTON   ? ATOMIC ENERGY (?)   ┼┼┼┼ RAILWAYS (Additional railways under construction into Northern Siberia)

░ Shaded area = main agricultural belt. North of shaded area = main timber belt. South of shaded area = desert and mountain zone. Along Arctic coast = tundra.

Chapter XLI

INDUSTRIALIZATION

END OF N.E.P.

It has been argued that political consolidation, crowned by the constitution of 1936, was gained at the cost of economic and social reaction, beginning with the N.E.P. in 1921. However, the Soviet government never lost sight of the socialist program, the execution of which alone could give permanence to the new society; and in many essentials, the N.E.P. was abandoned before 1925. It had achieved much. Transportation had been brought back to the prewar level, industries had showed steadily improving production curves, foodstuffs had returned to the markets, and confidence in the organizing abilities of the government had increased.

On the other hand, the N.E.P. had restored a considerable amount of private enterprise; under it speculation in essential commodities had hampered a steady flow of goods, the quality of industrial work had been inferior, the stability of budget and currency was still endangered, and an oversized bureaucracy lacked experience and, despite its numerous controls, failed to co-ordinate the national economy. The private entrepreneur had recovered almost one-tenth of the wholesale trade and approximately one-half of the retail trade, but he feared renewed expropriations and thus lacked a feeling of security.

Although industries had steadily gained over agricultural activities, they were still insufficient to provide, in a hostile world, much needed equipment for the country's defense. Medieval and modern production methods still existed side by side.

THE FIRST FIVE-YEAR PLAN

Political, Cultural, and Strategic Aspects.   In order to overcome the difficulties and to end the mixed private and socialist economy, it was decided to reorganize the planning commission of the N.E.P. and to appoint eleven members who were to work out a co-ordinating plan for all economic activities in all parts of the empire. During the years 1925 to 1928 this commission (*Gosplan*) drew the first "Five-Year Plan" (*Piatiletka*), which constituted less a final ukase than a program subject to revision while in progress. Politically, the Five-Year Plan envisaged the strengthening of a socialist society through elimination of resurgent private enterprise. Independent entrepreneurs were to be eliminated through taxation and government competition. Credit facilities were to be withheld from them, freight service for their goods restricted, high rents exacted, and personal discrimination imposed—extending even to their children, who were excluded from universities. Likewise, private enterprise in agriculture was to be curbed and the liquidation of the so-called "kulaks," who formed the wealthier part of the peasantry, was started. Culturally, the plan provided for improved working and living conditions, for extended educational facilities, and for reduction of illiteracy. It laid a new basis for the scientific investigation of Russia's resources and potentialities. Strategically, it outlined better distribution of defense installations throughout the empire and aimed at emancipation from foreign countries and from foreign basic materials.

Economic Aspects.   But the most important section of the plan dealt with economic issues. It stipulated the method and provided the means for the industrial transformation of the country. The over-all productivity of labor was to be increased and definite quotas were set which were to be reached within a specified period. Coal mining in the Donets basin was to be speeded by mechanization, as was steel and iron production. New metallurgic plants were to be erected in Krivoi Rog, in Zaporozhe, on the Kerch peninsula, and in Siberian Kusnetsk. There were to be a pig-iron and rolled-metal combine at Magnitogorsk, more oil wells in the Caucasus, and truck and tractor works in Stalingrad. Automobiles were to be manufactured in Nizhnii Novgorod on the basis of a contract with Henry Ford, who was to supply rts and technical advice. Prospecting for oil was to be carried in Asia. The plan provided further for electrification, the importance of which had been emphasized by Lenin. The largest European power plant was built in connection with a new dam across the Dnieper at Dnieprostroy. Thousands of kilometers of roads with stone surface were to be laid, and a railroad (*Turksib*) connecting Turkestan and Siberia was to be completed.

Execution of Plan. With great enthusiasm, the execution of the gigantic Five-Year Plan—duly propagandized—was undertaken; and, owing to the great exertions of all and in spite of the depression in capitalist countries, its fulfillment could be announced in 1932, one year ahead of schedule. The Turksib railroad was opened on May 1, 1930, the Dnieprostroy dam in 1932, and great accomplishments could be registered in all other undertakings. Yet, there was much criticism, and the official figures given out to substantiate the advance made were assailed as to their correctness. Failure of the transportation program was only too evident; and the low productivity of the laborer, his wastefulness, and the poor quality of his work were criticized. His lack of interest, a result of low and almost equal wages for all, and the excessive costs of production owing to his laxity were pointed out. Too much centralization hampered local initiative; the bureaucracy caused unnecessary delays and through its distrust antagonized skilled technicians, who because of existing shortages generally had to be recruited from former bourgeois circles or from abroad. Actually, some of these technicians were accused of sabotage, others of treason; they were tried, and this action led to severe international repercussions. Furthermore, the existing tension between peasant and industrial worker was not sufficiently alleviated, for the former felt that he still carried the chief burden of the national economy without benefiting in equal measure from the fruits of the country's industrialization. Food, fuel, and many amenities of life were still lacking everywhere, particularly because a large percentage of the national income was reinvested in capital assets; thus living standards were not raised. Ideologically, doubts, supported by the Trotskyite opposition, prevailed regarding the possibility of permanent socialist success unless the communist system were to be adopted by all nations of the globe.

SECOND AND THIRD FIVE-YEAR PLANS

Second Plan. The government, although proud of its achievement, was by no means blind to criticism; and a new Second Five-Year Plan was drafted after careful consideration of the first *Piatiletka's* shortcomings.

AIMS. Besides the political goal of furthering a classless, socialist society, the main aims of the Second Plan consisted in the improvement of living standards through increase in consumer goods, rationalization of work, and improvement in the quality of goods. The pace of introducing innovations was slackened; but better equipment, standardization, mechanization, further electrification, and greater mastery of production techniques were to make possible the doubling of the output of goods. A geographic redistribution of industrial centers was planned through the construction of plants close to raw-material sources in the Caucasus, Siberia, and central Asia; special funds were set aside for the erection of steel mills, coal mines, and power stations east of the Urals. Money was also allocated in proportionately greater amount for improving the transportation system through the electrification of railroads, the opening of new waterways (such as the White Sea-Baltic, the Moscow-Volga, and the Volga-Don canals), and the manufacture of increased numbers of motor vehicles, airplanes, and steamboats.

In addition, the Second Five-Year Plan provided for the doubling of real wages and a reduction in prices, so as to improve standards of living. Food rations were actually abolished in 1935; but, as a result, prices rose and soon equaled those formerly paid on the free market. The educational system was extended, vocational schooling was improved, and polytechnical training was made compulsory. Model schools were built in each district, and research institutes were endowed with sufficient funds. The circulation of newspapers was raised. A better health service was instituted through erection of *crèches* (nurseries), health resorts, and sanitariums, and plans were worked out to replace private housekeeping by large "socialized" housekeeping through the introduction of a catering system and through the sale of semiprepared food or part-ready meals.

RESULTS. After five years, the government published figures indicating the successful accomplishment of the plan; it stated that the desired quotas had been reached and that productivity of the average laborer had been doubled. Socialism had made further progress, for private producers and traders accounted for not more than 6 per cent of the total Russian production and turnover. However, one specific development caused alarm. In response to Stalin's speech on May 4, 1935, calling for greater individual productivity, a worker by the name of Stakhanov had cut several times as many tons of coal as required of each miner; and soon thereafter a peasant woman, Maria Demchenko, had raised far more per hectare than her expected quota. This seemed to indicate the possibility of increasing the industrial and agricultural output through greater exertion of each citizen. Consequently, the year 1936 was proclaimed a "Stakhanov year." Stakhanovite clubs were founded by those who greatly exceeded their quotas; and the state supported them through bonuses, privileges, and special rewards. "Shock brigades" formed from these clubs were to set the working pace, "socialist competition" was extolled, and over-all quotas for the average worker were substantially raised. As in capitalist countries, wages for the workers were more and more differentiated, according to the amount of work performed; distribution of ration cards was used by factory managers as a spur for production and discipline; and efficiency standards were revised.

Third Plan. As a result, a vigorous countermovement set in. "Star performances" were bitterly condemned since they often did not affect the average output but instead led to the production of faulty goods and the misuse of tools. Discontent among workers increased, and justified fears were voiced regarding the re-emergence of a privileged group within the proletariat. The Third Five-Year Plan, approved by the Party in 1939, but beginning to function in 1938, reflected these sentiments.

Unsolved Problems. This Third Plan—which, because of the war, could not be fulfilled—is of importance only inasmuch as it throws light on earlier shortcomings and subsequent trends. It differed essentially from former plans in that the industrialization program, though again emphasized, was "decelerated" and "gigantomania" was denounced. The need remained for greater individual productivity and rational working methods. The plan accentuated again an increase in consumer goods, stimulated textile production, and tried to remedy the unsatisfactory housing situation. Two problems found special attention: labor discipline and defense needs. In order to further the former, nonsteady workers were deprived of their preferment for living quarters, social insurance was reduced for them, and absences from work were punished by loss of vacation. Leaves for women during pregnancy were shortened; managers who did not enforce government decrees were subjected to heavy fines. As to the other problem, defense, up to one-quarter of the national income was set aside for military purposes, new oil resources were developed, factories were relocated in remote regions, and regional self-sufficiency was increased. Vigilance was strengthened not only against "wreckers" in factories, but also against possible saboteurs within the ranks of the planning commissions.

SUMMARY

Achievements. As a whole, the three Five-Year Plans transformed Russia from an essentially agricultural country into a country with a balance between agriculture and industry. Hitherto unknown skills and advanced tools were introduced; Russia was raised to a leading place in most essential industries; backward regions were developed; and a vastly improved transportation system, though overcrowded, brought material and cultural assets to and from all parts of the empire. The plans strengthened the socialist, classless state and constituted the world's chief experiment in a state-planned economy.

Shortcomings. But in a world which moved everywhere towards industrialization, reform, and better social conditions, they fell short of the aim of securing the Russian workingman living standards commensurate with his effort. Furthermore, despite guarantee in the constitution, they failed to provide for the acceptance and spread of individualistic freedom which the theory of the communistic state demanded. In many respects, the development followed the pattern set by tsarist Russia; for geography, geology, and climate, and the Russian man with his attitudes and traditions composed a background which, materialistic and purely economic thinking notwithstanding, could not be changed beyond a degree compatible with normal processes of growth.

PROBLEMS

1. Compare the aims of the First and Second Five-Year Plans.
2. Discuss the main difficulties in completing the work outlined by the plans.
3. Discuss the reaction of the plans on the concept of a communist state.

CHAPTER XLII

AGRICULTURE AND TRADE

SOVIET AGRICULTURE

Agriculture *vs.* Industry. The industrial transformation between 1925 and 1939 was paralleled by agricultural changes which equaled the industrial innovations in economic importance and surpassed them in social significance. The tension between industrial and agricultural workers—the one representing the proletariat with Marxist tendencies, the other constituting the backbone of individualism and private property—was such as to endanger the whole Soviet structure. A process of leveling was necessary to reconcile the diverging classes and to distribute equitably the economic burden. The Trotskyites had recognized the problem early; and the Party under Stalin, though disavowing its precursors, followed their lead when outlining the first *Piatiletka.*

DISSATISFACTION OF PEASANT. Essentially, the Revolution had disappointed the peasant. By 1905 he had possessed in full private ownership about 40 per cent, and by 1914 more than 50 per cent, of the cultivable land. He had since seized the estates of crown, church, and nobility, but had then been deprived of his new acquisitions and of all he had previously owned by the fundamental laws of 1918 which permitted no personal ownership whatever. Not even the *usus fructi* was unequivocally accorded him; for by fixing prices and requisitioning grain and by taxation and socialization of farms, the state deprived him of his freedom of action. Committees of Poor Peasants—sometimes directed by those who had remained poor through laziness, drunkenness, or inability—interfered with successful agriculturists. As a result, many peasants began to produce for their own needs only, and though their own consumption increased and their social level was raised, the country as a whole suffered direly. The government found itself forced to intervene; and since the newly founded national (Soviet) farms yielded too little to provide for the needs of the country, quotas were fixed by which the peasant had to contribute to the national food supply. Wherever these quotas were not met, grain was collected from him by force. This regulation —ruthlessly enforced—led to grave disturbances and ultimately to counterrevolutionary movements. It was therefore changed in 1921: the N.E.P. allowed again, within limits, private trade in agricultural products and reintroduced taxation instead of compulsory grain delivery.

NEED FOR RURAL REFORM.   The N.E.P., however, failed to offer a solution to the agricultural problem as such, for the gulf between the interests of worker and peasant remained unbridged. The wealthier peasant, the kulak—better off than his neighbor whether by virtue of greater ability and industry or by virtue of shrewdness and skill at exploiting others—began to prosper again; and, leasing more land, he threatened the concept of a classless society. Backward methods of production persisted and coercive measures with regard to collective farming hindered expansion of the sowing area. The First Five-Year Plan, therefore, undertook the task of industrializing agriculture, transforming the peasant into a laborer, and stamping out the main protagonist of individual farming, the kulak.

Collective and Co-operative Farming.   For this purpose, large mechanically equipped farms were created on which the land was cultivated collectively or co-operatively. Peasants who accepted the new system jointly owned and used all facilities except expensive machinery, which was rented from so-called "tractor stations." A collective farm (*kolkhoz*) or a co-operative farm (*artel*) was required to raise and deliver to the state a certain amount of produce, the type of produce being to a large extent fixed by over-all planning commissions. Wheat, rye, oats, potatoes, sugar beets, and industrial crops were predominant. What was harvested above the quota had to be used to meet the financial obligations of the *kolkhoz* or the *artel* and to pay the tractor station. The then remaining surplus could be sold on the free market and the income used for distribution among the members or spent on cultural and other improvements. Speculation in grain was forbidden.

KOLKHOZ AND ARTEL. A *kolkhoz* represented an economic and social unit which drew up budgets, paid taxes and expenses, set aside reserves, and divided the common income according to the amount and quality of work performed. It consisted, on an average, of seventy-five families, each of which could maintain personal ownership in house, garden, fowl, and a few animals. A specific measure of productivity on the common land was fixed for the individual farmer, who was obliged to invest between 100 and 150 days' work to meet his quota. Production above the required quota increased the peasant's share in the *kolkhoz's* profit or reduced his required working time, so that industrious peasants had extra time for attending to their own gardens and for extending their hours of leisure. Strict discipline, enforced by fines and premiums, was observed; "labor brigades" under the command of "brigadiers" attended to the daily requirements. Outside help, except for experts, could not be hired; negligent members could be expelled, but voluntary withdrawal was also possible, although it involved loss of the share in the common land. *Artels* allowed for somewhat more private initiative and for the individual care of household, beehives, poultry, truck garden, some cattle, and one sow. A general meeting of the members decided most common problems.

Collectivization. Enthusiastic young men were sent to extol the value of collectivization and preach the advantages of large, scientifically administered farms. Apart from the propaganda, special privileges were extended to those who joined, consisting of lower taxes and postponement of debt payments. Where these inducements were not sufficient, force was employed. In 1930 a law was passed which made it possible to legally confiscate land, houses, and other possessions of all who could be considered "kulaks"; these were brutally expelled from collectivized regions. So great was the official ardor that Stalin himself had to warn against excesses and to insist on the individual's right to join or not to join collective farming. By the end of the First Five-Year Plan, about three-quarters of the arable land was under cultivation by collective or co-operative farms. In some regions the percentage was higher, as in the Ukraine, the

Caucasus, and the lower Volga region. In the less-fertile northern parts, collectivization was undertaken on a smaller scale, perhaps because the government planners needed agriculturists with personal initiative and individualistic spirit to help increase the agricultural production of these not sufficiently exploited regions.

EFFECTS OF COLLECTIVIZATION. The results of collectivization were in many respects gratifying. Modern cultivation and cattle-raising methods could be introduced; the burden of the individual was lightened through the use of machinery; agricultural output reached prewar standards in 1930 and surpassed them thereafter. Industrial crops were grown and found ready markets in the numerous processing factories. Politically, collectivism enabled stricter supervision of the individualistic agriculturist; for the state could exercise control through tractor stations upon which each *kolkhoz* depended for its needed machinery. The desired leveling process could thus be carried on.

COMPLETION OF COLLECTIVIZATION. The Second Five-Year Plan prescribed the doubling of agricultural production, which was to be achieved through completion of collectivization, additional tractor stations, and better scientific methods. Production quotas were substantially raised. New crops were to be introduced, deserts exploited, marshes drained, and virgin regions tested for agricultural possibilities. Those kulaks who had managed to survive the liquidation of their class were now permitted to return if they were deemed politically reliable, and they could become members of the collective farms.

Situation at Outbreak of World War II. Using all available resources, the Second Five-Year Plan resulted in increased food production, in the extension of the area under cultivation, and in adequate supply of industrial crops. Collectivization reached a high of 90 per cent of all existing farms. With the introduction of some modern bakeries, meat-packing houses, and refrigeration methods, a start was also made toward better distribution and higher average consumption.

As production was still not sufficient to raise living standards substantially and as the needs and hopes of the people were still unsatisfied, the Third Five-Year Plan called for increased discipline and continued vigilance against laxity, and it aimed at including most of the cattle-raisers in the collective system. But war interrupted the fulfillment of this plan.

SOVIET TRADE

Domestic Trade. The spirit of radicalism, compromise, and socialist planning, which was mirrored by the successive phases of industry and agriculture between 1918 and 1939, was also reflected in the development of trade in Bolshevist Russia. During the period of civil war and intervention, trade—together with all other economic functions—had stagnated and did not revive until the era of the N.E.P. in 1921, when co-operatives, and later private companies, were allowed to function again. But as in industry and agriculture, reaction set in after 1925. State-owned "syndicates," co-operatives, and *kolkhoz* markets found increased government support and favors and began to monopolize many wholesale and retail trading activities; within three years, private trade declined from 40 per cent of the total to about 15, and this trend continued thereafter. Price ceilings were imposed on private companies, advertising was banned, and competition was limited; yet prescribed standards were required to be maintained. Nevertheless, a certain amount of private retail trade survived; for, despite much higher prices and manifold handicaps, buyers were attracted by better service, by the greater variety of goods offered, and by their availability without rationing.

Foreign Trade.

ORGANIZATION. Unlike trade within the country, external trade was forbidden to private enterprise and remained an exclusive state monopoly. The urgent task of achieving the greatest possible self-sufficiency (autarchy), the need for careful planning of imports so that they would satisfy the demands for industrialization, and the possibility of using the country's growing buying power for political ends and revolutionary objectives actuated the government to keep its hold on foreign trade. A People's Commissariat for Foreign Trade took charge of exports and imports, trade treaties were concluded, and, if necessary, concessions to foreign capitalists were granted.

PRACTICE. During the first two Five-Year Plans, a change was gradually effected with regard to the type of exports and imports. Raw materials such as furs, timber, oil, and such agricultural products as wheat had always constituted the bulk of the country's foreign trade; and in the first years after the Revolution these commodities continued to lead among Russia's exports. Often they were sold at very low prices in order to pay for imports urgently needed for economic as well as political reasons, and this led to bitter accusations of dumping and to grave international tension. In time, successful attempts were made to shift to manufactured goods, which could still be sold at low prices because of the living standards within the country, but which better benefited the country's economy. However, the level of foreign trade before the Revolution was reached at no time after it. The total volume remained low, and toward the beginning of the Third Five-Year Plan it was further reduced when political considerations brought a shift from Germany and England, Russia's former best customers, to the United States, which offered less promising markets.

PROBLEMS

1. Discuss the introduction and significance of collective farming.
2. Discuss the status of agriculture as a result of collectivization.
3. Discuss the importance of foreign trade monopoly for the Soviet system.

CHAPTER XLIII

LIFE IN THE U.S.S.R.

THE FAMILY

Revolutionary Legislation. The effect of the upheaval of 1917 on the daily life of the average Russian was overwhelming. Existing ties, denounced as bourgeois, were dissolved; and the family as a social institution was undermined. In December, 1917, a decree was published (and in 1918 this was followed up by a marriage law) which stipulated that only civil marriage carried legality. Marriage formalities were reduced to registration; and divorce was facilitated— a simple notification from one marriage partner to the other, and, if necessary, an agreement regarding the care of the children being all that was demanded. Illegitimate children gained equal rights with legitimate ones. Abortion was legalized in 1920.

Need for Reversal of Policy. Immediate practical results were felt in the relationship of parents and children. Homes of rich and poor were broken up and political disagreements between the older and the younger generations, combined with economic changes, added to the disintegration of society. Roaming bands of orphans and fugitive youths became a public nuisance and menace. Famines, poor housing conditions, and—most of all—shifting, redistributing, and relocating millions of people menaced all familiar institutions and altered many moral values. The Soviet government found itself faced with the necessity of creating a new and stable basis for social relationships by re-establishing and then by bettering prewar living conditions. But poverty and internal ideological struggles prevented efficient measures, and it was not until the late 1920's that a definite program was adopted. By then, the mores of the people had overcome the appeal of political ideologies; since no law could change the fundamental concept of monogamy, and since promiscuity was checked by forces inherent in nature and in pre-established social conventions, normal family life slowly returned.

Re-establishment of Family. In 1935 the whole socialist theory of the family was revised; under pressure of economic and demographic factors and despite the denunciations of those who feared an interruption in the development towards a socialist society, the family was again recognized as the foundation of the state. Abortion, which at one time had reached a level 50 per cent higher than births, was forbidden unless medical reasons made it necessary. Laws were promulgated in 1936 providing bonuses and tax exemptions for large families. The divorce rate was checked by law in the same year; and in 1944 further stringent conditions were imposed, including high fees and an investigation into the reasons for divorce. Common-law marriages no longer received the protection extended to legal marriages.

Position of Women. In line with the professed ideals of the Soviet government, attempts were made with the changes in family relations to improve the social position of women and to guarantee them equality with men. Local laws among "backward" ethnic groups allowing polygamy and child marriage were abolished, and prostitution was fought everywhere. Positions in all professions were opened to women and their pay was raised to equal that of men. For the sake of employed mothers, nurseries (*crèches*) and kindergartens were founded and mothers were guaranteed their normal wages for a period of six to eight weeks before and after childbirth (this time span was considerably reduced in the period from 1930 to 1944). Yet the percentage of women engaged in working for a living did not increase until industrialization was speeded up in the interest of national defense, when the labor shortage was painfully felt. The Communist party then began to exercise pressure upon all who were not otherwise engaged, and women undertook to seek employment, preferably in light industries. During the Second World War more than half of all persons employed were female; in the medical field, their numbers reached almost 75 per cent of the total.

PLANS FOR THE FUTURE. Likewise, steps were contemplated to raise the position of the housewife and to ease her burden. Plans were laid even to build whole "socialist cities, free of drudgery," with communal kitchens, dining rooms, and laundries. But this program could not be executed; and owing to collectivization in rural districts, urbanization in both European and Asiatic Russia, and the constant arbitrary shifting of populations, the housing situation rather deteriorated and the burden of the housewife remained a heavy one.

EDUCATION

Uniform School Laws. While the concepts of family life were undergoing constant changes, the Soviet government found it doubly necessary to pay attention to the education of the young generation. In 1918 was promulgated the first Soviet Uniform School Statute, which reduced the customary discipline of tsarist schools, deprived the church of all influence, and emphasized manual instead of intellectual training. But relaxation of discipline in the period of civil war led to an exodus of pupils from the schools and also to a great decline in the number of educational institutions—two factors which combined to lower the already deficient scholastic standards. Only after political stabilization was achieved in 1923 could a new statute of the "Uniform School" be worked out to check the growth of ignorance. It emphasized the teaching of social relationships and reduced emphasis on mastery of facts and methods. A program of "complex themes and projects" was outlined, paralleling so-called "progressive" trends in other countries; but it did not work because broad concepts, such as nature or society, were made topics for discussion among pupils who had not acquired the most elementary tools of learning. The same year, 1923, brought a reorganization of universities. Like the school program, it led to a lowering of former scholastic standards, for discrimination was exercised against the intelligentsia and their children, regardless of ability, and preference was given to Communist workers. Moreover, strict ideological supervision hampered the free development of professor and student.

End of Experimentation. The years 1925 to 1930, consequently, led to a revision of the entire educational system. Political indoctrination was reduced and, despite lack of competent teachers, emphasis was placed instead on reading, writing, arithmetic, language, geography, and literature. Compulsory primary education, planned in tsarist times but unfulfilled because of the outbreak of war, became a fact for almost all of Russia, regardless of race or religion. The introduction of a simplified alphabet helped to carry out this program. Discipline also was reintroduced; and physical culture received special attention, with stress on co-operative sports which simultaneously served military demands.

Ideological Reversal. After the promulgation of the Second Five-Year Plan, history also came again into its own and constituted a focus of national interest; ideological perspectives were sacrificed to factual knowledge. For the higher schools children of skilled personnel gained equal attendance rights with Communists; in universities, although technical training was still favored, the traditional faculties were re-established and served to promote an understanding of scientific and technical methods as well as of the relationship of science to human life and society. By 1936, the former authority of the teacher returned, grading and examinations were revived, and strictest discipline was insisted upon. Even school uniforms again appeared.

Schools after 1941. During the Second World War, coeducation in elementary schools of cities was to a large extent abolished, because the authorities came to consider the physical growth and intellectual needs of girls and boys as too divergent. Only in institutes of higher education, where students enrolled at the age of fifteen, was coeducation maintained. Thirteen universities with about seventeen thousand (graduate liberal arts) students, three hundred and eighty professional schools, and many local universities and lecture courses provided Russia proper with the facilities needed for educating the elite of the coming generation. These facilities were open to all; but unless stipends, which were generally available for good students, were provided, a special fee had to be paid. After completion of their training in technical schools, students were often obliged to serve for a number of years at whatever place the state authorities decided to use their skills.

Adult Education. Inasmuch as the family had been deprived of much of its significance and many of its tasks, and inasmuch as the church had lost its dominant position, various new institutions had to be created to supplement the educational work of schools and universities. The *Comsomol* (Communist youth organization) attended to ideological indoctrination as well as to physical training of the young; beginning in 1936 it also took a growing interest in raising the cultural level of its members, in teaching them discipline, and in strengthening their moral fiber. Adult and evening schools were opened in all parts of the country and, conducted in languages of the various nationalities, brought the elements of education to all Soviet citizens, young and old. Press, radio, motion pictures, and lectures of all kinds were devoted to the spread of learning, information, and social theory. Museums were sponsored everywhere; and thousands of libraries were founded, with a total of some one hundred and fifty million popular books and almost as many volumes for research.

LIVING CONDITIONS

Wages and Prices. Naturally, the Soviet government was aware of the close relationship of family life, education, and general living conditions. Its efforts to improve these, however, met with great difficulties. The Revolution had ruined the high standards of the upper class without improving immediately the economic situation of the workingman, although his social position was changed promptly. Wages rose, it is true, but so did prices—except for rents; goods fixed at low prices could be purchased only within the allotted scanty rations and often necessitated waiting in long queues. Up to 40 per cent of the total wages were used for taxes, trade-union dues, social insurance (old age, funeral), and educational projects; wages were withheld at the source for these purposes. The withheld wages served also to build sanitariums and to provide free medical and dental care, although if specialists were called in, they were allowed to charge an extra fee.

Working Hours. An eight-hour working day was introduced after the Revolution, and during the times of reconstruction this was lowered to seven. Unemployment disappeared by 1930; thereafter a shortage of labor arose which caused the government to exercise economic and other pressure on people so that they would accept jobs wherever needed under the Five-Year Plan and stay on the job. Experiments were also made with the abolition of Sundays and the introduction of uninterrupted workday weeks; factories were operated without pause, and workers labored in shifts of five or six days, followed by a holiday which differed according to the shift. But this plan caused confusion and dissatisfaction, ruined industrial machinery by overworking it, and made impossible common enjoyment of holidays. The number of working days per year was scarcely less than in prewar times, and two weeks' yearly vacation just balanced the loss of the religious holidays celebrated in tsarist times. In 1940 the week with six eight-hour days and a Sunday was reintroduced.

Political Supervision. Since political reliability could not be expected from every worker, strict supervision was exercised; and this often poisoned the atmosphere. Office workers and intellectuals from tsarist times, even though most of them served loyally, worked under particularly adverse conditions; only with difficulties could they find security in the new society. Those who were considered unreliable were without compunction shifted to distant regions; families were broken up, productive work was interrupted, and intense misery resulted. Labor camps in Siberia and in Arctic regions were filled with many who would have willingly co-operated at the places for which they were trained; and under the pretext of tasks necessary for society as a whole, involuntary work with all its attendant distress was enormously increased. As time went on, supervision was not relaxed but augmented, and both the Second and the Third Five-Year Plans provided for special vigilance and strictest control.

SUMMARY

However harsh the measures undertaken, they were generally explained by the needs arising from a period of transition linking a capitalist and a socialist era. Modernizing Russian family life, spreading education to all classes and all nationalities of the empire, opening schools and professions to married and unmarried women, and adopting new standards of working conditions on a basis of equal rights and opportunities—these achievements, notwithstanding difficulties, shortcomings, and coercion, were considered the basis for a better future which a coming generation, trained by a new society in a different spirit, would achieve.

PROBLEMS

1. Discuss the influence of the Bolshevist Revolution on family life.
2. Discuss the influence of the Revolution on educational standards.
3. Discuss the position of women in the U.S.S.R.

CHAPTER XLIV

SCIENCE, RELIGION, AND ARTS

SCIENCE

Conflict between Science and Religion. In twentieth-century Russia, which found its inspiration in Karl Marx's materialistic conception of history, a conflict between scientific and metaphysical thinking was inevitable. This was not altogether a continuation of the nineteenth-century European conflict between science and religion, which had resulted from widespread implicit faith in the progress of mankind through a deeper understanding of the laws of nature and their application to human affairs. The conflict in Soviet Russia was more of a practical than a philosophical nature; science was promoted as a means rather than as an idealistic goal, and religion was fought as a material obstacle rather than as an outmoded attitude.

Science in Tsarist Times. When the Communists took over Russia, the study of the natural sciences flourished and the Academy of Sciences enjoyed high rank in the world. Founded in 1725, its fame had rested during its initial stages mainly on foreign, particularly German, scholars; the physicist Euler and the botanist Steller were among its most celebrated members. The first Russian of great repute was Lomonosov, and it was after him that the

Academy became a truly national institution. During the nineteenth century, its members Petrov and Lenz held distinguished places in physics, Ber (Baer) and especially Pavlov (nervous reflexes) in biology, Mechnikov in physiology, Chernyshev and Vernadsky in geology, Belopolsky in astronomy, and Soloviev and Kluchevsky in history. In addition, many outsiders, such as Mendeleyev, who developed the atomic table, enjoyed equal or greater fame.

Soviet Academy of Sciences. Lenin recognized the importance of maintaining existing standards. Science was furthered in every way, and the geologist Karpinsky was elected president of a reformed Academy. But only after the consolidation of the country following the period of civil war was it possible to continue the great tradition. Branches of the Academy were set up throughout the country to train scientific personnel, stimulate interest, and broaden the basis of technological studies. Various divisions were created for natural sciences, history, literature, economics, and other fields. By 1939 there existed some one hundred and fifty institutions, museums, and observatories. Eminent men emerged or continued their studies begun in tsarist times; the historians Pokrovsky, Volgin, and Tarle, the physicians Bogomolets, Burdenko, Filatov, and Stern (first woman member of the Academy), the physicist Kapitsa and the chemist Semënov, T. Lysenko in agriculture, and many others in all fields of science contributed to the advancement of mankind's understanding of natural and social forces.

Academic Freedom. The state took an interest in their work and—through the establishment of laboratories and research institutes and through "authors' certificates," prizes, honors, orders, and cash premiums for inventors—endeavored to stimulate the greatest possible productivity. On the other hand, the state supervised the attitudes of its scientists and the political significance of their work. If their views or teachings were contrary to the accepted ideology, they were removed or their work was disavowed. In 1929 almost one-third of the members of the Academy, including some of its most distinguished men, were purged, and again a few years later the work of others was interrupted and their books were revised or disappeared from the market. Thus science both profited and lost through state interference; but as a whole the achievements in Soviet Russia, though not reaching in originality and scope the level of the United States or Germany, kept up with the standards of Western countries.

Arctic Institute. One of the special fields of Soviet scientific endeavor was the Arctic regions, their possibilities, problems, and resources. In 1930 a separate institute was created to continue work which had been carried on from the time of Peter the Great. This comprised investigating the wealth in iron, zinc, gold, and furs of Russia's Arctic regions and the cultures of the inhabitants; it comprised also establishing communication lines and transportation centers for the dawning air-borne age. Under the direction of Professor Schmidt, and often with the help of involuntary labor, considerable advance was made. Ports were founded and the northeastern passage became a regular trade route. Attempts were even undertaken to develop the Arctic parts for agricultural production, but—partly because of inadequate and inefficient personnel—progress was slow.

RELIGION

Materialism *vs.* Religion. Whereas Soviet activity in the field of sciences was vigorous from the very first, no matter whether it was stimulated by imperative needs for technological progress or by conscientious promotion of man's scientific understanding of the world surrounding him, Soviet attitude toward religion was vacillating and the pronouncements of the leaders were contradictory. As heirs to atheistic materialism, the Soviets found themselves from the beginning in a paradoxical position in a country strongly subject to religious influences, whether Orthodox, Catholic, Protestant, Mohammedan, or Jewish.

Attack on Orthodoxy. After the overthrow of Tsarism, the Synod of the Orthodox church, which Peter the Great had introduced and which under Pobedonostzev had exercised such unwholesome political influence, was abolished by the provisional government. It was replaced by a patriarchate in Moscow such as had existed before Peter's time, the metropolitan Tikhon becoming the first holder of the office. True to the liberal concepts of the February Revolution, full equality was guaranteed to all faiths. But upon seizure of power by the Communists, the new ideals and values propagated by a militant materialism clashed with traditional religious beliefs. The Orthodox church, which comprised seven-tenths of the population, was the first to suffer, but the Catholics with their Roman connections soon found themselves no less exposed. Fearful disorders occurred; churches were desecrated, church lands were confiscated, and church control of education as well as of politics was eliminated. The Orthodox church and its patriarch Tikhon raised their voices in outraged protests, denouncing the internal atheistic trends and the Soviet's political orientation in external affairs, and crowned their opposition by the excommunication of all who adhered to Bolshevism.

DISSOLUTION OF SYNOD. Their opposition was in vain. The new constitution provided for complete separation of state and church and for prohibition of political interference by the Orthodox. It deprived the clergy of citizenship rights and, in 1921, banned all public religious instruction for children under eighteen years of age. Theological seminaries were closed, church publications were forbidden, and acts of brutality were committed against clergymen, monks, and nuns. Many perished, others were exiled, and churches and cloisters were closed. In the following year, the surrender of all church treasures, including sacred objects, was demanded for famine relief; and when in some instances the surrender was refused, the patriarch and many bishops were arrested, the Synod was dissolved, and more prelates, Orthodox as well as Catholic, were tried, killed, or banished.

LEAGUE OF ATHEISTS. But despite propaganda and oppression, the people continued to visit the remaining churches. For this reason as well as for fear of repercussions in international relations, the government found itself compelled to make compromises. Gradually permission was granted to religious societies to lease buildings for worship. Thereupon, the patriarch issued a statement abjuring his former attitude and exhorting his flock to obey the state as God-ordained authority. Later, he severed connections with the bitterly antagonistic churches of the émigrés abroad. These acts led to abatement of religious persecution by the Soviets, and in 1927 a provisional synod was authorized which entered into negotiations with the government to obtain greater religious freedom. But the assault on religion was continued by a League of Militant Atheists formed in 1925. Under its auspices and under Communist pressure, polls were held and, "by request of many communities," churches were closed wherever possible. Universities, newspapers, cinemas, and trade-unions held religious institutions up to ridicule, and the spreading of science was used as counterweight against "religious superstition."

Revival of Orthodox Church. Enjoying full though unofficial support from the authorities, the atheist movement grew, numbering three million members in 1930 and five million in 1934; yet, it did not succeed in winning over the masses or in erecting an efficient bulwark against a religious revival. The persecution of the church served rather to purify the organization, and those who despite all threats held firm to their beliefs constituted a firmer and stronger fundament than the church had previously possessed. The government could not fail to recognize the inefficacy of the antireligious drive; and spurred by the threat arising from an emerging Hitler power in Germany which made national unity imperative, a completely new course was charted. In 1936, the "historical mission of Christianity" was officially recognized, support was withdrawn from the Militant Atheists, tolerance was propagated, religious feast days were reintroduced, church bells sounded again, and although public religious instruction of children was still prohibited, the new constitution eliminated the existing disabilities of the clergy.

WAR AND RELIGION. Further concessions were made when war broke out in 1941. True to its stand through the ages, the Orthodox church promptly supported the national cause against the foreign invader and offered prayers for Soviet victory. In order to rally all forces, the government re-established full freedom of the churches, and in September the chief atheist newspaper was discontinued. Two years later the metropolitan of Moscow, Sergius, was for the first time received by Stalin, and thereupon elected patriarch, thus filling a position vacant since the death of Tikhon almost a score of years earlier. A "Department for Orthodox Church Affairs" was established under the Council of the People's Commissars and began to constitute, as of old, a link between state and church. Religious seminaries were reopened and a reconciliation was effected with the Orthodox religious groups of émigrés. When in January, 1945, after Sergius' death the metropolitan Alexis was enthroned as patriarch, the Orthodox church gained a recognized place within the new Russian society.

TRIUMPH OF CHURCH. After the miscarriage of the official drive against Orthodoxy in the first ten years of Communist rule and the indirect fight carried on through the atheist movement during the second decade, the Marxist attitude towards religion was thus abandoned. Significantly enough, it was not on the basis of international brotherhood, which formed the great principle of both Christianity and Communism, but on the ground of national interest that the reconciliation was effected.

ARTS

Communist Trends in the Arts. During the years of its struggle against the church, the Soviet government never lost sight of the people's desire for pageantry as well as spiritual nourishment and, partly as a measure against religion, fostered interest in music, theater, art, and literature. Even during the years of civil war, it sponsored artistic and literary activities in line with the tradition of tsarist times. A special organization, the "Proletcult," and a "Trade-Union of Art Workers" were founded to stimulate artistic creation and align it with political trends. But accent on social consciousness in accord with the basic concepts of the new state often stifled the free and full development of artistic expression, and state sponsorship and censorship contributed their share to limiting the artist's initiative. On the other hand, commercialism in art, including film and radio, was eliminated; the appeal to the sensational was suppressed, and new forms emerged, exploiting the educational and technical possibilities of the new means of expression. In general, those endeavors were promoted which were of a co-operative rather than of an individualistic character; city planning had precedence over single buildings, the theater ensemble over the star.

Literature. The development of all arts in Soviet Russia followed, as a whole, political trends. In the period up to 1921, destructive, negative, and revolutionary productions prevailed; from 1921 to 1933, experiments in new forms of expression were carried on; the period of 1934 until 1941 witnessed a revival of the national tradition; and the years since 1941 reflected war and victory. Yet, not many men of genius sufficient to represent the spirit of the era emerged. In the field of literature, M. Gorky (1868–1936), A. Blok (1880–1921), and Alexis Tolstoy (1882–1945), all prominent before the Revolution, remained the chief exponents. Among the younger generation, Konstantin Simonov, Vera Tuber, Alexander Korneichuk, and others were applauded, but none as yet has gained fame beyond the Soviet borders. The drama, whose foremost masters in tsarist times, Pushkin, Gogol, Turgenev, Leo Tolstoy, Chekov, and Gorky, were all primarily novelists, possessed no one who equaled the early leading figures or even matched the lesser talents of the nineteenth century, Pisemsky and Ostrovsky. Even in quality of performance, the theater after 1918 had difficulty in challenging the standards of earlier periods. Radio and film, however, perhaps because they were more expressive of the modern age, showed great accomplishments, the film benefiting particularly from inspired authorship and eminent directors such as S. Eisenstein.

Music. In the field of music, two composers of pre-Revolutionary days, the popular Myaskovsky and Prokofiev, retained their high rank; but here a member of the younger generation, D. Shostakovich, succeeded in sharing and later surpassing their fame.

Painting and Architecture. In painting, little of durable value was created. Upon assumption of power, the Bolshevists dissolved the Academy of Fine Arts and nationalized all great art collections; but productively, they added little to existing treasures. Far more was achieved in the realm of architecture, where gigantic undertakings in industrial expansion, in city planning, and in public buildings with their accent on functional ends set tasks worth while in themselves and commensurate with the spirit of the age. Here it was also possible to evoke interest and cultivate talent among the many nationalities of the Union, whose advancement remained one of the chief concerns of socialist rule.

PROBLEMS

1. Discuss the attitude of the Soviet government toward the advancement of science.
2. Discuss the causes for the collapse of the Communist fight against the church.
3. Describe the contributions of Soviet art.

CHAPTER XLV

FOREIGN RELATIONS I: EUROPE

The vast expanse of Russia and her enormous resources in natural wealth and manpower made it possible for the Soviets to carry out at home the experiment of socialism which the Revolutionary leaders originally considered feasible only if undertaken on a world-wide scale. But in her foreign policies, Russia had to adapt herself to the pattern imposed by the international community of nations and the traditions of capitalistic powers.

SOVIET OBJECTIVES

The predominant objectives of Russian foreign policies up to 1934 were the preservation of the Soviet system in Russia and the spread of communist ideology abroad. Territorial aggrandizement, Pan-Slav ambitions, and imperialistic aims were denounced and rejected; the ways of traditional diplomatic intercourse were likewise temporarily given up, and economic agencies, trade headquarters, and information bureaus attended to many diplomatic functions. Opportunities for the furtherance of communism were seized as they offered themselves, giving Soviet foreign policies a constantly changing and unfathomable appearance.

ANGLO - RUSSIAN RELATIONS SINCE 1856

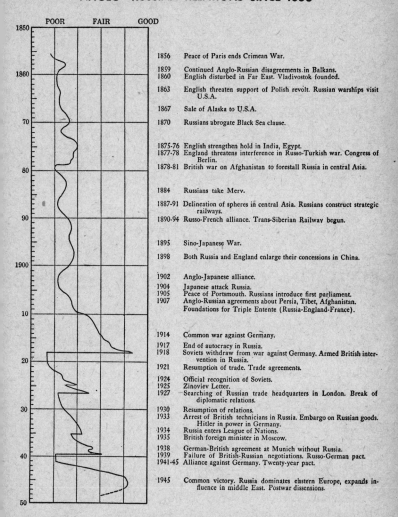

	POOR	FAIR	GOOD	

1856   Peace of Paris ends Crimean War.

1859   Continued Anglo-Russian disagreements in Balkans.
1860   English disturbed in Far East. Vladivostok founded.

1863   English threaten support of Polish revolt. Russian warships visit U.S.A.

1867   Sale of Alaska to U.S.A.

1870   Russians abrogate Black Sea clause.

1875-76   English strengthen hold in India, Egypt.
1877-78   England threatens interference in Russo-Turkish war. Congress of Berlin.
1878-81   British war on Afghanistan to forestall Russia in central Asia.

1884   Russians take Merv.

1887-91   Delineation of spheres in central Asia. Russians construct strategic railways.
1890-94   Russo-French alliance. Trans-Siberian Railway begun.

1895   Sino-Japanese War.

1898   Both Russia and England enlarge their concessions in China.

1902   Anglo-Japanese alliance.

1904   Japanese attack Russia.
1905   Peace of Portsmouth. Russians introduce first parliament.
1907   Anglo-Russian agreements about Persia, Tibet, Afghanistan. Foundations for Triple Entente (Russia-England-France).

1914   Common war against Germany.

1917   End of autocracy in Russia.
1918   Soviets withdraw from war against Germany. Armed British intervention in Russia.

1921   Resumption of trade. Trade agreements.

1924   Official recognition of Soviets.
1925   Zinoviev Letter.
1927   Searching of Russian trade headquarters in London. Break of diplomatic relations.

1930   Resumption of relations.
1933   Arrest of British technicians in Russia. Embargo on Russian goods. Hitler in power in Germany.
1934   Russia enters League of Nations.
1935   British foreign minister in Moscow.

1938   German-British agreement at Munich without Russia.
1939   Failure of British-Russian negotiations. Russo-German pact.
1941-45   Alliance against Germany. Twenty-year pact.

1945   Common victory. Russia dominates eastern Europe, expands influence in middle East. Postwar dissensions.

ANGLO–RUSSIAN relations have been tense except for brief periods of co-operation against a common enemy. Rivalry began in the time of Peter the Great when Russia started to build a navy on the Baltic and to change the balance of power in Europe. In the 19th century it was sharpened by Russia's growing influence in the Balkans and her advance to the Mediterranean, as well as by rivalry in the Far East and central Asia. In the 20th, the reorganization of the British empire and questions of economic and strategic domination in the Middle East have not relieved the tension.

FIRST PHASE: ISOLATION

Versailles.   The first period of Soviet rule was marked by isolation: civil war, foreign intervention, and geographical seclusion made normal intercourse with other nations virtually impossible. The professed communist aim of world revolution and self-determination of all peoples also contributed to the exclusion of the Soviets from international decisions; furthermore, the organization of the Comintern as a means for achieving their ends prevented participation in the undertakings of the capitalist and imperialistic world whose diplomats were busy rearranging the political map of Europe. The Soviet government was denied a seat at Versailles, although the communist problem as such and Western fears of Russia's future aspirations influenced the decisions of the Versailles statesmen and the treaty which they contrived.

SECOND PHASE: REOPENING OF CONTACTS

First International Treaties, 1921.   It was the conclusion of the Civil War and the adoption of the N.E.P. in 1921 which ended Russia's isolation and introduced a new phase into Soviet foreign relations. A number of important treaties were completed—particularly with neighbors—and diplomatic activities were resumed. Peace with Poland, commercial arrangements with Germany and Sweden, and friendship treaties with Turkey, Persia, Afghanistan, and Outer Mongolia were concluded. Russia's voice was also heard in other international questions, such as the neutralization of the Aland Islands.

Relations with Western Europe.   But in its relationship with Western European nations and America, the Soviet government made little progress. Although it offered substantial economic advantages and succeeded in opening commercial intercourse with England and Italy, its demands for outright diplomatic recognition, its repudiation of prewar debts, and its communistic orientation and propaganda prevented the re-establishment of normal relations. In 1921, the Russians were again excluded from an international congress—the Washington Disarmament Conference; and when in the following year they were invited to a conference held at Genoa, they found few common interests with their former allies.

RAPALLO, 1922.   In their political isolation the Russians turned to the other great isolated nation of Europe, their former enemy, Germany. Exposed to the demands of foreign oil concessionaries, hindered in their international policies by Western diplomacy after Versailles, and defeated in their proposals for general disarmament by Allied opposition under French leadership, they made advances to Germany. Their proposals were well received, for Germany's foreign office under Minister Rathenau envisaged the resumption of Bismarck's policy, which had held friendship with Russia the pivot of German security. In exchange for *de jure* recognition by Germany, a treaty was concluded at Rapallo, near Genoa, which provided for close economic and political collaboration. Together, the two countries soon exercised influence of great importance in international affairs. When the French in 1923 marched into the German Ruhr and when the Allies decided to hand over the territory of Memel to Lithuania, the Soviet government showed its political orientation by denouncing both acts and by further strengthening its economic ties with Germany.

RECOGNITION BY WESTERN EUROPE, 1924. In order to prevent exclusive co-operation of Russia and Germany, the Western powers thereupon began more serious negotiations with Russia; and in 1924, although the United States still held aloof, England, Italy, and France extended official recognition to the Soviet government and supplemented their move by trade treaties. A number of smaller countries including Norway, Austria, Greece, Hungary, and Mexico followed their example.

LOCARNO, 1925. This second phase of Soviet foreign policy, which essentially constituted the struggle for recognition begun in 1921, drew to a close in 1925. It had brought advantages to the Communists, who now enjoyed both official recognition and economic relations with most European powers as well as close co-operation with Germany. But by 1925—the year of the Locarno Pact—it became evident that the Rapallo system was not to last and that Soviet isolation persisted. Already before the conclusion of the Locarno Pact, recurring incidents had alarmed the Russians. A diplomatic agent, M. Vorovsky, had been murdered in Switzerland and no satisfactory action was taken by the Swiss government; in Germany, the Russian trade headquarters had been raided in search of political propaganda material; and in England, a storm was raised over the so-called "Zinoviev letter" which purported to contain instructions by the Russian minister Zinoviev to the British Communist party and was interpreted as official Russian interference in British internal affairs.

Furthermore, the French and English persisted in their opposition to disarmament. After the Locarno Pact, Germany, although concluding a nonaggression agreement and continuing her commercial connection with Russia, even extending credit of three hundred million gold marks, politically veered away and began to reorient herself towards the Western world. This was followed by her entry into the League of Nations and her participation in conferences at Geneva, from which the Soviets felt excluded as long as the Vorovsky affair was not satisfactorily settled.

Threat of Renewed Isolation. Facing an increasingly united Western world, the Russians thereupon began to turn their attention to eastern Europe and central Asia, and to advocate as a countermeasure an Eastern Bloc or "Eastern Locarno." But at first they were not successful; for in 1926 a totalitarian government under Pilsudsky was established in Poland, which instead of accepting Russian advances allied itself with Rumania and tried—though without success—to form an anti-Soviet alliance with the Baltic states. The Russians thus found themselves stalled in their external policies, and the report of the government submitted to the All-Soviet Congress in 1927 reflected the fears of the Soviet leaders. It depicted the situation as critical, with England a persistent opponent and France an ally of hostile and reactionary Poland and Rumania. It called attention to the raids upon the Soviet embassy in China and upon the Soviet trade headquarters in London (which led to a temporary rupture of diplomatic relations with Britain), to the murder of the Communist leader Voikov in Poland, and to incidents in Persia, Geneva, Italy, and Greece—all, it was asserted, inspired by imperialistic headquarters in Paris and London. It denounced the League of Nations as an organ of French and English imperialism and as no instrument of peace; it deplored the failure of disarmament and the resultant needs for military preparedness which reacted unfavorably on the internal progress of Communism. Except for a precarious friendship with Germany, Turkey, and Persia, the leaders thus found no comfort in the international situation.

THIRD PHASE: INTERNATIONAL COLLABORATION

Reversal of Policies. It was under such conditions that the Soviets entered the third phase of their international relations, which consisted in an abatement of their propaganda for world revolution and in increased collaboration with other nations. While continuing

GERMAN - RUSSIAN RELATIONS SINCE 1870

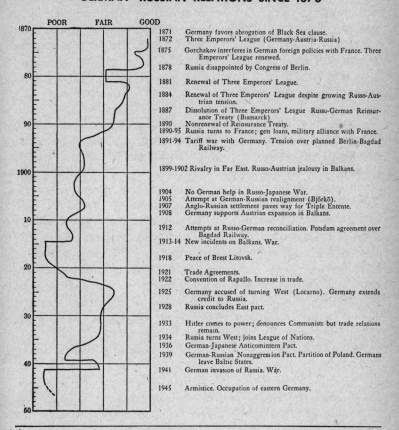

POOR	FAIR	GOOD

1871 Germany favors abrogation of Black Sea clause.
1872 Three Emperors' League (Germany-Austria-Russia)

1875 Gorchakov interferes in German foreign policies with France. Three Emperors' League renewed.

1878 Russia disappointed by Congress of Berlin.

1881 Renewal of Three Emperors' League.

1884 Renewal of Three Emperors' League despite growing Russo-Austrian tension.

1887 Dissolution of Three Emperors' League Russo-German Reinsurance Treaty (Bismarck)
1890 Nonrenewal of Reinsurance Treaty.
1890-95 Russia turns to France; gets loans, military alliance with France.
1891-94 Tariff war with Germany. Tension over planned Berlin-Bagdad Railway.

1899-1902 Rivalry in Far East. Russo-Austrian jealousy in Balkans.

1904 No German help in Russo-Japanese War.
1905 Attempt at German-Russian realignment (Björkö).
1907 Anglo-Russian settlement paves way for Triple Entente.
1908 Germany supports Austrian expansion in Balkans.

1912 Attempts at Russo-German reconciliation. Potsdam agreement over Bagdad Railway.
1913-14 New incidents on Balkans. War.

1918 Peace of Brest Litovsk.

1921 Trade Agreements.
1922 Convention of Rapallo. Increase in trade.

1925 Germany accused of turning West (Locarno). Germany extends credit to Russia.
1928 Russia concludes East pact.

1933 Hitler comes to power; denounces Communists but trade relations remain.
1934 Russia turns West; joins League of Nations.
1936 German-Japanese Anticomintern Pact.
1939 German-Russian Nonaggression Pact. Partition of Poland. Germans leave Baltic States.
1941 German invasion of Russia. War.

1945 Armistice. Occupation of eastern Germany.

THIS chart should be read in conjunction with that on page 267 showing trends in Anglo-Russian relations. It indicates that good German-Russian relations meant general peace for Europe, as a rule, and that bad ones were to be interpreted as an alarm signal. Two critical moments came, first, in 1890, as a result of the dismissal of Bismarck and non-renewal of the Reinsurance Treaty, and, second, in 1934, as a result of the consolidation of Nazi power over Germany. In view of Russia's persistent need for industrial goods and Germany's continuous demand for grain and raw materials and of the normal absence of territorial competition, the lack of harmony cannot be explained by diplomatic disputes, Pan-Slavism and Pan-Germanism, tariff wars, etc. It was rather extraneous issues—the Balkan situation and a European balance-of-power system—which have determined the relationship of the past three decades.

their policies towards Germany, they relented in their opposition ·to England and established satisfactory commercial relations; they also began to modify their attitude towards France, despite her alignment with Poland and Rumania. Both England and France welcomed the change. Resigned to Soviet refusal to honor prewar debts and to Russian insistence on making proselytes for Soviet political doctrine, they now considered the re-entry of Russia into the concert of nations as at least a step in the direction of stabilization and the reconstruction of the European continent.

Kellogg Pact and East Protocol. In August, 1928, Russia added her signature to the Kellogg Pact, although with reservations; for without disarmament she considered it ineffectual. Finally, in February, 1929, she realized her plans for an Eastern Locarno, and the "East Protocol" (Litvinov Pact) to outlaw war was signed by the Soviet Union, Poland, Latvia, Estonia, and Rumania, and later by Turkey, Persia, and the city of Danzig. The pact was a demonstration rather than an effective weapon, and needed practical supplementation such as was achieved only later through nonaggression pacts with some of the participants. Yet, it reassured the Soviets and constituted a victory in their drive for security, making possible a less intransigent attitude in their over-all policies.

Normalization of Foreign Relations. This phase of Soviet postwar diplomacy lasted until 1934. In addition to the East Protocol and the normalization of foreign relations, it brought resumption of Russo-English relations in 1929 and a nonaggression pact with France in 1932. Litvinov replaced Chicherin, who had headed the Soviet foreign office through the years of the N.E.P. and the East Protocol, and emphasized the continuity of Soviet foreign policies in the direction of watchful co-operation. Small incidents as they occurred in Poland or Finland were more easily disposed of now, and a *modus vivendi* was found even with regard to Japan and other so-far hostile countries. Indeed, foreign affairs were gradually subordinated to the great tasks set by the Five-Year Plan, and in a time when the economies in the capitalist countries suffered the greatest setback, nothing seemed so beneficial for the advancement of Soviet aims abroad as successful and constructive activity at home.

Realignment. In 1933 Adolf Hitler came to power in Germany. At first his advent did not mark a departure from the path already followed by Germany. Although vigorous verbal attacks were launched against the communist system, economic relations with Russia remained in effect untouched. Yet, as a precautionary measure, Russia's attitude towards France became increasingly conciliatory, and special efforts were made to preserve satisfactory relations with neighboring countries and with England. More important events occurred, however, in non-European countries. In America, a change of administration in the United States brought, finally, official recognition of the Soviet government there—a move not imitated by the Central and South American republics, which withheld recognition until the years of the Second World War. In the Far East, on the other hand, war clouds gathered, and renewed Japanese restlessness constituted a peril to the Soviet system.

SUMMARY

The development of Russian foreign relations with Europe from 1918 to 1934 thus shows successive phases of isolation, struggle for recognition, end of isolation through the Rapallo Treaty, and a renewed feeling of isolation following the Locarno Pact. This situation was relieved by continued economic co-operation with capitalist countries and ultimately, in 1929, by the "East Protocol." Not until Hitler began actively and aggressively to influence international relations in 1934 was another change called for.

PROBLEMS

1. Discuss the significance of the Russo-German alignment after Rapallo.
2. Discuss the factors impeding a rapprochement of Russia and the Western European nations.
3. Describe the relationship of Russia and her neighbors.

CHAPTER XLVI

FOREIGN RELATIONS II: ASIA AND AMERICA

CENTRAL ASIA

Abrogation of Imperialism. Russia's international relations in Europe were essentially governed by forces beyond Soviet control; in relations with Eastern countries, however, it was the Soviet government which held the initiative. Promptly upon their assumption of power the Communists denounced the imperialistic policies of their predecessors and voluntarily abrogated the advantages which Russia had secured at the expense of weaker nations in Asia, including those advantages gained by the Anglo-Russian Agreement of 1907. They gave up the former protective attitude towards Oriental peoples and renounced banking rights, collection of debts, monopolies, and all other one-sided privileges. Then as soon as civil war ended in 1921, the government, true to its promise, on a basis of equality concluded treaties of amity with Persia, Afghanistan, Mongolia, and Turkey. The last-named power obtained the fortress of Kars, taken by Russia in 1878. In exchange, Turkey released Batum, which was first incorporated into Georgia; and in 1922 when Georgia, together with parts of Armenia and Azerbaijan, formed the Transcaucasian

274

Republic and entered the U.S.S.R., Batum returned to Russian possession.

Rise of Russian Prestige. The Soviets were greatly strengthened by their policy of equality and co-operation, and thus succeeded indirectly in reducing English influence. The propagandistic value was particularly felt in Persia and Afghanistan, the two countries most resenting British interference. Russian prestige was also enhanced in Turkey, where Russia refrained from participating in the demilitarization of the Straits undertaken by the Western powers in 1923.

Trade Agreements. Once political understanding was reached, trade agreements followed. Treaties were concluded in the years 1924 to 1927, and in every instance proved highly successful. By 1927 Russia held second place in a vastly expanded Persian trade, and a strong upswing in commerce with Turkey could be noted; Afghanistan and Mongolian trade showed a corresponding rising curve, as did Sinkiang (Chinese Turkestan), with which an agreement was made in 1925.

Political Effects.

ADVANTAGES. Russian economic relations in central Asia were favored by special conditions. Geographically, Russia was more closely connected than any other power with the areas there, and raw materials produced by them were welcome for Siberia's industrialization. The foreign-trade state monopoly could therefore be relaxed for central Asia, and free private trading on a primitive bartering basis was permitted with benefit to the native populations; special tariffs were applied to goods reaching Russia across her eastern borders. Moreover, political resistance to Soviet ideological infiltration was slight in the "backward" East, where indeed one of the neighbors, Mongolia, herself abolished private property, expelled formerly dominating Chinese merchants, and began large-scale nationalization. In Sinkiang, likewise, Chinese influence and financial domination were reduced.

LIMITATIONS. After 1931, the pace of the initial successes could not be sustained; rising nationalism and religious revival checked the progress made by the Soviets. Reversals were also noticeable in economic relations with Turkey; Persia introduced high protectionist tariff walls; and world depression exercised an adverse influence even in remote central Asiatic countries. Yet, as a whole, the decade from 1921 to 1931 had fundamentally changed the economic status and the political balance and opened satisfactory prospects for the Soviet future.

FAR EAST

Far Eastern Republic. While the Communists made steady progress in central Asia, they were unsuccessful in the Far East, where their social theories clashed with more firmly established societies. The creation of a separate state in Siberia during the Civil War and its continuation as a "Far Eastern Republic" after Admiral Kolchak's death in 1920 had reduced Russian prestige and continued to influence Soviet policies adversely even after the collapse and liquidation of the "Far Eastern Republic" in 1922.

China. The greatest difficulties were encountered in China. Russia had to deal there with several warring factions. The Kuomintang party, Sun Yat-sen, the Christian General Wu, Marshal Chang Tso-lin of Manchuria, and after his death his son, each took a different attitude toward the Soviet regime in Russia and strove to use the communist ideal or communist peril as a tool for exercising pressure and gaining hegemony in internal Chinese affairs. Under these circumstances, Russian offers of friendship, renunciation of imperialistic aims, and conclusion of trade agreements remained unfruitful, and their sincerity was challenged by the various factions. Furthermore, Russian ideological and economic penetration into Sinkiang and into Mongolia, both of which were used as centers to spread communist propaganda, constituted a potential threat to China's territorial status and security.

CHINESE EASTERN RAILWAY. Among the many issues, one problem was of special importance. It concerned the ownership and management of Russia's Chinese Eastern Railway. Notwithstanding the enormous influx of Chinese settlers into railroad territory which had occurred after the construction of the line by the Russians in 1896, and notwithstanding her own over-all position with regard to other pre-Revolutionary imperialistic ventures, Russia asserted here her full prewar rights. Negotiations were protracted; and although in 1924 a treaty established diplomatic relations with the Chinese government, provided for equal rights, and arranged joint management of the railroad, no permanent settlement was reached. For the railway constituted a problem influencing the national status of

China as well as the most diverse international interests. Apart from the Chinese government, France, Britain, the United States, and Japan all considered the line a paramount asset strategically and economically; and, fearing for their own positions, they sought to forestall the expansion of Russian power and of communist ideas. Under their influence, and as a result of antirevolutionary intrigues, the 1924 treaty was cancelled; in 1926 Russian directors of the railway were taken into custody by Chinese agents and Soviet property was confiscated; in 1927 the Russian embassy was searched by Chinese soldiers; and in 1929 the Soviet consulate in Harbin was raided and delegates assembling for a meeting of the Third International were arrested. Diplomatic relations were broken, and only after prolonged negotiations at Nikolsk Ussuriisk were they restored in December, 1929. The *status quo* with regard to the Chinese Eastern Railway was re-established, but this arrangement postponed rather than solved the problem. Eventually the solution came in an unexpected direction as a result of the Sino-Japanese conflict in 1931.

Japan. The intervention of Japan on the Asiatic continent meant a threat to Russia. Russia and Japan had been hostile from the very beginning of the Bolshevist regime, and Japan had been a leading interventionist in the early period of Soviet rule. She had invaded Siberia, trying to secure a permanent foothold there, first with the help of Admiral Kolchak, later through the autonomous Far Eastern Republic. But in 1922, after the Washington Disarmament Conference, she was forced to withdraw; and in 1925 official relations were established with the Soviet government. Japan consented not only to refrain from interference in Siberia, but also to abandon her occupation of Russian northern Sakhalin, though she retained fishing rights and oil concessions there.

SALE OF CHINESE EASTERN RAILWAY. The existing status was disturbed anew in the early thirties when Japan started to intervene actively in China. Her successes brought an aggressive and militarily strong power instead of a disunited China to Russia's back door and made it necessary for the Soviets to take vigorous countermeasures. A second track was laid for the Trans-Siberian railway, industrial centers were shifted eastward, immigration was furthered through reduction of taxes and corn deliveries, and the Far Eastern army under Marshal Blücher was greatly strengthened. Simultaneously, negotiations with Japan were undertaken which in 1935 led to a fundamental change. In order to keep peace, Russia liquidated the most persistent object of contention in the Far East by selling her share of the Chinese Eastern Railway. Ownership was transferred to the Japanese-sponsored country of Manchukuo, and the Soviets received a payment of one hundred and seventy million yen. This transaction altered the balance of power in the Far East and affected the interests of various great powers, but again failed to constitute a permanent solution.

UNITED STATES

United States Hostility. While the Soviet government struggled to maintain its position in Asia, changes occurred in America. The key to the American situation was held by the United States, which had recognized the Kerensky government on March 22, 1917, but failed to open diplomatic relations with the Bolshevists. For almost five years she continued—despite the extinction of the provisional government—to regard Kerensky's ambassador, Boris Bakhmetev, as official Russian representative, refused to receive the Soviet envoy, C. A. K. Martens, and threatened his deportation. In the meantime, in order "to guard military stores," she participated in the Allied expedition for intervention; in August, 1918, she sent expeditionary forces to Vladivostok and in September, 1918, to Archangel. These forces stayed on after the armistice with Germany was concluded and, under the pretext of enabling the Russian people "to choose their government freely," aided anti-Revolutionary armies. Only in June, 1919, and April, 1920, respectively, were they withdrawn from Archangel and Siberia.

First Relations. While the expeditionary forces were still in Russia, William C. Bullitt was sent to the Soviet government to report on the situation. His visit did not lead to the resumption of official relations; and only limited private trade was allowed in July, 1920. In the following year American relief was extended to the suffering people under Herbert Hoover's direction, and in 1922 the Soviets were permitted to establish an Information Bureau in Washington.

Commercial Intercourse. Thereafter, considerable trade developed, exports to Russia climbing between 1922 and 1930 from thirty to more than one hundred million dollars (after that declining) while imports jumped from one to fifteen million. The needs of the Soviet government for agricultural and industrial machinery

U.S. - RUSSIAN RELATIONS SINCE 1860

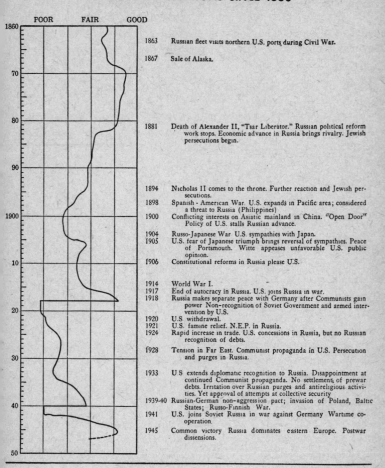

1863	Russian fleet visits northern U.S. ports during Civil War.
1867	Sale of Alaska.
1881	Death of Alexander II, "Tsar Liberator." Russian political reform work stops. Economic advance in Russia brings rivalry. Jewish persecutions begin.
1894	Nicholas II comes to the throne. Further reaction and Jewish persecutions.
1898	Spanish - American War. U.S. expands in Pacific area; considered a threat to Russia (Philippines)
1900	Conflicting interests on Asiatic mainland in China. "Open Door" Policy of U.S. stalls Russian advance.
1904	Russo-Japanese War. U.S. sympathies with Japan.
1905	U.S. fear of Japanese triumph brings reversal of sympathies. Peace of Portsmouth. Witte appeases unfavorable U.S. public opinion.
1906	Constitutional reforms in Russia please U.S.
1914	World War I.
1917	End of autocracy in Russia. U.S. joins Russia in war.
1918	Russia makes separate peace with Germany after Communists gain power. Non-recognition of Soviet Government and armed intervention by U.S.
1920	U.S. withdrawal.
1921	U.S. famine relief. N.E.P. in Russia.
1924	Rapid increase in trade. U.S. concessions in Russia, but no Russian recognition of debts.
1928	Tension in Far East. Communist propaganda in U.S. Persecution and purges in Russia.
1933	U.S. extends diplomatic recognition to Russia. Disappointment at continued Communist propaganda. No settlement of prewar debts. Irritation over Russian purges and antireligious activities. Yet approval of attempts at collective security
1939-40	Russian-German non-aggression pact; invasion of Poland, Baltic States; Russo-Finnish War.
1941	U.S. joins Soviet Russia in war against Germany. Wartime co-operation.
1945	Common victory. Russia dominates eastern Europe. Postwar dissensions.

AMERICAN–RUSSIAN relations of the past were determined essentially by absence of common interests—permitting the growth of either country without affecting the other. The Alaskan problem was liquidated before becoming an obstacle to friendly relations. Far Eastern regions possessed sufficient inherent strength to withstand an imperialistic clash of the two countries, and American isolation prevented the rise of dangerous international issues. In the 20th century, Russia (which had previously touched United States interests primarily in the Pacific area) began to assume greater importance in the Atlantic and European sector. Ideological as well as practical political issues began to concern the United States after the weakening of France, England, and Germany as outposts of the civilization to which America belongs.

accounted for the amount of exports, while imports from Russia, although including some ore shipments, remained essentially confined to luxury items such as furs and caviar and therefore never reached considerable figures. Yet, notwithstanding trade developments, official recognition was persistently denied by the successive United States Secretaries of State—Hughes, Kellogg, and Stimson—partly because of Soviet repudiation of prewar debts and confiscation of American private property, partly because of Soviet government-sponsored communist propaganda in the United States. Public opinion essentially supported official United States policy, but it was governed less by financial considerations than by religious issues, political ideology, and aversion to state planning and interference.

Diplomatic Recognition. Not until November, 1933, after the Democratic party had taken over the administration of the United States, was a diplomatic settlement reached. In exchange for official recognition, the Communist government promised to refrain from propaganda in the United States and to safeguard the lives and peaceful work of Americans in Russia. Bullitt was now sent as official representative to Moscow, and Alexander Troyanovsky came to Washington. Yet, relations remained half-hearted; religious persecution and party purges irritated American sentiments, no satisfactory arrangement regarding prewar debts was reached, and, contrary to Soviet guarantees, propaganda for world revolution did not subside.

PROBLEMS

1. Compare Soviet relationships to Asiatic nations with tsarist ones.
2. Discuss the importance of the struggle over the Chinese Eastern Railway.
3. Discuss the difficulties prevailing in Russo-American relations.

CHAPTER XLVII

ROAD TO WORLD WAR II

COLLECTIVE SECURITY

Nazi Peril. The year 1934, which brought the consolidation of Hitler's power in Germany, marked a turn in Russian foreign policy. Nothing could be expected of a Germany which outlawed its Communist citizens, appealed to all anti-Soviet forces abroad, and indifferently watched the deterioration of existing political bonds. Moreover, Germany rejected a Soviet proposal for the guarantee of the independence of the Baltic states, which Russia considered indispensable for her own security. Faced by the specter of renewed isolation, the Soviet government turned with determination to European neighbors and to the West, and found response from an apprehensive world. Small nations like Czechoslovakia, Rumania, and Bulgaria, which so far had challenged the Soviet system, hastened to recognize it now; nonaggression pacts with Poland, Latvia, Estonia, and Finland were prolonged by ten years; political and economic bonds with France were strengthened to forestall the surrender of France to German influence; and ultimately Russia joined the League of Nations.

League of Nations. At its inception the League had been intended by its founders, among its manifold purposes, as an "al-

281

ternative to Bolshevism"; and Russia, which had not been invited to the drafting of the Covenant, described it in the words of Lenin as "an alliance of world bandits against the proletariat." She essentially feared not the League but the forces behind it, and from the outset was antagonized by Persian, Finnish, Georgian, and other complaints which together with Soviet Far Eastern policies were made topics of denunciatory discussion before the League assembly. But after the adoption of the N.E.P., Russia, although refusing membership, co-operated to a limited extent. She permitted the League's relief work under Fridtjof Nansen and later participated in the League's conferences on public health and the prevention of epidemics. Although after the murder of Vorovsky her attendance at Geneva meetings was deemed impossible, Russian co-operation, wherever economically or propagandistically advisable, was forthcoming and could be witnessed in connection with questions of labor standards and in international economic and financial policies.

SOVIET ENTRY INTO LEAGUE. Politically, however, Russia oriented herself with nonmembers, such as Germany and Turkey; and not until Germany's entry into the League and the growing need for credits from the West was closer co-operation with the League itself —though not full membership—considered. In 1927, Litvinov was for the first time dispatched to Geneva to attend a disarmament conference. Chiefly for propagandistic reasons, he made sweeping proposals; and though upon rejection of his plan he suggested less drastic measures, his excessive zeal antagonized rather than persuaded the other members. In 1932, another disarmament conference was held, which was again attended by the Soviets but with no better results. After Hitler had come to power, a change in the attitude of the Russian delegation occurred: its members were increasingly willing to compromise on international issues, and in 1934, in view of the circumstances, the Soviet Union formally joined the League. It thus officially attested its desire to shift from isolation and independent action to collective security together with capitalist countries.

Participation in Collective Security. The results of this new trend in Russian foreign policies were evidenced in the year 1935. The deterioration of relations with Germany was officially avowed and Germany was accused of violating the Versailles Treaty, notwithstanding the fact that this treaty previously had been bitterly denounced by the Russians themselves. In March the British foreign minister Eden made a personal call at Moscow to discuss collective security; two months later the French minister Laval journeyed to Russia and concluded a Franco-Russian "East Pact"; and after him, Czechoslovakia's foreign minister Beneš arrived for the signing of an assistance treaty. Thus, Russia began to dominate the international scene. But since common fears rather than mutual interests constituted the link, the Soviet government took care to strengthen its position through independent measures as well. As the capitalistic world, beset by depression and fascism, seemed to be approaching its gravest crisis, special stress was laid upon ideological propaganda; the Comintern received increased unofficial encouragement, and utmost support was given to other organizations such as the Profintern, the Antifascists, and the League of the Godless.

CHECKS TO COLLECTIVE SECURITY. Such action, in turn, influenced adversely collaboration with the Western powers, whence protests soon were voiced against the proselytizing activities of the Communists. Instability of relations with the West thus continued to prevail, and consequently Russia took steps to renew her former neighborly relations with Germany. This was achieved not only by a new trade treaty, but also by an invitation to Germany to join the Franco-Russian "East Pact." Yet, collective security remained the watchword and the bonds with Western Europe were not severed. Common action for security was advocated in the case of Italy's aggression in Abyssinia and adherence was pledged to the Montreux Convention regarding the Straits and to the U.S.A.-Franco-English Three-Power Naval Treaty.

Growth of International Tension. Two new areas of friction emerged in 1936. The one, Spain, where fascists undertook to overthrow the republican government, soon became the most serious international issue testing the respective alignments of the great powers. Most European countries intervened on one side or the other, splitting the Continent. The Soviet government lent its forces—first financially, later militarily—to the republicans. The other area, the Far East, developed similar threatening aspects when, despite the recent sale of the Chinese Eastern Railway, clashes with infiltrating Japanese occurred on the Manchukuo frontier. The Soviets found themselves compelled to strengthen further their army there, and a new treaty for mutual aid and consultation was concluded with the Mongolian republic. Before the year ended, the interconnection of

the two events and their significance—at least for Russia—became
evident when in November Germany, which in its anticommunist drive
had encouraged and supported the revolt in Spain, concluded an "Anti-
Comintern Pact" with Japan. Soviet Russia thus found herself threatened from two sides and was forced to seek collective security with redoubled energy, through co-operation at Geneva as well as outside the
League of Nations. She also concluded a nonaggression pact with China
and held conferences in Moscow with the foreign ministers of Sweden,
Latvia, and Turkey. Still, the dangers to the socialist commonwealth
from the side of capitalism abroad continued to increase. Italy officially joined the German-Japanese Anti-Comintern Pact in 1937;
the propaganda of the Comintern alienated the Western powers and
America; the republican cause in Spain—unsupported except by
Russia and a few thousand volunteers from other countries—declined despite Litvinov's urgent appeals in Geneva; and the Japanese
steadily advanced in China and Manchukuo.

COLLAPSE OF COLLECTIVE SECURITY

Munich, 1938. In the fall of 1938 came the collapse of the
policies painfully pursued by Russia on the road to collective security
through co-operation with Western powers. When Hitler threatened
war because of alleged aggressive acts on the part of Czechoslovakia,
England and France deserted the cause and without consulting Russia submitted to the Nazi leader's demands. Not only did they participate (at Munich) in a decision over Czechoslovakia from which
the Soviets were excluded, but by permitting the partition of the
country—treaties notwithstanding—they caused a breach in the existing defense system of Russia. The latter found herself once more
isolated; her obligations toward Czechoslovakia were automatically
cancelled by France's refusal to come to the Czechs' aid, and although
refusing recognition of Germany's acts the Russians were in no
position to avert their execution.

German Nonaggression Pact, 1939. A half-year later, the incorporation of the rest of Czechoslovakia into Germany revived hopes
in Russia for collective security as the Western nations now realized
the impossibility of ever satisfying Nazi greed. In April, 1939, negotiations between Russia, France, and England were undertaken for
a military alliance. But Western inability to gauge the respective
threats of Nazism and communism, combined with lack of military
preparedness, resulted in the breakdown of the parleys. Litvinov, the

fundamental principles of his foreign policies collapsing, thereupon resigned; his successor, Molotov, renewed negotiations, but when they led again to failure the wheel was thrown in reverse. Instead of a Western alliance, a trade and nonaggression pact with Germany was concluded in August. The world was shocked by the sudden change of Russian policies and, paralyzed, watched the outbreak of war on September 1, 1939.

Invasion of Poland. The first act consisted in a German invasion of Poland and the prompt defeat of that country. Sixteen days later, in view of the end of the Polish state and the concomitant dissolution of treaty obligations, Russian troops invaded Poland from the east. They occupied almost half of the country and divided it with Germany; through an amity treaty with Hitler, a new common Russo-German borderline was established. This act ended the period of collective security and introduced a last phase in Russian international relations where the accent was placed on the individual nation's military power and its unrestricted use for survival.

Invasion of Finland. The division of Poland was supposed to serve Russian security and to stop any further German advance eastward, particularly in the direction of Russia's Baltic harbors—which would have constituted a most serious menace; for since the times of Ivan the Terrible and Peter the Great, access to the Baltic Sea was justly considered a basic principle for Russian independence. Well aware, however, of the possibility for just such a German push, the Soviets tried to forestall it by pacts with Lithuania, Latvia, Estonia, and Finland. With regard to the three Baltic states, negotiations led to "mutual assistance agreements" in October, 1939; but those with Finland broke down and, after a number of frontier incidents, an attack was launched on this country on November 30, in order to secure by force advantageous military outposts in the event of an attack from the west. Because of this act of aggression, which was interpreted as a chauvinistic desire for aggrandizement and dissemination of communistic principles, the Soviet Union was expelled from the League of Nations. But she carried on with war, and after a protracted campaign, which divulged many military shortcomings, Finland was conquered and forced to cede her eastern provinces together with the fortress of Viipuri (Viborg) as well as rights to ports and fortifications along her south shore.

Absorption of Baltic States. The gains in the Baltic area still did not seem sufficient to guarantee the Soviet position and therefore new, "friendly" governments were imposed on Lithuania, Latvia, and Estonia. In July and August, 1940, the three nations were transformed into Soviet Republics and entered the Soviet Union. These changes were recognized by Germany in the following January, and an agreement was made for population exchanges and frontier revisions.

Outbreak of German War. The Nazis, however, contrived to break the agreements and, aside from fundamental political and ideological differences, failed to settle many practical issues in other regions, such as questions referring to the Balkans and the Danube area. The Soviet government was aware of the danger and worked feverishly to strengthen its military position. In Asia, a neutrality pact was concluded with Japan and fishery rights were granted her; in America, negotiations were undertaken with the only remaining nonbelligerent power, the United States. Internally, Stalin was named chairman of the Council of People's Commissars in order to collect all forces, and the army was reorganized on the basis of the experience of the Finnish war. On June 22, 1941, the expected and inevitable happened. In accordance with the logic of Nazi doctrine German armies invaded Soviet territory; Rumania, Finland, and later Slovakia and Hungary followed, and also Italian and Spanish contingents joined the Nazi forces. Thus began the struggle for survival of the Soviet system.

PROBLEMS

1. Discuss the attitude of Soviet Russia toward the League of Nations.
2. Trace the rise of Russia's international position, 1934–1939.
3. Discuss the actions of Russia toward her Western neighbors, 1939–1941.

CHAPTER XLVIII

WORLD WAR II

RUSSIAN ARMY

Birth of Russian Army. War found Russia militarily well prepared. From their accession to power, the Bolshevists, in the midst of a hostile world, had given due attention to the defensive strength of the country and the preservation of its military tradition. This tradition can be traced back to the time of Ivan the Great, who had put an end to the disorganized nomadic and feudalistic fighting methods of the Middle Ages. Conscious of Russia's special geographical conditions, Ivan preserved some of the fundaments of warfare which had proved valuable through the centuries. As he was provided with sufficient manpower in his vast realms, he employed large armies so that by sheer weight he could overpower the enemy; he fostered the art of guerrilla warfare; and he knew how to take advantage of climatic conditions—of long and arduous winter seasons when rivers and swamps were frozen and allowed swift movements of appropriately equipped Russian forces, whereas heavily armored enemies were frustrated. And he likewise adopted methods which Tartar and other invaders in their long and successful campaigns had shown to be of special value in the wide, sparsely populated stretches of the Eurasian plains. Mobile Cossack units and lightly armed cavalry from Ivan's time supplemented the heavy cadres previously in use. Under Ivan III's grandson, Ivan the Terrible, artillery was modernized and strengthened, constituting from then on a weapon of pride to the Russians. Also, a special well-disciplined force, the Streltsi, was created as a bodyguard directly responsible to the Tsar.

Army under Peter I.   In the following century, when the Ukraine was incorporated, Zaporogian Cossacks increased the military power of Russia. Their absorption into the army made changes necessary which were carried out by Prince Golitsyn, Regent Sophia's lover, and especially by Peter the Great. The most important reform consisted in the abolition of the "tables of rank," by which positions of command had been accorded nobles on the basis of hereditary rank and seniority, but which were now replaced by a system of promotion based on ability. Furthermore, the Streltsi, who like the ancient Roman praetorian guards had gained undue political influence, were wisely suppressed. Peter replaced them by "imperial guards," the Preobrazhensky and Semenovsky regiments, which were composed of strictly professional and disciplined troops created after European models. Peter also began the establishment of a navy— the result of his experience at the siege of Azov, his successful acquisition of ports on the Baltic Sea, and his personal interest in maritime affairs and in shipbuilding.

Army in Later Eighteenth Century.   Although the navy was allowed to decay under Peter's successors, the Russian army gained in strength and importance during the eighteenth century. Under Anna as well as under Elizabeth, Catherine, and Paul, it was regularly reorganized and matched contemporary standards of Western Europe; military dress, discipline, tactical training, mechanical equipment, and particularly artillery were consistently improved. Toward the end of the century, a gifted leader emerged in the person of Suvorov, whose Turkish and later Italian and Swiss campaigns, notwithstanding many mistakes and the ultimate failure of the latter, showed strategic as well as tactical ability hardly inferior to that of Napoleon.

Napoleonic Era.   Peculiarly enough, the Napoleonic Era with its long warfare, which brought such terrible defeats as Austerlitz and Friedland and such victories as the campaigns of 1812 and 1813, produced little progress in the military field. Russian over-all strategy of 1812 was based on resistance, reliance upon geographical conditions, and almost medieval fighting methods rather than on scientific studies commensurate with those of the period. Thus, the campaigns turned out to be costly and the war was unduly prolonged, and the severe criticism of later generations seemed justified.

Modernization of Army. Innovations, however, were introduced by Alexander I after the fall of Napoleon. With the help of the able artillery general Arakcheyev, "military colonies" were introduced which marked a radical departure from prior ways of recruiting troops; but corruption and antiquated social conditions checked their success and retarded the evolution of military science. The weakness of both army and navy and of their commanders was demonstrated in the Crimean War, and the need for radical reform became evident. It was carried out in 1874 when, after the completion of fundamental social reforms, compulsory military service was introduced. It showed tangible results in the war of 1878 and in World War I. But the auxiliary services remained inefficient and leadership incompetent, and the valor of the individual soldier could not compensate for the shortcomings of organization and strategy.

Creation of "Red Army." When the Bolshevists seized power, a thorough change was made in the organization and direction of the military forces, and many of those in command were eliminated, if for no other reason than their social status. "Revolutionary Order Number One" abolished all distinctions of rank. Although a number of tsarist commanders were retained, new, politically reliable leaders were also appointed; and all were subjected to the supervision of political commissars and soldiers' councils. Furthermore, a new military force was improvised in 1917 as *"avant-garde* of the proletariat," and war-weary soldiers and reluctant peasants were demobilized. The Red Army proper came into being on February 23, 1918, and under the able direction of men like Trotsky gained in strength and efficiency. During the Civil War it saved the Bolshevist government.

Mechanization of Army. After the end of civil war and intervention, in 1921, the Red Army was reduced from five and a half to one and a half million men, and by 1925 it amounted to no more than six hundred thousand. Trotsky was replaced as chief of staff by M. Frunze, and the term of military service was lengthened. In the meantime a new officers' corps, indoctrinated with Revolutionary ideas, was trained; its authority was gradually increased; and ultimately regular officers' ranks, including that of marshal, were reintroduced. Military orders were likewise renewed; and in 1931 the gradual numerical strengthening of the forces was begun, resulting in 1936 in a military establishment of no less than two million men. During this period industries were keyed to the needs of defense; the equipment was bettered; a modern artillery and aviation corps was built up; and, after many disappointing years, even the tank corps and the air force began to live up to modern requirements. The constitution of 1936 provided again for compulsory military service, and great efforts were made to evoke a new feeling of national pride. In 1937 Revolutionary Order Number One was officially revoked, and in the same year, purges were carried out to rid the military forces of all possible traitors; suspicious leaders were tried and executed— Marshal Tukhachevsky among them.

THE WAR

Preparations against Nazis. The organization of the Soviet military forces was thus completed when the Second World War broke out. But experience in the field was still lacking. Incidents on the Manchukuo border had not taught the art of large-scale operations, and the occupation of eastern Poland in 1939 put no problem to Soviet military leadership. It was the Finnish war undertaken in November, 1939, which constituted a true test, and it divulged grave shortcomings: initiative was lacking, bureaucracy hampered action, equipment was sometimes faulty, and the Finnish defenses on the Mannerheim Line were broken at last only by overwhelming numbers. The following year was, therefore, used for a correction of exposed deficiencies and for the adaptation of new methods which Soviet military analysts observed abroad in the triumphant campaigns of the Germans. The commanders were, however, circumspect enough to prepare for defense as well as attack. They modified their tactics according to experience derived from foreign invasions incurred in previous centuries on the part of Tartars, Poles, and French, and they prepared for a possible assault from the west as well as the east.

Nazi Strategic Plan. The blow fell in June, 1941. At a time chosen because no other front except a minor one in Libya existed for them, the Germans invaded Russia with some two hundred divisions. Their aim was to gain in a lightning thrust three objectives: to seize Leningrad after a quick advance through the Baltic countries and to isolate Russia from the Baltic Sea; to gain Moscow over a central route, as formerly used by Napoleon, and to disrupt the converging Russian transportation system; and to grab the coal- and food-producing regions of the south and deprive the Russians of fuel and provisions. They hoped to find support from a discontented population.

Nazi Failure. In every direction, the Germans came within sight of their objectives, but in none did they gain them. Leningrad was reached on August 21, 1941, and besieged in vain until January, 1944. The main blow against Moscow was slowed down near Smolensk and an unsuccessful three-month battle for the capital began on October 13, 1941. On the same day, in the south, a siege of Sevastopol was started; but the fortress was not taken until June, 1942, and it was recovered in May, 1944. The *Blitzkrieg* thus bogged down; contrary to Nazi calculations, winter overtook the German armies, which like all invaders suffered intensely, and in the next year their strength was insufficient to continue the threefold thrust. The onslaught, therefore, was largely confined to the south, where the whole Black Sea Coast, the Ukraine with the Donets coal basin, and parts of the Caucasus region were occupied. But the key to the southern defense system, the city of Stalingrad, which dominated the vital lower Volga basin with all its communication lines and which was besieged in September, 1942, could not be taken. A Russian army under Marshal Zhukov defended the city heroically in a bitter five-month struggle which turned out to be decisive for the outcome of the war. A whole German army corps was captured and the remaining Nazis began their retreat. In the following summer, 1943, they staged a temporarily successful counteroffensive near Kursk; but despite the fact that Russia's allies failed to establish a second front and confined themselves to aerial blows, Russian progress—efficiently furthered by American Lend-Lease aid—could not be halted.

Russian Victory. Deliverance came in the year 1944: in June, the Allied invasion of Normandy opened the long-expected second front, and in September, Finland, Rumania, and Bulgaria capitulated. The Germans were forced farther and farther back, although they continued to defend themselves with great fortitude; their retreat from the Baltic countries, central Russia, the Donets basin, and the Ukraine was slow, and terrible devastation was wrought in the abandoned regions. The advance of the Russian armies to Warsaw, which was taken in January, 1945, Königsberg, which was captured in April, and the Oder River, which was crossed in the same month, was extremely difficult and asked for utmost valor, skill, and perseverance. The final battle of Berlin was most savage, and not until May 8, 1945, did the Germans capitulate.

War against Japan. As it later became evident, no systematic co-ordination of German and Japanese strategy existed throughout the war. No Japanese attack in the Far East endangered the military operations on Russia's western front, nor did it become necessary to divert forces in men or material for action in the East. Notwithstanding the German-Japanese alliance and the Anti-Comintern Pact, treaties for fishery rights and others were successfully negotiated between Russia and Japan, and thus a comparatively small force sufficed to guard Russia's eastern border. Not until August 8, three months after the defeat of Germany, did hostilities break out in the Far East, and then they happened owing to Russian and not to Japanese action. As Japan had suffered decisive defeats before and the weapon of the atomic bomb had been loosed upon her, determined fighting with Russia was confined to a brief interlude and quickly ended with Japan's surrender on August 14, 1945.

Thus closed World War II.

PROBLEMS

1. Trace the historical development of the Russian army.
2. Discuss the chief objectives of the German drive into Russia in 1941.
3. Discuss the relations of Russia and Japan during World War II.

CHAPTER XLIX

THE POSTWAR ERA

Unlike the other belligerents of World War II, the Soviets at no time during the struggle lost sight of their ultimate aims. They were sure that if they were to survive at all, they would emerge with enormous prestige and power and that they would be in a position to achieve long-desired ends. Wisely maintaining a comparatively independent position throughout the war and using successfully every opportunity for securing definite commitments from their allies without conceding much themselves, they prepared for the postwar period.

PREPARATIONS

Wartime Diplomacy.

EASTWARD SHIFT. At the beginning of the war, under the impact of the first Nazi assault, many concessions were made to gain the full support of a suspicious world, such as the acceptance of the Atlantic Charter, the signing of the "Declaration by the United Nations" (January 1, 1942), a twenty-year assistance pact with England (May, 1942), lend-lease agreements with the United States (June, 1942), and ultimately the formal dissolution of the Comintern by its executive committee (May, 1943, but revived in new form in October, 1947); but soon after the German advance was stopped, a different course was taken. It found its expression in cleverly timed denunciations of the Allies for failing to open a long-promised second front, in territorial claims on Baltic regions and Bessarabia, and in a neutral policy toward Japan. As a result, Russia's allies found themselves constantly involved in political as well as military negotiations, which gave ample proof of a new distribution of power; for as never before in the history of the Western world, the point of gravity was shifted eastward into spheres of Russian predominance: In December, 1941, Eden, British Foreign Secretary, visited Moscow; in August, 1942, Churchill met Stalin there; in October, 1943, both Eden and Hull, Secretary of State of the United States, traveled to Moscow; in November, President Roosevelt and Prime Minister Churchill went to see Stalin in Teheran, the most easterly meeting point yet of any great international conference. In October, 1944, Churchill was again in Moscow; in December, the Frenchman de Gaulle visited there; and in February, 1945, Churchill and Roosevelt once more traveled east to meet Stalin at Yalta in the Crimea.

RELATIONS WITH WESTERN NATIONS. Through these conferences the direction of Russia's postwar policies was established. They consisted, on the one hand, of international co-operation, which was demonstrated by participation in a postwar food conference at Hot Springs, Virginia (May, 1943), a United Nations Monetary Conference at Bretton Woods (July, 1944), a Security Conference held at Dumbarton Oaks (August and September, 1944), and the first United Nations Conference, held at San Francisco (April, 1945). On the other hand, and notwithstanding all their international-mindedness, the Soviets also pursued an independent policy. It was shown by such instances as their refusal to take part in an International Civil Aviation Conference, whereby their intention was emphasized to guarantee the security of the Union through independent military preparations—a policy later implemented by the installation of "friendly" governments in surrounding territories. Thus it may be said that the prewar Soviet policy, which had envisaged combining collective security with independent national action, was consistently and logically continued.

RELATIONS WITH NEIGHBORS. With such an aim in view, the Soviets began comparatively early in the war to denounce the principles of the Atlantic Charter, whose binding character was later abrogated also by the very men who had drafted it. Then, too, demands for general recognition of the absorption of the Baltic States into the Soviet Union were made; and in April, 1943, the U.S.S.R. broke relations with the then existing Polish government. As time went on, the struggle between Russia and her allies over the form of a new Polish government friendly to Russia increased and came to a climax when, in January, 1945, a Communist-dominated counter-government, formed at Lublin, was officially recognized by the Soviets. As to Czechoslovakia and Yugoslavia, both instituted regimes primarily acceptable to Russia, and treaties of amity were concluded with them. Japan, too, bowed to her mighty neighbor, even before Russia joined in the hostilities, by consenting to a withdrawal from long-held coal and oil concessions in northern Sakhalin.

RELATIONS WITH ENEMIES. The only part of Soviet policy which remained unclear and vacillating throughout the war was that toward her enemies. The desire for impressing particularly Germany and Finland with the advantages of the Soviet system, and the realization that at all times co-operation between Germany and Russia had brought great benefit to both sides, conflicted with the general desire to avenge Nazi invasion and destruction, with the fear of Western influences in the new Germany, and with the hope for annexations and reparations. A "Free German Committee," founded in Moscow in 1944 and composed of German refugees and war prisoners including high ranking generals, was only half-heartedly supported; and eventually a stern, oppressive policy was promoted. As to Finland, Rumania, Bulgaria, and Hungary, it was subsequently decided to bring them entirely into the Russian orbit, and only Italy was left to the Western powers.

Wartime Economy. Just as wartime diplomacy was keyed to postwar aims, so was the Soviet wartime economy made part of postwar planning as soon as the first great shock was overcome. With confidence and foresight, what was undertaken under the pressure of the moment and what often seemed an undesirable measure, was turned into a productive move and into a positive good. Thus, the Russians profited by the great eastward transfer of industrial plants, necessitated by the German occupation of the Donets basin and other industrial regions, in order to establish new permanent centers in the Urals, Siberia, and central Asia, whereas the old centers were scheduled to serve after their recovery as additional facilities. The loss of raw-material sources, including agricultural produce, became the starting point for increased surveying activity and led to the discovery and development of new and strategically safer regions.

The destruction of homes and plants was made the beginning for reconstruction along more modern lines; and even the wrath of the people over the devastations wrought by the intruder as well as their dismay at the scorched-earth policy of their own government was turned into productive channels, and women, Stakhanovites, and all other patriots exerted themselves doubly in their effort to build new industries and collective farms.

The price in human effort and material goods was extremely high, but under the pressure of war the Russian people provided the necessary manpower and carried—through extra work, taxes, and loans—the financial burden. Without the help of foreign contingents, they fought the war on Germany's eastern front; they built the new industries through their own efforts; and notwithstanding the substantial aid donated through lend-lease by the United States—aid that may well have meant the decisive balance at the critical stages in 1942 and 1943—the bulk of the military requirements was provided by the Russian peoples.

Wartime Social Policy.   While Soviet diplomacy and economy profited at least indirectly from the war, the impact of the struggle on social conditions within the U.S.S.R. was not uniformly in line with the desires and ideology of the Soviet state, nor were its consequences foreseeable. For the sake of unity, the Orthodox church was reinstated; for the sake of efficiency, political commissariats in the army were abolished; officer-ranks were accentuated; and "patriotism" was extolled—all of which conflicted with the international tendencies of Marxist teachings. Contact with intelligent and prosperous capitalistic enemies as well as allies influenced the political outlook of many soldiers and administrators; elements of doubtful loyalty came to the fore; the policy of racial toleration was endangered by ruthless population shifts, such as that of the so-called Volga-Germans who in two centuries of faithful work had contributed so much to the development of the Volga region, and of other groups, some in central, others in eastern Asia. The many changes heralded a major shift in the sociological structure of the Union.

SOVIET ATTITUDE AND ACTION

Postwar Diplomacy.

EXTENSION OF SOVIET INFLUENCE.   When the hostilities ended in 1945, the fruits of the wartime effort were conscientiously harvested. Territorially, enormous acquisitions were made: the Baltic States, Finland's Karelia and her Arctic shore line, eastern Poland, parts of Germany's East Prussia, Czechoslovakia's Ruthenian lands, Rumania's Bessarabia, and Japan's Southern Sakhalin and the Kuril Islands were annexed. In addition, a strong Soviet hold was established on Finland, eastern Germany, Czechoslovakia, Hungary, Yugoslavia, Albania, Rumania, Bulgaria, and in Asia on Manchuria and northern Korea. Soviet power was also felt—often through the activities of Communist parties—in outlying regions, such as western Germany and Sweden, France and Italy, India and China, and particularly Greece, Turkey, and Iran.

CONFERENCE OF POTSDAM. The conflict resulting from this development found its reaction in the councils of the nations and was sharpened by the American development of a process for the release of atomic energy, which gave the United States an unheard-of advantage in the military field. From the conference which was held, after the hostilities in Europe were ended, at Potsdam in July and August, 1945, and where two of the three chief participants, the United States and England, were represented by new men (President Truman, who had replaced Roosevelt after the latter's death, and Prime Minister Attlee, who had succeeded Churchill in the midst of the conference after a landslide vote for the Labor party), discord was increasingly felt. The destruction of German industrial power, irreconcilable with the annexation of German agricultural lands in the east and the Soviet desire for reparations, but agreed upon at Potsdam, and the dissensions regarding the political future of Germany gave but one evidence of the inherent weaknesses of the compromises, even where they referred to former enemies.

PREPARATION OF PEACE TREATIES. After Potsdam, the heads of the three strongest powers did not meet again; only the foreign ministers came together, and their conferences—complicated by the admission of a powerless but vociferous France—failed to settle existing differences. Not less than eight meetings took place: at London and Moscow in 1945; at Paris and New York in 1946; at London, Moscow, Paris, and again London in 1947. Except for peace treaties for the minor allies of Germany, which were the result of many unsatisfactory and perhaps dangerous compromises, no major issue was settled by them.

Postwar Economy. While the international scene was thus characterized by dissension and failure, domestic problems were attacked with a uniform will and success. In 1945, a new Five-Year Plan provided, like the earlier ones, in the first place for an increase in heavy industry and therewith for the strengthening of Russia's defenses. As the published statistics of 1947 indicate, this part of the program made quick progress. The plan further provided for the rehabilitation of war-damaged regions and for the incorporation of the economies of the acquired territories into that of the Union. The contributions of each region to the country's economy were carefully apportioned, and everywhere scientific research was pushed. Since wars at all times have tended to reduce the productivity of victor and vanquished alike, care was taken to provide incentives for hard work. An eight-hour day was reintroduced and the customary provisions for better housing and living conditions were made.

Postwar Social Problems. In a sense, the new Five-Year Plan reflected tensions within the Soviet Union. There were soldiers who, having seen the comparatively prosperous conditions of the average peasant and industrial worker in central Europe, came back—just as those after the Polish wars or after the Napoleonic invasion— not only with booty but also with unwelcome ideas. There were members of national groups, "displaced persons," whose refusal to return to their annexed countries meant a threat to future loyalties. There were officers who had too long enjoyed the privilege of commanding positions and the distinction of rank; their readjustment to civilian life was a challenge to the "classless society." There was also considerable unrest and dissatisfaction in many sections, as for instance in the Ukraine, where Nazi ideas had not infrequently reflected the wishes of some of the population; punishments and purges followed in the wake of victory.

The Iron Curtain. The political, economic, and sociological issues combined determined the Soviet government to maintain its aloofness toward the outer world while reorganizing within. It therefore impeded contact of foreign powers with all peoples and countries within its sphere, i.e., east of a line which ran approximately through the center of Germany down to the Adriatic Sea and separated "like an iron curtain" eastern from western Europe. In Russia herself, many changes were made; Nicholas M. Shvernik succeeded Kalinin (who soon thereafter died) as chairman of the presidium of the Supreme Soviet; the "people's commissariats" were replaced by "ministries," as in Western countries; the administration was streamlined and action was taken against increasing graft, speculation, corruption, and crime; a thoroughgoing financial reform was carried out; the ruble was devaluated, rations were abolished, and prices in state stores were revised and equalized. Renewed emphasis was placed on the spreading of the communist doctrine, which was, however, modified by national aspirations; and armies and foreign representation of their own were allowed to constituent Union Republics, three of which (Russia, White Russia, Ukraine) held also separate seats in the United Nations.

In February, 1946, the first elections to the Supreme Soviet since 1937 were held; 99 per cent of the voters came to the polls and almost all endorsed the candidates on the ballot.

PROBLEMS

1. Discuss the rise of Soviet prestige during World War II.
2. Trace Russia's attitude towards Germany during and after World War II.
3. Describe the changes of the sociological status in Russia as a result of the war.

CHAPTER L

RUSSIA AND "ONE WORLD"

Democracy. Peace and security—the longings of the peoples after the destruction of war—were sadly undermined by the division of the world into two camps—a division which was evidenced by the "iron curtain." Not even the word "democracy," which had been a prime mover in the struggle against Nazism and fascism, retained a common meaning; ideologies separating the totalitarian and socialist from the liberal and capitalistic world clashed anew once the enemy had been defeated.

Fourth Five-Year Plan. The Soviet government took special care to combine its campaign against the capitalistic world with positive and constructive endeavors at home. It adapted its ideological position to its changed political role, propagandized the advantages of socialism, and at the same time worked diligently on the economic reconstruction of the country and on social improvements. After the successful currency reform of December, 1947, which put the ruble on a sound basis throughout the Soviet area and simultaneously strengthened socialist trends through a new levelling process, the Soviets succeeded in repeatedly reducing prices, increasing industrial output, and raising the buying power of the average citizen. Agricultural productivity reached the prewar level by 1949; and industries, though lagging

300

in some branches, such as timber and oil, achieved considerable advances over prewar standards in steel and some other vital commodities. The whole economy was keyed to the fulfillment of the fourth Five-Year Plan within four years, and wherever shortcomings were found, stern self-criticism was applied. Enormous loans were successfully launched, the cultivated acreage was increased, reclamation projects were undertaken, houses were built, and a greater number of wage earners were put on a competitive piecework basis for individuals or groups. However, much of the advance was made possible only by subordinating the aim of higher living standards to that of strengthening the state, by constant planning and strict supervision, limiting personal freedom, and by forcing war prisoners, draftees from occupied areas, and political dissenters from Russia herself into involuntary labor in Siberian mines, lumber camps, and industries. The Communist party, which had greatly swelled during the war years, was carefully screened and repeatedly purged, and a number of changes occurred in both government and political leadership. During 1948 and 1949, Zhdanov, head of the Cominform, died; Molotov, the foreign minister, was succeeded by Vishinsky; and the minister of foreign trade, the chief of staff of the army, the chairman of the state planning commission, and many minor officers were replaced.

Cosmopolitanism vs. Patriotism. Special attention was paid to the ideological orientation of the people. In line with Soviet foreign policy, enthusiasm was fostered for all things Russian, and disdain and fear of "Anglo-American" concepts were spread. Soviet patriotism was preached as the road to equality and brotherhood of men; it was described as true internationalism, based on the rule of the working class, and was contrasted with "bourgeois cosmopolitanism," which was said to infringe on the ideals of state and folk and to render impossible national self-determination. Russia waged a bitter fight against the international control of the Catholic world by the papacy, which countered, in July, 1949, by excommunicating all active Communists.

"Cosmopolitanism" was particularly denounced in the intellectual field. Scientists, economists, musicians, and architects were warned against it; historians were asked to turn from Pokrovsky's teachings, which had belittled Russia's past and were now regarded as an early communist error; linguistic, physical, and astronomical studies were made to follow the fundamental political doctrine. In biology, Michurin and Lysenko's theories of the determining influence of environment on living beings as against the heredity theories of Mendel and

Morgan were proclaimed as the only valid ones according to the teachings of materialism, and all biologists had to conform to them. In line with these tendencies, much emphasis was given to Russian contributions to the intellectual heritage of the world, and the telephone, radio, submarine, and many other discoveries and inventions hitherto accepted as European or American were claimed for Russia.

The Communist Appeal in the West. The emphasis on the Russian national tradition and the many ideological compromises made for the sake of securing practical advantages for Russia proved to be obstacles to the spreading of the Communist doctrine. The strong amity movement toward Russia after the end of the war was interrupted. Most free elections of subsequent years in Italy, France, the Scandinavian countries and other West-European nations revealed that communist parties in these countries were unable to maintain their earlier appeal for the masses. In Germany and Austria—and beyond their borders—the behavior of the Russian troops, the exploitation of prisoners and workers through forced labor, the spoliation of the countries, the transfer of vital peacetime industries and the redistribution of land ownership, and the shifting of populations after annexations disheartened even those who had been sympathetic to Russia. Only a few and eventually unsatisfactory economic agreements could be made with Western European countries, such as Switzerland, Sweden, France, and lastly England.

The Communist Appeal in the East. A different development, however, took place in the East. Although in the Near and the Middle East, demands reminiscent of Pan-Slav imperialism spread fears in Turkey, Iran, and many Mohammedan countries, communism became of major significance in India, Burma, China, Indonesia, and the Malay peninsula. Likewise, in eastern Europe communism made considerable gains. With the help of Soviet military power communist governments friendly to the Soviet Union were established between 1945 and 1947 in Poland, Hungary, Rumania, and Bulgaria, and in February, 1948, through a coup very disheartening to the Western powers, also in Czechoslovakia. These various countries were bound together by the organization of a mutual "Information Bureau" (Cominform), which in 1947 took the place of the former Comintern, and by a Council of Economic Mutual Assistance founded in January, 1949. Only Yugoslavia under Marshal Tito, though ideologically communistic, gained an increasing amount of independence from Moscow, constituting thereby a dangerous gap in the structure of

Socialist unity and paving the way for heretical nationalistic developments within the Communistic world.

Opposition to Communism. The expansion of Russian power
in the East and the growing resistance of the West gave an opportunity to the United States, as the chief representative of the forces
opposing the Soviet ideology, to take action at least in those parts
which were not occupied by Russian forces and which because of their
maritime position were deemed of special strategic importance. Soviet
infiltration in Korea, in Iran (which, in addition to its wealth in oil,
was important because it dominated the approach to the Indian
Ocean), and into Greece and Turkey (which controlled the approaches to the Mediterranean) was vigorously and successfully opposed through economic and military aid. Notwithstanding Soviet protests, a policy of aid for the preservation of strategically important
smaller countries ("Truman Doctrine") was aggressively pushed. In
June, 1947, the program of resistance was expanded by a proposal
(Marshall Plan) that all nations of Europe should combine to work
out a plan for the re-establishment of economic prosperity, and the
United States supported the execution of the plan by economic aid.
The Soviet government—fearing that this proposal would lead to a
decline of communist strength through economic recovery and, possibly, to virtual domination of Europe by the United States—refused
its participation after brief consultation with England and France;
and the smaller nations in the Soviet sphere followed her lead. Finally,
between February and July, 1949, a military alliance was formed by
the United States and the countries bordering on the Atlantic Ocean,
the "North Atlantic Pact" (including Italy, but not Spain), which
guaranteed mutual protection and envisaged the supply of arms by
the United States.

Discord in the United Nations. The struggle necessarily soon
engulfed the young United Nations organization, where two blocs
faced each other and where decisions on most critical issues were made
impossible by the fundamental opposition of the postwar aims of the
United States and the U.S.S.R.; for both countries possessed in effect
the right to veto decisions in the Council. Russia, which generally was
backed by a minority only, made extensive use of this right; through
her actions, the fate of many extraneous issues spanning the whole
globe—from Argentina to Palestine, from Indonesia to Iran—was
deeply affected. Particularly critical disputes occurred in connection
with plans for the control of atomic energy, so that the commission

dealing with the problem had to give up its work in May, 1948; the Russian government continued thereafter to insist on a complete ban of atomic weapons, although it demanded a veto right over any possible control agency. The U.S.S.R. exploded an atom bomb in the fall of 1949. The Russian development of atomic weapons had little apparent influence on the proposals of the United States and the U.S.S.R. for atomic control, but it did influence representatives of the smaller nations to intensify their efforts to find a compromise solution.

"One World." By 1950, the lines were clearly drawn between East and West. Each tried to consolidate its holdings and to protect them by armed might. However, each also made vigorous attempts to add to its sphere the two major areas separating East and West—Germany and China, whose places in the society of nations continued undefined though their peoples and potentialities, of course, remained. As to Germany, Russia endeavored early in 1948 to compel Western concessions through a blockade of Berlin, and thus to gain greater influence; but in May, 1949, in the face of determined Western resistance, the attempt was given up and the foreign ministers of East and West met once more—the first time since 1947—in order to try to reach agreements on general policies. They failed in this, however, as well as in their negotiations on a peace treaty with Germany. With regard to China, on the other hand, Russia secured a decisive advantage through the triumph of the indigenous Communist party, which conquered in eastern China the more industrial and commercial regions of the country. Thus, the existing rift between East and West was increased; and the chief problem, which was to be the key for all future internal and external policies of the Soviet Union, remained unsolved—the question of "one world or two."

PROBLEMS

1. Trace the advance and the reverses of communism in postwar Europe.
2. Discuss Russia's attitude and actions against "cosmopolitanism."
3. Discuss the issue of "democracy" between the victorious powers.

COLLEGE OUTLINE SERIES

Barnes & Noble, Inc., *Publishers*

[*Continued on next page*]

[Continued from preceding page]

CHRONOLOGICAL TABLE

325—Council of Nicea: Christianity recognized in Roman empire.
375—Beginning of the Great Migration of Peoples.
476—End of Roman empire.
485—Foundation of Frankish kingdom.
711—Mohammedans invade Spain.
768–814—Reign of Charlemagne.
c. 855–885—Cyril and Methodius convert Slavic tribes.
862—Ruric made ruler of Novgorod.
907—Oleg's expedition against Constantinople.
936–973—Otto the Great, German Emperor.
967–971—Sviatoslav's expedition against Byzantine Empire.
988—Christianity adopted by Vladimir I.
1015—Death of Vladimir I.
1017—Church of St. Sophia begun in Kiev.
1019–1054—Reign of Yaroslav the Wise.
1037—Kiev becomes metropolitan see.
1043—Last expedition against Byzance.
1054—Catholic-Orthodox schism.
1066—Battle of Hastings: Norman invasion of England.
1073–1085—Pope Gregory VII.
1099—First Crusade: Jerusalem taken by Christians.
1113–1125—Reign of Vladimir II.
1139–1174—Reign of Andrew Bogolubsky.
c. 1147—Founding of Moscow.
1158—Swedes begin occupation of Finland, Germans and Danes that
        of Livonia and Estonia.
1215—Magna Carta issued.
1216—Death of Pope Innocent III.
1223?—Battle of the River Kalka.
1226—Death of St. Francis.
1236—Second Tartar invasion.
1240—Battle of the Neva: defeat of Swedes.
1240—Kiev taken by Tartars.
1242—Battle of Lake Peipus: defeat of Teutonic Knights.
1252–1263—Reign of Alexander Nevsky in Muscovy.
1274—Death of St. Thomas Aquinas.
1295—Model Parliament in England.
1320—Kiev falls under Lithuanian Rule.
1321—Death of Dante.
1325–1341—Reign of Ivan I Kalita.
1325—Moscow becomes metropolitan see.

1339–1453—Hundred Years' War between England and France.
1348—Black death in Europe.
1359–1389—Reign of Dimitri Donskoy.
1380—Battle of the Don.
1386—Union of Poland and Lithuania.
c. 1400—Andrew Rublev in Novgorod.
1408—Re-establishment of Tartar rule over Russia.
1438–1439—Council of Florence: attempts to unify Catholics and Orthodox.
c. 1450—Printing press with movable type invented in Germany.
1453—Fall of Constantinople to the Turks.
1462–1505—Reign of Ivan III the Great.
1471–1496—Conquest of Novgorod and its destruction as trading center.
1480—Battle of the Oka River: end of Tartar rule.
1485—Incorporation of Tver.
1492—Discovery of America.
1492—End of Mohammedan rule in Spain.
1505–1533—Reign of Basil III.
c. 1510—Climax of Renaissance in Italy and Germany.
1510—Conquest of Pskov.
1514—Conquest of Smolensk.
1517—Beginning of Reformation (Luther).
1519–1522—First voyage around world (Magellan).
1532—Machiavelli, *The Prince.*
1533–1584—Reign of Ivan IV the Terrible.
1534—Break between England and Rome (Henry VIII).
1552—Conquest of Kazan.
1553—Discovery of North Cape route to Russia.
1554–1556—Conquest of Astrakhan.
1556—Abdication of Emperor Charles V.
1558–1603—Reign of Queen Elizabeth in England.
1558—Beginning of Livonian War.
1565—Oprichnina founded.
1568—Beginning of Netherlands War of Independence.
1581—Yermak's first expedition into Siberia.
1582—Peace of Yam Zapolie.
1584–1598—Reign of Feodor I, last tsar of Rurik family.
1588—Defeat of Spanish Armada.
1589—Moscow becomes a patriarchate.
1595—Establishment of "Uniate church" in Ukraine.
1597—Legalization of serfdom in Russia.
1598–1605—Reign of Boris Godunov.
1604—Appearance of "False Dimitri." Beginning of Time of Troubles.
1604–1608—Cossack revolts in Ukraine against Poland.
1605–1606—Dimitri as Tsar.
1605—Gunpowder Plot in England.
1606–1610—Reign of Basil IV Shuisky.

1607—English colony established at Jamestown, Virginia.

1608—Appearance of "Second False Dimitri."

1611–1612—The Poles in Moscow.

1613—Election of Romanov family to the throne.

1613–1645—Reign of Michael I.

1616—Death of Shakespeare.

1618–1648—Thirty Years' War.

1618—Russians reach upper Yenisei River in Siberia.

1619–1633—Philaret, Patriarch of Moscow.

1620—Landing of Pilgrims at Plymouth, New England.

1625–1649—New Cossack revolts in Ukraine against Poland.

1632—Russians reach Lena River in Siberia.

1637—A "Siberian Department" established in Moscow.

1643–1715—Reign of Louis XIV in France.

1645—Russians reach Pacific Coast of Siberia.

1645–1676—Reign of Alexis I.

1648—Peace of Westphalia.

1649—Charles I beheaded: Puritan Commonwealth established in England.

1649—Publication of new Russian law code.

1652—Nikon becomes Patriarch of Moscow.

1653—Convening of last Zemsky Sobor.

1654–1656—Church council in Moscow for sake of reform: beginning of the Schism.

1660—Restoration of Stuarts in England.

1661—Peace of Cardis with Sweden.

1667–1671—Revolt of Stenka Razin.

1676–1682—Reign of Feodor II.

1681—Pennsylvania granted to William Penn.

1682–1725—Reign of Peter I the Great.

1682–1689—Regency of Sophia.

1683—Vienna besieged by Turks.

1687—Newton, *Principia.*

1688—"Glorious Revolution" in England: Bill of Rights.

1689—Russo-Chinese Treaty of Nerchinsk.

1689—Peter seizes government.

1690—Locke, *Essay concerning Human Understanding.*

1696—Capture of Azov.

1697—Kamchatka reached by Russian explorers.

1697–1698—Peter's trip through Europe; suppression of Streltsi.

1700—New calendar introduced.

1700–1721—Great Northern War.

1700—Defeat at Narva.

1703—Founding of St. Petersburg.

1709—Battle of Poltava.

1710–1711—Russo-Turkish War: loss of Azov.

1713—St. Petersburg becomes capital of Russia.

1713—Peace of Utrecht: end of Louis XIV's wars of aggression.

1716—Invasion of southern Sweden.

1718—Death of Alexis, son of Peter.
1721—Peace of Nystad.
1721—Patriarchate abolished in Moscow; Holy Synod established.
1722–1723—War against Persia.
1725—Academy of Science founded in St. Petersburg.
1725–1727—Reign of Catherine I.
1727—Russo-Chinese Treaty of Kyakhta.
1727–1730—Reign of Peter II.
1730–1740—Reign of Anna I.
1731—Ladoga Canal completed.
1733–1735—War of Polish Succession (Stanislaw Leszcyński).
1737—Charting of northern Siberian coast line.
1738—Russian ballet school founded.
1738–1739—War with Turkey.
1739—Treaty of Belgrade: coast on Black Sea gained.
1740–1741—Reign of Ivan VI; regency of Anna Leopoldovna.
1740–1786—Reign of Frederick the Great of Prussia.
1741–1762—Reign of Elizabeth.
1741—Discovery of Bering Straits.
1743—Ostermann exiled.
1743—Peace of Abo: Sweden cedes Viborg.
1745—Capture of Louisburg (King George's War).
1755—Moscow University founded.
1755—Lomonosov, *Russian Grammar.*
1755—Lisbon earthquake.
1756–1763—Seven Years' War (French and Indian War).
1757–1762—Russian participation in Seven Years' War.
1758—Academy of Fine Arts founded.
1762—Reign of Peter III.
1762—Nobility freed from compulsory service.
1762–1796—Reign of Catherine II the Great.
1762—Rousseau, *Le Contrat Social.*
1763—Peace of Paris: British gain French colonies in America and
          India.
1764—Secularization of church lands and property.
1765—Death of Lomonosov.
1767–1774—Commission for the Study of Reforms.
1768—Outbreak of war with Turkey.
1772—First Partition of Poland.
1772–1774—Pugachev Revolt.
1774—Treaty of Kuchuk Kainardji.
1775—End of Cossack autonomy in the Ukraine.
1776—Declaration of Independence of United States.
1776—Adam Smith, *Wealth of Nations.*
1778—Death of Voltaire.
1780—Armed Neutrality against England during American Revolu-
          tion.
1781—British surrender at Yorktown.
1781—Kant, *Critique of Pure Reason.*

1783—Annexation of Crimea.

1785—Charter for Russian nobility and merchants.

1787—Adoption of American Constitution.

1787–1790—Russo-Swedish War.

1787–1792—Russo-Turkish War: campaigns of Suvorov.

1789—Outbreak of French Revolution.

1792—Treaty of Jassy.

1793—Second Partition of Poland.

1793—Execution of Louis XVI; beginning of Reign of Terror in France.

1795—Third Partition of Poland.

1796—Odessa founded.

1796—Napoleon's first campaign in Italy.

1796–1801—Reign of Paul I.

1799—Suvorov's Italian and Swiss campaigns (War of Second Coalition).

1801—Russian suzerainty formally recognized by Georgia.

1801–1825—Reign of Alexander I.

1801–1809—Thomas Jefferson, President of United States.

1802—Philharmonic Society founded.

1803—Expedition around world.

1804–1815—Napoleon I, Emperor of France.

1805—Defeat at Austerlitz.

1806—Napoleon's Continental System begun.

1806—Outbreak of war with Turkey.

1807—Defeat at Friedland.

1807—Treaty of Tilsit: alliance with France.

1807—First steamboat service (Fulton on Hudson).

1808—Congress of Erfurt.

1808–1809—Russo-Swedish war.

1808–1809—Constitutional reforms proposed by Speransky.

1809—Treaty of Frederikshavn with Sweden: acquisition of Finland.

1809—Opening of official relations with United States.

1812–1814—War of 1812 (United States and Great Britain).

1812—Peace with Turkey at Bucharest: acquisition of Bessarabia.

1812—Napoleon's invasion of Russia.

1813–1815—Wars of liberation of the Germanies.

1813—Battle of the Nations at Leipzig.

1813—Persia cedes Baku; incorporation of Georgia.

1814—Occupation of Paris.

1815—Congress of Vienna; Holy Alliance founded.

1816–1819—Emancipation of peasants in Baltic provinces.

1818—Constitution for Poland.

1819—Colombia first independent South American republic.

1820—Missouri Compromise.

1821—Outbreak of Greek War of Independence.

1822—Congress of Verona.

1823—Monroe Doctrine.

1825–1855—Reign of Nicholas I.

1825—Dekabrist Rising.
1826–1828—War against Persia; expansion in Caucasus region.
1826—Death of Karamzin.
1827—Battle of Navarino.
1828—Outbreak of war with Turkey.
1829—Peace of Adrianople.
1829–1837—Andrew Jackson, President of United States.
1830—Railroad with locomotives opened from Manchester to Liverpool.
1830—July Revolution in France; revolution in Belgium.
1830–1832—Revolution in Poland.
1831—Death of Hegel.
1832—Completion of *Faust;* death of Goethe.
1832—First Reform Bill in England.
1832—First commercial treaty with United States.
1833—Treaty of Unkiar Skelessi.
1837—Death of Pushkin.
1837–1901—Reign of Queen Victoria in England.
1840–1842—British Opium War against China.
1841–1844—Emerson's *Essays.*
1846–1848—Mexican War.
1848—Gold Rush to California.
1848—Marx and Engels, *Communist Manifesto.*
1848—February Revolution in France; revolutions in Germanies, Austria, Italy, Hungary.
1848—Death of Belinsky.
1849—Suppression of Hungarian revolution.
1851—St. Petersburg–Moscow railroad opened.
1852—Louis Napoleon (Napoleon III), French Emperor.
1853—Occupation of Sakhalin and Korea.
1854–1856—Crimean War.
1855–1881—Reign of Alexander II.
1855—Fall of Sevastopol.
1856—Peace of Paris.
1856—Death of Glinka.
1857–1867—Herzen, *The Bell.*
1857—Indian Mutiny against Britain.
1859—J. S. Mill, *On Liberty.*
1860—Founding of Vladivostok; Treaty of Peking.
1861—Italy becomes kingdom; death of Cavour.
1861–1865—United States Civil War.
1861—Emancipation of serfs.
1862—Financial reform.
1863—Educational reform.
1863—Secession from Academy of Fine Arts.
1863—United States Emancipation Proclamation.
1863–1864—Revolt in Poland.
1864—Judicial reform; introduction of Zemstvos.
1865—Assassination of Lincoln.
1865—Capture of Tashkent.

1866—Attempt on life of Alexander II.

1867—Reduction of protective tariffs.

1867—Sale of Alaska to United States.

1868—Capture of Samarkand.

1869—Karl Marx, *Das Kapital,* Vol. I.

1869—Opening of Suez Canal.

1870—Outbreak of Franco-Prussian War; German victory at Sedan.

1870—Abrogation of Black Sea clauses of Treaty of Paris.

1870—Municipal reform.

1871—German empire proclaimed (Bismarck, Chancellor).

1871—Communist uprisings in Paris (*La Commune*).

1872—Three Emperors' League founded (Germany, Austria, Russia).

1873—Conquest of Khiva.

1874—Introduction of universal military service.

1875—Southern Sakhalin ceded to Japan; western Kuril Islands ac-
         quired.

1875–1876—New uprisings in Balkans.

1876—Death of Bakunin.

1876—Annexation of Kokand.

1877—Reintroduction of protective tariffs.

1877–1878—War against Turkey.

1878—Treaty of San Stephano.

1878—Congress of Berlin.

1878–1881—Second British war against Afghanistan.

1878–1881—Terrorist activities.

1878–1884—Populist movement.

1881—Assassination of Alexander II.

1881—Death of Musorgsky.

1881—Death of Dostoyevsky.

1881–1894—Reign of Alexander III.

1882–1886—Payments and burdens of emancipated serfs reduced.

1882–1890—Social legislation (child labor, working hours, factory
         inspection).

1883—Triple Alliance formed (Germany, Austria, Italy).

1883—United States Civil Service Act.

1883—Social Democratic party founded (Plekhanov).

1884—Merv taken.

1885—Revolution in Bulgaria.

1887—Reinsurance Treaty with Germany.

1890—Resignation of Bismarck.

1890—Anti-Jewish legislation enforced.

1891–1892—Franco-Russian alliance: French loans for Russia.

1891–1903—Trans-Siberian railroad constructed.

1894–1895—Sino-Japanese War.

1894–1917—Reign of Nicholas II.

1896—Treaty with China regarding Trans-Siberian railroad in Man-
         churia.

1896–1897—Strike movement.

1898—Hawaii annexed by United States.

1898—Spanish-American War: Philippines acquired by United States.
1898—Port Arthur leased.
1898—United States Open-Door Policy proclaimed.
1899—Hague Peace Conference.
1899—Finnish legislature abolished.
1899–1902—British Boer War.
1900—Boxer Rebellion.
1901–1909—Theodore Roosevelt, President of United States.
1901—Russo-Persian treaty.
1902—Anglo-Japanese Alliance.
1903—Menshevist-Bolshevist split in Social Democratic party.
1903—Abolition of joint-tax liability of peasants.
1903—Pogroms in Kishinev, Gomel.
1903—German-Turkish agreement regarding Bagdad railway.
1904—Anglo-French Entente Cordiale.
1904–1905—Russo-Japanese War.
1904—Assassination of Plehwe.
1905—Fall of Port Arthur; naval Battle of Tsushima.
1905—Demonstration under Father Gapon: Bloody Sunday.
1905—Peace of Portsmouth.
1905—Meeting of Tsar Nicholas with Emperor Wilhelm II of Germany.
1905—First Moroccan crisis.
1905—Union of Sweden and Norway dissolved.
1905—October Revolution.
1906—First Duma.
1906—Stolypin's agrarian reform; dissolution of *mir*.
1907—Second Duma.
1907—Second Hague Peace Conference.
1907—Anglo-Russian convention: foundation for Triple Entente.
1907—Russo-Japanese convention.
1907–1912—Third Duma.
1908—Convention with Austria at Buchlau.
1910—Potsdam agreement with Germany regarding Bagdad railroad.
1910—Russo-Japanese treaty.
1910—Death of Tolstoy.
1911—Turko-Italian war.
1912—Outbreak of Balkan wars.
1912–1916—Fourth Duma.
1913–1921—Woodrow Wilson, President of United States.
1914—Assassination of Archduke Francis Ferdinand at Sarajevo.
1914–1918—World War I.
1914—Defeat at Tannenberg.
1914—First Battle of Marne.
1915—Defeat in Galicia.
1915—Fall of Warsaw.
1916—Brusilov offensive.
1916—Assassination of Rasputin.
1917—February Revolution; abdication of Nicholas II; provisional government.

1917—United States enters World War I.
1917—Kerensky offensive.
1917—July uprising of Soviets.
1917—Russia becomes a republic; renewal of Patriarchate.
1917—Bolshevist October Revolution (Lenin, Trotsky, Stalin); Kerensky government overthrown.
1917—Armistice with Central Powers.
1918—Constituent Assembly dispersed.
1918—Brest-Litovsk Peace Treaty with Central Powers.
1918—Outbreak of civil war; Allied intervention in Russia begins.
1918—Red Army created.
1918—Death of Nicholas II.
1918—First Soviet Constitution (Fundamental Law); creation of Federation of Soviet National Republics.
1918—End of World War I; revolution in Germany.
1919—Treaty of Versailles; League of Nations founded.
1919—Third International (Comintern) established.
1919—Foreign trade monopoly established.
1920—Recognition of Soviets by Estonia.
1920—End of Allied intervention.
1920—End of civil war; death of Kolchak; withdrawal of Denikin and Wrangel.
1920–1921—War against Poland.
1920–1922—Famine.
1921—Washington Disarmament Conference.
1921—Peace of Riga; cession of White Russian lands to Poland.
1921—Institution of N.E.P.
1921—Friendship treaties with Turkey, Persia, Afghanistan.
1922—Conference at Genoa; Treaty of Rapallo with Germany.
1922—End of Far Eastern Republic.
1922—Fascist regime established in Italy (Mussolini).
1922—Arrest of Patriarch Tikhon; dissolution of Synod.
1922—Stalin becomes secretary of Communist party.
1922—Union of Soviet Socialist Republics (U.S.S.R.) created.
1923—French invasion of Ruhr.
1923—Revised Fundamental Law published.
1924—Death of Lenin.
1924—Treaty with China.
1924—Recognition of U.S.S.R. by England, Italy, France.
1924—Incident of Zinoviev letter.
1924—Trotsky stripped of power.
1925—Locarno Pact.
1925—Recognition of U.S.S.R. by Japan.
1925—Fourteenth Party congress: announcement of industrialization plan.
1926—Pilsudski dictatorship established in Poland.
1926—Trotsky expelled from Politburo.
1927—Raid on Soviet trade headquarters in London; relations with England broken.
1927—Tenth Jubilee of Revolution.

1928—First Five-Year Plan inaugurated.

1928—Briand-Kellogg Peace Pact.

1929–1933—Herbert Hoover, President of United States.

1929—New York stock market crash; beginning of Depression.

1929—East Protocol signed.

1929—Resumption of relations with England.

1929—Trotsky expelled from U.S.S.R.

1929—Raid on Soviet consulate in Harbin; Treaty of Nikolsk Ussuriisk.

1930—Turksib railroad opened.

1930—Liquidation of kulaks.

1931—Mukden incident; Japanese invasion of Manchuria.

1931—Trial of Industrialist party.

1932—Dnieprostroy Dam opened.

1932–1937—Second Five-Year Plan.

1933—Hitler becomes German Chancellor.

1933–1945—Franklin D. Roosevelt, President of United States.

1933—Recognition of U.S.S.R. by United States.

1934—Russia joins League of Nations.

1934–1938—Party purges: execution of Zinoviev, Kamenev, Bukharin, Rykov, Tukhachevsky.

1935—Italy invades Ethiopia.

1935—Sale of Chinese Eastern railway.

1935—Franco-Russian alliance.

1936—Outbreak of Spanish civil war.

1936—Stakhanov Year.

1936—Stalin Constitution: revision of Fundamental Law.

1936—Death of Gorky.

1936—German-Japanese Anticomintern Pact.

1937—Outbreak of Sino-Japanese war.

1937—Italy joins Anticomintern Pact.

1938—Third Five-Year Plan started.

1938—Germany annexes Austria.

1938—German-French-English agreement at Munich concerning Czechoslovakia.

1939—Annexation of Czechoslovakia by Germany.

1939—Collapse of English and French military negotiations with U.S.S.R.

1939—Nonaggression pact with Germany.

1939—Outbreak of World War II.

1939—Annexation of eastern Poland.

1939—Mutual assistance pacts with Estonia, Latvia, Lithuania.

1939–1940—War against Finland.

1939—Expulsion of U.S.S.R. from League of Nations.

1940—Incorporation of Baltic republics into U.S.S.R.

1940—Collapse of France.

1941—Stalin becomes Premier.

1941—Russo-Japanese neutrality pact.

1941—Nazi invasion of Russia.

1941—U.S.S.R. accepts Atlantic Charter.

1941—United States enters war against Japan, Germany.

1942—United Nations Declaration signed.

1942—Siege of Moscow raised.

1942—Fall of Sevastopol.

1942—Twenty-year alliance with Great Britain.

1943—Re-establishment of Patriarchate.

1943—Siege of Stalingrad raised.

1943—Capitulation of Italy.

1943—Anglo-Russian-United States conference in Moscow.

1943—Teheran Conference.

1944—Siege of Leningrad raised.

1944—Bretton Woods Conference.

1944—Allied invasion of Normandy.

1944—Alliance with France.

1944—Armistice with Rumania, Bulgaria, Finland.

1945—Yalta Conference (United States, England, Russia).

1945—San Francisco Conference.

1945—Berlin taken.

1945—Potsdam Conference.

1945—Atomic bomb destroys Hiroshima.

1945—Russian declaration of war against Japan.

1945—Surrender of Japan: end of World War II.

1946—Initiation of Fourth Five-Year Plan.

1946—Discord in United Nations over Iran and Greece.

1946—Proposals in United Nations for atomic energy control.

1947—Peace treaties signed with Finland, Italy, Bulgaria, Rumania,
   Hungary.

1947—Marshall Plan for economic rehabilitation of Europe

1947—Currency reform.

1948—Establishment of a communistic government in Czechoslovakia.

1948–1949—Berlin blockade.

1949—Excommunication of Communists by the Pope.

1949—Defeat of Nationalist China by the Chinese Communists.

1949—Dissolution of political ties with Yugoslavia.

BIBLIOGRAPHY

The following bibliography has been compiled with four aims in view: (a) to include only such books on Russia as are easily accessible; (b) to provide a comparatively wide choice of such books as long as they are written in English; (c) to cover all periods and phases of Russian life; (d) to lead to material containing further detailed bibliographical material for the interested student.

BIBLIOGRAPHIES:

Kerner, Robert J., *Slavic Europe,* Cambridge, 1918
Walsh, Warrens B., *Reader's Guide to Russia,* Syracuse, 1945

PERIODICALS:

American Slavic and East European Review
Russian Review
Slavonic and East European Review
Soviet Russia Today

GENERAL HISTORIES:

Eckardt, Hans von, *Russia,* New York, 1932
Kliuchevsky, V. O., *A History of Russia,* 5 vols., New York, 1911–28
Pares, Bernard, *A History of Russia,* New York, 1947
Platonov, S. F., *History of Russia,* New York, 1925
Pokrovsky, M. N., *Brief History of Russia,* 2 vols., New York, 1933
Simmons, Ernest J., ed., *The USSR,* Cornell, 1947

SPECIAL HISTORIES:

Elnett, Elaine, *Historic Origin and Social Development of Family Life in Russia,* Columbia, 1926
Hrushevsky, Michael, *A History of the Ukraine,* Yale, 1941
Kerner, Robert J., *The Urge to the Sea,* California, 1946
Masaryk, Thomas G., *The Spirit of Russia,* 2 vols., New York, 1919
Mavor, James, *An Economic History of Russia,* 2 vols., New York, 1914

Mirsky, D. S., *Russia, a Social History,* New York, 1930

Vernadsky, George, *Political and Diplomatic History of Russia,* Boston, 1936

ASIATIC RUSSIA:

Asakawa, K., *The Russo-Japanese Conflict,* New York, 1904

Golder, Frank A., *Russian Expansion on the Pacific,* Cleveland, 1914

Krausse, Alexis, *Russia in Asia,* London-New York, 1899

Lobanov-Rostovsky, Andre, *Russia and Asia,* New York, 1933

Taracouzio, Timothy A., *Soviets in the Arctic,* New York, 1938

Vladimir, *Russia on the Pacific and the Siberian Railway,* London, 1899

CHURCH HISTORY:

Casey, Robert P., *Religion in Russia,* New York, 1946

Danzas, J. N., *The Russian Church,* London, 1936

Heard, Albert F., *The Russian Church and Russian Dissent,* New York, 1887

Stanley, Arthur P., *Lectures on the History of the Eastern Church,* New York, 1907

RUSSIA AND AMERICA:

Dulles, Foster R., *The Road to Teheran,* Princeton, 1944

Tompkins, Stuart R., *Alaska: Promyshlennik and Sourdough,* Oklahoma, 1945

Zabriskie, Edward H., *American Russian Rivalry in the Far East,* Pennsylvania, 1946

HISTORIES BY PERIODS:

Alexinsky, Gregor, *Modern Russia,* New York, 1913

Curtin, Jeremiah, *The Mongols in Russia,* Boston, 1908

Karpovich, Michael, *Imperial Russia, 1801–1917,* New York, 1932

Kornilov, Alexander, *Modern Russian History,* 2 vols., New York, 1902–03

Malevsky-Malevitch, P., *Russia, USSR,* New York, 1933

BIOGRAPHIES BY PERIODS:

Waliszewski, Kasimir, *Ivan the Terrible,* Philadelphia, 1904

Graham, Stephen, *Boris Godunov,* Yale, 1933

Bain, R. Nisbet, *The First Romanovs,* New York-London, 1905

Schuyler, Eugene, *Peter the Great,* 2 vols., New York, 1884

Bain, R. Nisbet, *The Pupils of Peter the Great,* Westminster, 1897

Bain, R. Nisbet, *Peter III,* Westminster, 1902

Waliszewski, Kasimir, *The Romance of an Empress: Catherine II,* Philadelphia, 1894

Waliszewski, Kasimir, *Paul I of Russia,* London, 1913

Strakhovsky, Leonid, *Alexander I,* Boston, 1947

Graham, Stephen, *A Life of Alexander II,* London, 1935

Lowe, Charles, *Alexander III of Russia,* New York, 1895

Rivet, Charles, *The Last of the Romanofs,* New York, 1918

REVOLUTIONARY MOVEMENTS:

Kropotkin, Prince, *Memoirs of a Revolutionist,* New York, 1899

Mazour, A. G., *The First Russian Revolution, 1825,* California, 1937

Rodzianko, Michael, *The Reign of Rasputin,* London, 1927

Savinkov, Boris V., *Memoirs of a Terrorist,* New York, 1931

Stepniak, *Underground Russia: Revolutionary Profiles,* New York, 1883

Witte, Count Sergius, *The Memoirs of Count Witte,* Garden City, 1921

RUSSIAN REVOLUTION:

Bunyan, James, and Fisher, H. H., eds., *The Bolshevik Revolution, 1917–18,* Stanford, 1934

Chamberlin, William H., *The Russian Revolution, 1917–21,* New York, 1935

Denikin, A. I., *The Russian Turmoil,* London, 1922

Florinsky, Michael, *The End of the Russian Empire,* Yale, 1931

Kerensky, Alexander F., *The Catastrophe,* New York-London, 1927

Lenin, Vladimir, *Selected Works,* 12 vols., New York, 1935–38

Marcu, Valeriu, *Lenin,* New York, 1928

Mirsky, D. S., *Lenin,* Boston, 1931

Pares, Bernard, *The Fall of the Russian Monarchy,* New York, 1939

Souvarine, Boris, *Stalin,* New York, 1939.

Trotsky, Leon, *The History of the Russian Revolution,* New York, 1932

SOVIET PERIOD:

Dallin, David J., *The Real Soviet Russia,* Yale, 1944

Dallin, David J., *Soviet Russia's Foreign Policy, 1939–42,* Yale, 1943

Dean, Vera M., *Soviet Russia,* Boston, 1936

Fisher, Louis, *The Soviets in World Affairs,* 2 vols., London, 1930

Hoover, Calvin B., *The Economic Life of Soviet Russia,* New York, 1932

Lamont, Corliss, *The Peoples of the Soviet Union,* New York, 1946

Lawton, Lancelot, *An Economic History of Soviet Russia,* 2 vols., London, 1932

Malevsky-Malevitch, Peter, *The Soviet Union Today,* New York, 1936

Mikhailov, Nicholas, *Land of the Soviets,* New York, 1939

Scott, John, *Behind the Urals,* Cambridge, 1942

Stalin, Joseph, *Leninism,* 2 vols., London-New York, 1928–33

Trotsky, Leon, *The Revolution Betrayed,* New York, 1945

Williams, Albert R., *The Soviets,* New York, 1937

ART AND LITERATURE:

Brueckner, Alexander, *A Literary History of Russia,* London, 1908

Bunt, Cyril G., *History of Russian Art,* London, 1946

Kondakov, Nikodim P., *The Russian Icon,* Oxford, 1927

Miliukov, Paul N., *Outlines of Russian Culture,* 3 vols., Philadelphia, 1942

Seltzer, Thomas, ed., *Best Russian Short Stories,* New York, 1925

Simmons, Ernest J., *An Outline of Modern Russian Literature,* Cornell, 1943

Wiener, Leo, ed., *Anthology of Russian Literature,* 2 vols., New York, 1902–03

INDEX

4848